The Vulnerable Self

Confronting the Ultimate Questions

The Vulnerable Self

Confronting the Ultimate Questions

Avery D. Weisman, M.D.

Foreword by
John C. Nemiah, M.D.

 INSIGHT BOOKS

PLENUM PRESS • NEW YORK AND LONDON

Library of Congress Cataloging-in-Publication Data

Weisman, Avery D.
    The vulnerable self : confronting the ultimate questions / Avery
D. Weisman ; foreword by John C. Nemiah.
        p.   cm.
    Includes bibliographical references and index.
    ISBN 0-306-44501-8
    1. Existential psychotherapy.   2. Adjustment (Psychology)
I. Title.
    [DNLM: 1. Psychotherapy.   2. Adaptation, Psychological.   BF 335
W428v 1993]
RC489.E93W45   1993
616.89'14--dc20
DNLM/DLC
for Library of Congress   93-2600
                                                                   CIP

ISBN 0-306-44501-8

© 1993 Plenum Press, New York
A Division of Plenum Publishing Corporation
233 Spring Street, New York, N.Y. 10013

An Insight Book

Printed in the United States of America

To Lois

Foreword

In the many years that we have been friends, I have never known Avery Weisman to be at a loss for words or to spend one unwisely. He has always chosen them carefully, used them sparingly, and spoken them with precision. And he has required of others the same verbal economy that he imposes on himself. I can still hear the instructions he uttered on rounds one day to a resident about to recount a patient's history: "Make the presentation brief—no verbs!" The last phrase was spoken after a momentary pause, delivered with a slightly rising inflection that gave it emphasis, and accompanied by a trace of a smile that conveyed the affection he felt for all of us.

I dwell on the author's manner of communicating not only because it reveals a central characteristic of the man, but because of the light it casts on the pages that follow. A quick glance at his prose suggests an unusual simplicity in language and style; the common jargon of the clinical psychiatrist is nowhere in evidence. There is no mention of standard diagnostic entities, and there is little reference to the intricacies of the common mechanisms of defense, to superego functions, to ego strengths, or to unconscious processes. Instead we hear of the vulnerable self, of the ability to cope, of meaning and skepticism, of morale and despair, of tranquility and suffering, and of wisdom and fallibility.

The simplicity of Weisman's language is deceptive, however,

and we soon discover that the author is using the phraseology of existential psychiatry, although he does so without lapsing into the more recondite vocabulary of that approach to human ills. His concern is not with the standard, discrete psychopathological entities defined in the official *Diagnostic and Statistical Manual of Mental Disorders* but with the ubiquitous and equally profound (although not necessarily pathological) emotional distress inherent in human living, with its frequent losses, failures, bodily illnesses, and above all its transiency, imposed by the inevitability of death.

It is helpful for the reader to be aware right from the beginning of the nature of the author's subject, for he does not himself make it explicit. It is important as well to recognize that the author is not writing a book *about* existential psychiatry, but that throughout his text he is simply developing and presenting ideas within the framework of the existential paradigm. Unwary readers may therefore become confused, especially if they do not bring to the text a knowledge of existential concepts; indeed, those uninformed in that regard may find it helpful first to read Chapter 6, where the author provides a somewhat more formal, explicit, and clarifying description of the basis of the existential approach that is to be found in the rest of the book.

The author is not, however, your traditional card-carrying existentialist; far from it. Although his concerns are squarely focused on the universal enigmas of human existence, he does not offer the official answers of existentialism, or of any other philosophical school. He is, as he tells us, a "skeptical pilgrim" in the uncertain passage through life, saved from dogmatism by doubt, impatient with pat solutions. His is not a doubt that is truculent or abrasive, though, for it has been transmuted by his sensitive and empathic comic muse into a therapeutic instrument of great utility. Firmly but gently, and with kindly good humor, the author as therapist makes skeptical pilgrims of his patients, too, by persuading them to give up their entrenched patterns of denial and self-deception, and by enabling them to see that their seeming despair and inability to cope are often not inevitable but express submerged motivations that have been needlessly hidden from view. His skillfully told clinical vignettes of the middle-aged executive in Chapter 3 and of the librarian in Chapter 4 are graphic and convincing demonstrations of the insights that doubting the validity of surface behavior and conscious experience can bring to patients and therapists alike.

Although, as a clinician, I could have wished that the author had devoted more space to such descriptions of patients, I am aware that his intended boundaries are wider. As it is, he has given us a volume of many dimensions that will expand the knowledge and understanding of readers. In this panoramic view of the world of Weisman there is much of value for all of us.

JOHN C. NEMIAH, M.D.

Preface

I came to write this book as the result of a misapprehension. I wanted to start at a point following the last chapter of my previous book, *The Coping Capacity* (1984)—which, I believed, began at the point where an earlier book, *Coping with Cancer* (1979), had ended. In this way I hoped for a continuity, without giving much thought as to why continuity was desirable.

In reexamining the books and reviewing my recent writings, however, I learned that the serial plan was neater and more organized than its execution. There was, of course, some overlap and a degree of repetition, but I did not intentionally plagiarize myself. Instead I realized that all through the years, whether in developing clinical hypotheses or assessing so-called facts, I was occupied with certain themes and variations on them. The sequence therefore did not simply consist of end-to-end clinical reports but seemed to be an unfolding process of exploration, expansion, and evolution. Consequently, in the present book it has been possible to bring out some of the presuppositions that had been implied before and to go beyond mere explication into what I considered newer ground that psychiatrists, among others, seldom explore.

Most writers, I have noticed, modestly disclaim that their conclusions have any finality. In my case, however, lack of finality is built into the conclusions. The spirit of skepticism would not have it otherwise. Nevertheless, the courage to cope and to become provides a certain faith in the longitudinal enterprise called *significant survival,* or purpose in life. Although not easily defined, at least for the individual, the principles of such survival can be identified through confronting ultimate questions, or what I have termed *metaproblems.*

The following chapters represent separate versions of this enterprise. Call it an existential adventure, if you wish; I consider it a pilgrimage of sorts in which we must deal with suffering, vulnerability, coping, courage, meaning, morale, and mortality itself, as well as with related ideas in between. Be assured that this is not a rehash or review, abstract, footnoted, and full of cross-references. Rather, it is a reflection on some of the ultimate questions that puzzle us all, particularly at the end of the twentieth century, an era of discovery and despair, of suffering and trust (most of which has been betrayed).

I have been relatively removed from the up-close clinical scene for a few years. This has turned out to be advantageous. I have had a chance to develop distance and perspective about psychiatry, psychoanalysis, psychosocial research, and psychotherapy, all of which occupied so much of my life up until now, when I have begun other kinds of work.

It has been almost 50 years since I began psychiatric training at Massachusetts General Hospital. There have been many changes which are hard to specify. But I know that change has occurred, although many things have remained the same, particularly those things usually covered by the term, "human nature." Looking backward, it is hard to identify the changes that were most crucial and decisive, let alone when they occurred and the way in which the discipline of psychiatry has evolved since. I could, of course, ascribe most change to the rise of psychopharmacology. It is hard to serve two masters, and be an able and perceptive psychotherapist. Nevertheless, the simultaneous rise of consultation-liaison psychiatry has forced conscientious psychiatrists to heed the "psychosomatic" viewpoint, while struggling to find their distant identity.

Progress has to be a product of chronic optimism, even

though the years are not typified by unrelenting progress in any discipline. No metaphor is adequate to describe the wavering course of progress. It is certainly not a straight line, nor is it a roller coaster that just goes up and down, providing thrilling moments in-between. A spiral staircase goes up and around, with a different view of a narrow field. Perhaps that comes closer, although the existential enterprise that I try to describe in these chapters refuses to be circumscribed by the reigning dicta in psychiatry or any other discipline.

In addition to becoming a seasoned psychoanalyst over the years, I turned gradually to psychosocial research. Project Omega, a multidisciplinary study, investigated how cancer patients coped or failed to cope with their illness and its ramifications, from the first diagnosis throughout the course of the disease. Study of these gravely ill patients provided an excellent counterpoint to my hours behind the couch, as well as an opportunity to compare different patterns of coping that I found while doing psychoanalysis.

Accordingly, I have drawn clinical examples from both research and practice, and from both very ill patients seen in consultation or for study and relatively healthy people who consulted me about psychotherapy. This book is not significantly autobiographical in the sense of being personal. In my selection of topics and sensitivity to certain issues, though, I have been directed by my own inclinations. I maintain that the temperament of a therapist does more for the type of therapy he or she practices than training or theoretical predisposition. For example, the courage to cope is very important to me and, I believe, for other people. It is particularly significant, however, because I have never been sufficiently convinced of my own courage in the conventional sense. I am more certain of how important it is to identify relevant life tasks and underlying questions of vulnerability disclosed in more ordinary problems and confrontations.

I cannot pretend that the essence of the skeptical pilgrim is not in me, as it must be in other people, now and in the past. Paradox is all around us; inconsistencies permeate even the strictest attempts at rationality. There are many pilgrimages which are undertaken because of faith. But faith in what? The sad and embittered populations at century's end have been victimized by faith, and this is hard to call progress. Nevertheless, even skeptics can usually find a compatible course of action, consistent with "significant survival."

The vulnerable self is built into our humanity, and it shows itself through distress. But there is also a core of resiliency and sufficient resources that can, with some effort, become more authentic. The person who recognizes a vulnerable self that exists within a shell of complacency and conformity, along with unreasonable distress, should be able to understand the prototype pilgrim seeking enduring values. There are elements of rebellion, traces of unfulfillment, unasked (and somewhat terrifying) questions, and occasional flickers of demoralization in nearly everyone.

The skeptical pilgrim has an advantage. Familiar but not comfortable with his paradoxes, inconsistencies, avoidances, denials, and blind alleys that somehow connect, he knows well that he must account for his own vulnerability by making sense. With this start, combined with much tenacity, he takes heart over and over, thus coping more courageously and effectively than at an earlier time.

The confluence of opposites is necessary for deciding what something means or intends. There is no authenticity without an effort to understand what people believe, think they believe, and really act upon. Without such eclectic clustering, we are abandoned to unrelenting vulnerability. For example, we must believe that spirit and substance go together, as do body and mind, passion and principle, and so on. If there is room for rationality, then there is a place for magic and transcendence. It is only that terrible habit of dichotomizing and abstraction that splits things up into good and bad, right and wrong, and makes us believe that opposites can and should be indefinitely held apart.

I wonder what the ancients would have thought about psychotherapy, had they known how and why it is practiced today. It is difficult enough to know what they thought about anyway; we base our present understanding on how we interpret through analogies and unwitting contemporary paraphrases. Psychotherapy in some form or other has had many names through the centuries, but no society, I am led to understand, has been wholly without it. What that practice or format consisted of is less certain. Doctors and clergy, among others, have vied for the special prestige, as have shamans and other select figures. Indigenous practitioners are still with us, regardless of training, and manage to combine the desire to heal with magical expectations generated by the culture, which confers rationality, legitimacy, and authentication on them.

It takes no immense scholarship to realize that classical, biblical, and scholastic thinkers through the ages have in their distinct ways, confronted various versions of ultimate questions. Though there are many differences between these thinkers—also based on different ears, languages, idioms, and philosophy—I cannot imagine them so far removed from everyday life that issues of vulnerability did not occur to them; yet many were so preoccupied with pure thought, idealized existence, and the afterlife that it is possible. Culture and custom usually decide what is or is not valuable, and worth thinking about.

If we reach back to the Platonic era, it is easy to find that the central quandary was this: What is virtue, and can it be taught? If so, then how, by whom, and for what purpose? And given that courage is usually considered a virtue (although it is not always high on the list), can courage be taught? Is it a skill, an art, or a gift of the gods, like other virtues? Although I also wonder about virtue, values, and courage, my emphasis is on the vulnerable self, who suffers, copes, and reaches toward authenticity (along with sustenance, support, success, etc.). My view is that although we suffer from no lack of problems, suffering can be reduced, and perhaps coped with, by being armed with an acceptable meaning that maintains morale.

The ancients in classical times also questioned the purpose of education and laws. Plato, for one, believed in an ideal (called the Good) that would be the absolute measure of virtue. One of my questions that I answer in the negative, however, is about the hypothetical existence or nonexistence of a supervalue that will enable us to judge lesser values as good or bad, or as right or wrong. The source of most human problems can be traced to which values are relevant. Turn any problem on its head, and you will find a set of values that have been violated. As a rule, the person who embraces those values will have failed to live up to them and, hence, has a problem. Without a relevant value to offend, problems are not problematic.

I repeatedly point out as strongly as possible that confronting ultimate questions is not the private professional preserve of certain academics with a theological or philosophical inclination. It is a living issue of utmost practicality and pertinence, however remote it seems from everyday life. If vulnerability is intensified by not pursuing the meaning of various conflicts, if our morale sinks below what is tolerable, and if we avoid confronting the realities related to our mortality, our resiliency is pretty feeble, and our coping capacity very limited.

I illustrate my points using examples from psychotherapy and psychiatry, because that was my job for a long time. My recollections naturally turn to situations and experiences that impose an emotional rather than a physical threat, and that thus require courage of a different order. Any professional would do the same, using vocations, experiences, and idioms unique to a microcosm for more general encounters. Ultimate questions are always there, waiting to be identified and confronted. I find the pursuit exceedingly important because resolution might help enlighten us and perhaps even equip us to deal better with suffering and vulnerability. Not every instance of sickness happens in hospitals, and suffering is not restricted to battlefields and mean streets of our cities. In one form or another, evil is there to be coped with, whatever it is called these days. C. S. Lewis's Wormwood and Screwtape are members of the same family. The vulnerable self seems to be found almost anywhere that people have low self-esteem and high distress. Its dilemmas resemble each other.

If I now sound as if I have considered ancient questions and taken over some of the imagery of earlier times, this is the enduring quality of pilgrimages. Doctoring the sick and sick at heart is always relevant, although we are seldom sure of its direction, destination, method, or outcome. In this context, our pilgrim is not a crusader, not a religious devotee, and not a picaresque adventurer. Whether a pilgrim is skeptical is somewhat irrelevant. The only prerequisite is to recognize vulnerability, especially our own, but to retain hope that despite questioning all the remedies foisted on us, coping is plausible and practical.

There used to be jokes—probably still are—that poke fun at experts, authorities, and consultants. Having been all three from time to time, I have ample reason to poke fun, too. Given the difficult task of sometimes explaining the unexplainable, for instance, I am very skeptical about what various experts profess to accomplish. But I am committed to the pursuit of learning better how to cope with certain vexing difficulties. I am reasonably sure that practitioners of psychotherapy, for example, put their own stamp and style on the substance of what they elect to do. In so doing, they will try to work out their own past and unlived life, along with whatever skills and knowledge are at the service of patients and clients. Perhaps that is also true for other professionals in similar occupations.

The key issues everywhere, once the basic necessities are available, have to include the courage to cope and to heal the vulnerable self. When Dr. Erich Lindemann became chief of psychiatry at Massachusetts General Hospital in 1956, he asked me to develop a psychiatric consultation service. Because Dr. Lindemann's already significant accomplishments were in the field of social psychiatry and outreach into the community of sick people within social units (sometimes called families), it was clear that he wanted a more comprehensive approach to psychiatric consultations than could be reached with a few moments at the bedside, followed by an omniscient note scribbled in the chart. His invitation turned out to be opportune. I was able to consult about medical and surgical patients at periods of high vulnerability and to coordinate these observations with what I was learning in my psychoanalytic practice, which went on at a more leisurely pace.

The challenge of starting up a new service could not have been carried out, at least by me, without the good fortune of working alongside Dr. Thomas Hackett, then a fellow in psychiatry. We were to become collaborators and good friends until his premature death at age 59 in 1988. His death was a tragedy from which many of us have not yet recovered. I treasure his memory and grieve his loss.

Dr. J. William Worden was a key colleague in Project Omega; we worked together and produced publications that I believe still have value. I cannot mention everyone from whom I benefitted in professional work, and I ask for their understanding and willingness to be anonymous. But among colleagues who have special importance, I need to express my appreciation of Dr. Edwin Shneidman, a revered friend; Dr. Herman Feifel, an inspiring predecessor; Dr. Robert Kastenbaum, also, at one time, a close collaborator; and Dr. Harry Sobel, whose fresh ideas invigorated my own. Dr. Ned Cassem, the current chief of psychiatry at Massachusetts General Hospital, generously lent his support and wisdom, as well as making the facilities of a large institution available. He was also instrumental in naming the present consultation/liaison service after me.

This book could not have been completed in its present form without the advice and encouragement of Norma Fox and Frank Darmstadt, editors of Insight Books. Their experience and understanding helped crystallize what I had to say. Deirdre Donoghue did a masterful job of word processing.

These acknowledgments are far from complete. I have depended on many whom I have never met, but whose writings profoundly influenced me beyond what I could indicate in a list of references.

If compassion can be taught—in many ways, it is the opposite of arrogance—it is urgent to get some in a hurry as this century comes to a close. Multitudes are constantly terrorized, and count-less innocents have been brought to an undeserved death for obscure causes, and for none at all. We need no funeral oration to remind us that these sufferers never had a chance to become what they might, courage or not. Vulnerability cries out for relevance, relief, and resiliency.

AVERY D. WEISMAN

Contents

Foreword by John C. Nemiah, M.D. vii

Preface xi

Chapter 1

AUTHENTICITY: AN INTRODUCTION.................. 1

Chapter 2

THE ENIGMAS....................................... 21

    Sickness, Suffering, and Identity....................... 22
    Selfhood: Caught in the Act........................... 29
    Vulnerability: Being without Meaning.................. 31
    Two Kinds of Vulnerability........................... 36
    How Does "Making Sense" Make Sense? 40
    Three Virtues: Experience, Culture, and Wisdom 47

Chapter 3

THE SKEPTICAL PILGRIM 55

    An Uncertain Pilgrimage............................ 55

Though the Heart Has Its Reasons 59
Good Theories, Bad Theories, and Acceptability 62
Existential Vulnerability: Meaning without Being 75
The Self-Enclosed Personality 79

Chapter 4

THE COURAGE TO COPE 85

A Curious Virtue Called Courage 85
The Rationality of Courage 88
The Courage to Be..................................... 91
Existential Courage in Psychotherapy.................. 94
On Being Bad 99
Respect and Regard.................................... 102
Good and Bad Copers................................. 105
The Befitting 114

Chapter 5

SKEPTICISM IN PSYCHOTHERAPY 121

Psychotherapy for Skeptics 122
Beyond Morale....................................... 131
On Being a Therapist of Quality..................... 134
Flight from Fallibility 136
The Coinage of Therapy: Care, Concern, and Support .. 137
The Gist of Therapy: Counseling 139
An Existential Predicament 141
A Philosophical Aside................................ 142
Dealing with Dichotomy 149
Is There an Existential Psychotherapy?................ 153

Chapter 6

THREE METAPROBLEMS............................ 157

On Terminating Therapy 158

Metaproblems and Ultimate Questions   160
Three Metaproblems: Meaning, Morale, and Mortality . .   162

Chapter 7

THE PILGRIM WHO STAYED HOME.   197

Vulnerability and the Skeptical Pilgrim   197
Mystery Loves Company   201
Is There a Supervalue?   204
Options in Psychotherapy.   209
Impossible Goals, Proximal Problems, and Ultimate
  Questions   220

Chapter 8

CODA WITHOUT CONCLUSION   227

What a Vulnerable Self Needs Most.   228
Virtues of an Authentic Self   230
Skepticism and Ultimate Questions about Closure   235

FOR FURTHER READING.   241

INDEX.   245

It can be stated categorically that whenever a lengthening reaction is obtained by forcible flexion a contralateral extensor reflex develops simultaneously (JOHN FULTON, *Physiology of the Nervous System*, 1938).

Yes, there is hardly any doubt about it: for every resistance, there is an equal (almost) and opposite (nearly) counterresistance that balances silence and solitude. For example, in almost every encounter, facts are mistaken for factors, surmises confused with sentiments, analogies for causes, parts for the whole, and mere sounds for sensibility.

Now, if I were silent enough, what would I be thinking? And if I were not silent, why then am I now speaking?

Chapter 1

Authenticity:
An Introduction

It would have been gratifying (and a little intimidating) to offer a more personal and autobiographical document than the book you are about to read. But how I got from there to here—combined and interlaced with recollections of patients, colleagues, and many others along the way—however prudently and tactfully expressed, would have little compelling interest for anyone. Though I deeply believe that anyone's lifetime is itself a pilgrimage of sorts and that psychotherapy is a kind of adventurous enterprise, the existential event of being alive (here and now, as well as then and there) should not be confused with one person's viewpoint about a variety of topics and things. The human adventure itself has much more appeal, and in the present ambiguous state of psychotherapy, when almost anyone with a therapeutic bent can start practicing, the relation of existence to what is dealt with in therapy deserves further examination. If more theory is required, then it should be relevant to the human adventure; otherwise, therapy is a game without rules, reason, or a significant end point.

Times have changed: Psychodynamic psychotherapy, drawn from its celebrated predecessor, psychoanalysis, has fallen from the preeminence of just a few decades ago. Nowadays peer groups, psychopharmacology, and social engineering have

1

scraped away much of the authority and glamour once attached to so-called insight-oriented therapy. Far from becoming extinct, though, psychodynamic therapy has become a rather ill-defined but honorable adjunct to any number of procedures intended to relieve distress and sustain the perplexed.

I firmly believe that whatever healing properties psychodynamic therapy possesses are determined less by its theory and techniques than by the personality and temperament of the therapist. The early requirement insisted upon by Freud that analysts undergo periodic analysis was a powerful indication that to do therapy or analysis has its own inherent hazards. This, however, was only a negative reason for analysis; the more positive rationale was that psychoanalysis is a preparation for self-analysis that never ends. Analysts were supposed to examine themselves in no less rigorous fashion than that expected of their patients.

The requirement of a periodic return to analysis, including the invitation to become adept at self-analysis, has been followed by comparatively few psychodynamic therapists. Though analysts speak often about counter transference (i.e., how an analyst perceives distortions in his or her assessment of others and acts upon them), this is but clinical by-play, not at all comprehensive enough to qualify as a search for personal identity—or, as I call it, a quest for authenticity.

In the specialized hands of psychoanalysts, authenticity for the analyst (or anyone else, for that matter) has usually become encrusted with abstractions and hair-splitting speculations. As a psychoanalyst myself, I am grateful for many fine associations I have had over the years with others of similar training and practice; I have no intention of biting the hand that fed me and provided a certain amount of prestige. Nevertheless, we spent an inordinate amount of time in discussing and dissecting what to do, how to do it, and why it should be done this way and not another. Very little time was devoted to the truly personal ways in which the analyst reacted and responded. Even less time was spent in considering the impact of the existential encounter itself upon different ways in which the predominant therapeutic challenges were then formulated.

Temperament is a shorthand term for the *meaning* that an analyst, counselor, or therapist (I shall use the general term *therapist* for convenience) finds and imposes upon the clinical encounter. This meaning is predicated on the meldings of reason and passion, thought and emotion, and action and fantasy that go into how we ordinarily understand and cope with problems. Temperament also indicates how one determines, often instantaneously, what is and is not problematic, and therefore which meaning of many makes the most sense. In this respect, there are no universal or absolute truths that provide sure instruction; there are only situations that make sense for those involved. Making sense is a very primitive condition that is not to be confused with its sophisticated cousin, called understanding or comprehension. Making sense is inescapable; it is the reason and motive behind what we are inclined to do anyway, and is then given as the purpose for behaving as we must.

Considering my own temperament—fortified by what I will term experience, culture, and wisdom (which will be defined in due course)—I must now announce the concepts that are most important to me and that constitute the earliest forms in which my beliefs are cast. I shall, of course, do this insofar as I am able, but there is also a vast repository of things that I feel no particular conviction or passion about. These, too, are excluded more or less automatically from my beliefs. In psychotherapy, each therapist has his or her own contingent of concepts that attach themselves to what patients say and thus direct or skew the flow of other ideas or even the interpretation of events.

It is in this sense that temperament (how one sees the world) modifies meaning, the guidelines or tacit instructions for dealing with the world. Beliefs, therefore, may be based on reality, but reality itself is far more comprehensive. Because beliefs—and meanings of all sorts—are both subjective and objective, the wise therapist culls the differences and helps the patient recognize each variation. Take, for instance, the concept of freedom. For a therapist, freedom might mean the freedom to make intelligent choices among alternatives that the therapist (implicitly, of course) believes to be most beneficial. For a patient, however, freedom could be something very personal, such as getting a divorce: "If I were only free again, without a wife and family, who don't appreciate me anyway!" Getting these meanings together is a major task, just as getting to understand the meaning behind the same words is an obstacle. In the worst case, a patient might continue to think that freedom to choose means freedom to desert his or her family, an option that his guilt would never permit.

I am a skeptic about my work, and I like to include in this skepticism whatever is set before me as an established truth or reality. But because I, like everyone else, have abundant biases—including the notion that my biases are really valid principles—I could not question everything at every moment without falling into a slough of doubting compulsion. I cannot feel wholly cynical, however, and dismiss practically everything as fraudulent. For reasons that will become very clear, I believe in an enlightened skepticism that is not at all cynical (except about some matters that deserve it). Cynicism is not justified in large part because such virtues as hope, courage, and generosity seem to have an enduring quality that shows up when least expected, regardless of disappointments and misfortunes of all sorts. It is not necessary to make orotund pronouncements about "faith in human nature," whatever that means. It is only necessary to believe in contingency, not certainty—of that, I am pretty sure. This is the basis for enlightened skepticism, namely, looking out for contingency and conditions that make one cautious about generalizing too glibly.

There are passions of the heart that recognize no reason at all, and passions of the head that are equally intemperate and dogmatic. There are logical reasons and options that can be used to dampen almost any extreme, however, not because such reasons and options are logical or reasonable but because they resemble the unqualified sureness of instinct. Skepticism enables us to modulate extremes, and to avoid being swept away by either cardiac or cerebral passions. Most ideas thrive in an atmosphere of dichotomy, and good ideas flourish by virtue of opposition and antithesis.

Skepticism tries to use dichotomy, opposition, and antithesis not only to discover good ideas but to define what meanings are meant in various situations without becoming overheated by a passion for rationality. The chief reason for keeping rationality in check is about the same as that for keeping extravagant reliance on intuition in check: Unmodulated rationality or intuition undermines efforts to challenge beliefs that are only conventional and popular and does very little for recognizing the discouraging socially sanctioned answers to ultimate questions. Skepticism is not negativism, for that is a self-defeating attitude which camouflages itself as sometimes ultrascientific, religious, artistic, or whatever rewards excessively high, even unreachable standards.

Rationality for its own sake is meaningless, or at best legalistic. It has little to do with life as it is ordinarily lived and understood. I could cite many plausible reasons for believing as I do, and so could you. But your experience is primarily yours and is difficult to share with me. I would not, therefore, turn this book into a personal memoir or a professional textbook dealing with absolute events and clinical generalities, because both might well be illusory. From what I can observe about the world and the strange, paradoxical, and unjustified cruelties that are found in every direction, God does not deal in absolutes and generalities; hence, it would be presumptuous to pretend to be more certain than I am about many things. I cannot hide behind disclaimers of objectivity, however, and then sneak in other universal claims under the guise of intuition or subjectivity. In the field of human relations and in psychotherapy as we know it, certainty and dogmatism are insults to the intellect and perhaps injurious to the spirit as well.

In reading this book, therefore, you should investigate your own reasons for believing as you do, even with regard to cherished and enduring beliefs. That will become your story to know, just as this is mine to write, even in the absence of autobiographical details. You have a pilgrimage, and you live with ideas and impulses that are conceived through mixing passions and principles. My pilgrimage, which is mostly secular, has been both rough and smooth but reasonably orderly, considering the harrowing events that others undergo and survive. But comparisons are odious and misleading, because retrospective appraisals are interlaced with distortions, falsifications, and self-serving platitudes. Historical facts even at their most literal are low-level theories that serve an ulterior purpose. In doing psychotherapy, these are methodical problems that require careful attention; otherwise, it is hard to make sense and keep it that way.

Perhaps not everyone has had experience with psychotherapy or with counselors of various kinds. Perhaps it only seems like it. But in the last half of this century, there are few who have not had face-to-face contact with a counselor or some other putative expert on human behavior. From school counselors to lawyers, clergy, and psychiatrists, we have sought help or support, or guidance from one real or self-appointed expert or another in an effort to smooth out problems and regain a semblance of control.

What I offer is a viewpoint on *how we package and use our own experience.* I shall use the familiar idiom of psychotherapy, while avoiding professional jargon, as much as possible. I do this in the belief that psychotherapy, particularly of the psychodynamic or existential variety, is valid insofar as it fits into the scope of the human adventure as a personal whole. I do not instruct anyone in how to do psychotherapy, for several very good reasons. There are many books and manuals claiming to teach psychotherapy, and there are at least several hundred different bodies of practice that purport to be psychotherapy. I believe that although experiences can be shared and even put into a somewhat systematic framework, psychotherapy can no more be taught by manual and textbook than badminton. Any philosophy claiming to describe psychotherapy must reflect the principles of its advocates. Experience teaches us that when burnished by extensive repetition and scanty refutation, practice becomes sanded down into principles not far removed from dogma itself.

The idea that psychotherapy often bases itself on principles that establish themselves through redundancy is not unique; it is characteristic of most of our beliefs and self-guidance systems. It means that experience is largely what we have experienced and given a name to. Although it does not sharply discriminate what we have experienced from what we merely seem to recall experiencing, such a congeries of concepts can still make sense while not exactly qualifying as more than it is. Whatever pertains to what people actually do, think, or feel under various circumstances has to be relevant and worth examining. Anything less would be fraudulent. But we can hardly doubt that what they do, think, or feel is motivated by a drive to survive, make sense, cope effectively, and reach a decent quality of life.

A useful dictum for either philosophy or psychotherapy is, by definition, pragmatic and existential; otherwise, each can become lost in airy speculations anchored nowhere. Such dictums authenticate themselves in practice and acquire meaning only through the contexts in which they occur and are acted upon. Words are cheap unless their meaning signifies something useful and worth acting on. It is not necessary or even possible to deal with sharp definition; there are many ideas that seem indefinable (e.g., generosity, hope, loyalty, or health) but still guide us because they represent values we live by and strive for.

In this context *meaning* means something specific in that it refers to instructions about how to deal with something outside ordinary behavior. In other words, we inquire about what something means only when it is outside the ordinary run of behavior. Otherwise we pass it by with scarcely a look; if asked about it, our response would be perfunctory. I do not particularly care about the inner workings of a carburetor unless I have car trouble—that is, unless the car's behavior is abnormal. What then, I ask, does the bad behavior of my car mean? Could it be carburetor trouble? To be sure, human behavior and conduct are far less mechanical than the simple functions involved in internal combustion. But when fairly regular behavior or conduct constrained by values suddenly goes wrong, it is proper to inquire what this strange, aberrant behavior means. If it seems excessively outlandish or wholly irrational, then we ask how to make sense out of it.

An elderly, very proper man of 85 years who abruptly takes to urinating in public and seems oblivious to the stares of passersby is in trouble because his behavior is meaningless until it is assigned a context in which it makes sense, such as "incipient dementia." What this context means, however, is a set of instructions about how to deal with such behavior, or incipient dementia: "Don't let Dad go out alone, without an escort," or "The poor guy's losing it; don't scold him." Psychiatrists are frequently asked about the "why" of certain extraordinary or violent public crimes or deviations from the expected norm. Asking why is actually a plea for a context in which this behavior makes sense, not a rationale that makes it more acceptable. Fixing a meaning renders the act less troublesome to everyone else, because it then fits into a framework that already exists.

As a rule, we find out what people mean by asking them about it. We claim to expect them to tell the truth, though in reality we expect only their version of the relevant events. Do people mean what they say, then, and say what they mean? The answer is only sometimes, even when they try not to deceive or mislead. Self-deception and ordinary denial to make things stay as they were, or to enhance the image of the speaker, are very common. Shading the truth, if not outright distortion, is sometimes needed in order to survive; self-pity and faultfinding blame the world, not the self. In psychotherapy, it is axiomatic that patients tell us the truth—whatever that is—on the condition that to do so does not cause too much damage to self-esteem. We can expect the same from the therapist.

The central question is to find and achieve something close to self-authenticity. Let it be said that authenticity is a product of the vulnerable self and the responsible self; it is not, therefore, a state of sanctity or virtue that hardly ever is reached, like sainthood or righteousness. Authenticity demands clarity about what meanings are relevant, consistent, and acceptable in living and coping. We have many hypotheses that surround what we do, but most of what we mean and live by goes beyond what is already believed. An authentic person tries to avoid self-deception by having ways to challenge existing theories and suppositions. This is also what good therapists try to do when, through enlightened skepticism, they challenge axiomatic or accepted truths. Finding out what makes sense is an important existential task that, carried out along a lifelong continuum, will also make sense and be authentic enough to live for.

I take psychotherapy to be a mirror of what takes place in the world at large. Every field has its regulars and deviants, liberals and conservatives, and radicals and reactionaries, and psychotherapists are no different. Each new season brings forth a crop of new procedures and methods, all claiming originality and incredible effectiveness. At the moment, we are seeing the decline of what was enormously popular just a few years ago. Fashions and fads could not take hold even for an instant without claiming authenticity, validity, and, I suppose, an inside track toward enlightenment. For example, so-called holistic methods for relieving stress appeal to some patients who yearn for exotic truths (such as those found in Eastern religions) and a set of practices to bring them closer to a desired state of tranquility, if not insight. Some therapists immediately become adept at meditation, imagery, and so on, whereas others continue to practice what they were trained to do. Which camp therapists belong to, however, is determined by their temperament, not the quality of their results.

Therapists never tire of endless disputations about policies, philosophies, procedures, and other people. It amounts to new versions of old minutiae, not drastic innovations that revolutionize. Linking these newer versions of old minutiae, focusing on details of theory to magnify their importance, or simply creating a new fad is apt to give a free pass to respectful attachment or premature popularity. Word gets passed around, and to be up-to-date becomes chic; pressure groups grow, and thus schools are formed and become vanguards of their own publicity.

It may seem ultraconservative or even paradoxical to scorn

untested methods or methods that proclaim their effectiveness almost at inception, especially since other methods either have not worked very well or have not been thoroughly tested themselves. But such conservatism is as applicable to psychotherapies as it is to newer methods for treating cancer. Unfortunately, it is much harder to detect nostrums in psychotherapy than it is in cancer therapy.

Mankind has a long history, even a tradition, for searching out a panacea, fountain of wisdom, or absolute authority that will be permanently established and perpetually change life for the better by relieving life of its many ills. I do not fault such aspirations; the alternative is to accept what is and has been as inevitable. This is an ultimate question: Why is there suffering, and what can be done about it? Most ultimate questions come down to facing evil in all its forms.

Another ultimate question is that regarding one's purpose in life—or, as I also term it, the search for significant survival. This, too, takes many forms, including that found among those seeking improvement through psychotherapy. How much are people really prepared to change? Considering the distress that brings them to therapy, presumably most if not all would gladly give up the old, especially if it is inimical to getting along well. But this is not really an obvious conclusion. The familiar is sometimes preferred, painful as it is, to the unknown of potential changes. Therefore, change for the better is welcomed—provided that we are not expected to change very much. The question for an authentic self is always cushioned by acceptability; seeking truth is vague enough to be acceptable, except when it is painful. Thus we negotiate degrees of authenticity by swinging between the vulnerable self and the responsible self until we find a satisfactory amalgam of what is, could be, and what can be tolerated.

I take examples from psychotherapy and psychoanalysis not only because they have been my work for a long time, but because I see the issues that come and go during therapy as miniatures of what goes on in the world at large. How a patient copes with themes in therapy is not much different from how he or she deals with problems elsewhere. Some methods of coping have worked well, but others have been failures; otherwise, the patient would not be there in the first place. Patients who tend to be stoic and unresponsive to emotional events outside usually come into therapy describing their situation in a rather objective, flat, and circumstantial way. If they perceive problems, it is typically someone else's fault—their suspicion, irrationality, or unacceptable attitudes, not their own, except maybe for a thread of self-pity.

Although such reports can be distorted, they do represent a version of what problems exist and are most perplexing. In fact, unless therapy mirrors in diluted form some of the world outside and then encourages (and the implied sense of courage felt inward is correct) straight-on confrontation, it is a hoax, cruel, capricious, and irrelevant.

This does not imply that the ills of society, including the hypocrisies of everyday life and noise from the mean streets, are brought in bulk to the consulting room or onto the analytic couch. More attenuated versions or token examples must be considered. It does mean, however, that therapy is obliged to reflect the human adventure in order to be valid. After all, patients come from their own milieu and culture and return to it, values and expectations intact. But they are also forced to make sense, to look for reasons previously not considered, to question themselves, and to try to deal with distress and demoralization. By helping to make anxiety tolerable, or to make guilt work for rather than destructively against the patient, ways to cope may become stronger. If this is possible, then courage and hope will flourish. The central task is to face the fact of being alive and, just possibly, to discover persistent themes that lend purpose or significance to survival.

The parsimony principle should not be sold short. It keeps us honest and prevents proliferation of the inconsequential. Overly simple explanations of complex situations, however, lead to a kind of arrogance in both patient and doctor, just as in the dogmatic world outside.

Psychodynamic therapy, based on psychoanalysis, does rely on a few basic concepts, such as the reality of a dynamic unconscious, the repetition compulsion, transference expectations, and resistance to change. These are useful principles in helping therapists to understand both others and themselves better, and thus they advance the cause of authenticity. In its relation to the self (which means the inner core of subjectivity), authenticity means to become honestly aware of what is saliently positive or negative in how one reaches out to and is seized by reality. It is not merely, "I am," but "This is how I am, and why I see things this way."

But there is another principle I discovered while talking with cancer patients at various stages of their disease and with different kinds of distress. Though often too afflicted and demoralized to cope adequately with disease or its ramifications, these patients at the very moment of deepest vulnerability demonstrated a startling resiliency. Often it was difficult to tell when vulnerability receded, if indeed it did, and a renewed affirmation of courage and hope ascended. Left to this ambiguous plight, somewhere between the residue of life and the advent of death, I found it difficult to imagine a more existential situation. For example, I recall a man dying of lung cancer, complicated by alcoholism and liver disease, quietly talking with his wife one night in the hospital. There was little to do about his cancer and little left to say to him; he had been rather taciturn and overly factual, anyway. To my surprise, when I approached them the couple were busily discussing their children, showing an interest and affection that had not previously been expressed. They wondered about education, what the children's future would be like, and how to plan in the probable event of his early death. It was as if no limit on their relationship existed; they were simply two concerned parents talking about how best to deal with their children, in place of the turmoil that typified their previous life. Was this resiliency despite vulnerability also a belated case of authenticity, or was it just playacting as if nothing was wrong?

What might be true for certain cancer patients poised on the edge of despair and death might also be true for people threatened not by loss of life, but by diminished self-esteem, alienation, and loss of self-identity. Sickness unto death, or until death, can afflict anyone. The resurgence of resiliency among unlikely prospects reminds us over and over that good copers authenticate themselves with a wellness unto life, despite many kinds of problems.

Seeking a purpose in life or a set of values to depend upon has frequently been called a journey. But this scarcely gives a proper metaphor to the quest for overarching themes amid frustrating, baffling, and hostile events. Something that requires such dedication could be called a pilgrimage, except that a skeptic will have none of it if religion is included. Not all pilgrimages are religious, however, nor are they sanctioned by some authoritarian body. A wholly personal pilgrimage can be practical, though not very rewarding. It is down-to-earth, with no special way of visualizing some distant and exalted goal. This kind of pilgrimage is not so much a journey as a point of view that is set in motion by an inner calling rather than outside pressure.

A skeptical pilgrim, therefore, responds to a double mission. Though refusing a formal credo, he or she becomes a believer of sorts by seeking an ultimate justification for being alive, or more specifically by confronting ultimate questions whose very nature is to have no precise answers. He or she acts on this purpose, yet is an onlooker. Their goals are intentionally practical and short-term, although the larger purpose is couched in mysteries beyond words. Knowing that the heart has its unformed but persuasive reasons, they are also aware that the head, too, has its passions that thrust ahead with instinctual force. One without the other is difficult to imagine; it would make passion pointless and skepticism empty. In fact, I cannot picture an existence of pure reason or, for that matter, of amorphous emotion. Skepticism, properly applied, is a way of dealing with extremes. The loneliness of existence is such that even certainty is itself provisional.

Who are the skeptical pilgrims? They are always with us, knowingly or not, not exactly rebels, but defying stereotypes in their inner life. They speak in the idioms of their disciplines and era. Immersed in the intellectual formats of their times, they stand aside, noting how quickly styles change and how regularly the latter are confused with substance. Though a skeptical pilgrim has no cause to advance, in seeking substance he or she is unwilling to lend themselves to conformity and conventionality.

Courage and hope are among the positive virtues that skeptical pilgrims rely upon, whether in the immediacy of the here and now or in the ultimate questions of life and death. If their discipline happens to be psychotherapy (or its equivalent), they know that most of their colleagues heed only the negative, the pathological faults and fallibilities that get people in trouble long before they become patients. Most therapists ignore what patients do well: Positive virtues are seldom appreciated, and in psychodynamic therapy, what seems to be a positive virtue or accomplishment is regularly thought to be a sign of some unworthy, unconscious vice. By decoding the unconscious, altruism becomes narcissistic aggrandizement, courage is reaction formation against fear, and kindness is a special form of seeking domination.

Good copers hone their skills and strategies to the turf and times they inhabit. Making sense is an obligation that can be developed. Really good copers have a variety of feasible strategies that work well and thus entitle them to positive expectations. By turf and times, I mean the usual cultural and civic influences that slant people this way and not that; the skeptical pilgrim, the good coper, and everyone else are persuaded automatically by whatever is approved or disapproved in the society that they live in. Nevertheless, reality is relative, and so it determines what is and is not a critical issue, regardless of conventional beliefs.

The early promise of psychoanalysis in this century influenced both the culture and vocation of many people. It seemed to combine the rational and irrational in ways that could explain previously mysterious mental phenomena. Conflict, a congeries of wishes, fears, directives, and prohibitions, was construed as creating problems and symptoms that proper interpretation might wash away. Ultimate questions were also interpreted in terms of wishes and fears of father figures and dread of some personal disaster. Alas, this promise became fouled with journeyman dogmatism and sterile disputes that only in more recent times have shown indications of flaking away. And psychoanalysis has not yet recovered from therapeutic disappointment. From its dominant position in psychiatry, and perhaps in literature as well, psychoanalysis is now regarded as simply another powerful current in the river of contemporary thought. It has not solved the deeper problems of society, answered ultimate questions, or illuminated the darkness of human conflict; then again, no one else has.

Despite the output of innumerable experts and deep thinkers, we are still baffled by the enigmas that continue to agonize existence. The politics and economics of evil seem to be stronger than ever. Nevertheless, the healing and the holy professions go on, claiming to tell what is good, how to behave, which values are best, and what to do about various issues that plague us from birth to death and sometimes beyond. Ultimate questions of good and evil, sickness, poverty, war, and other issues, including the value of being alive in the first place, still abide. This is not the age of anxiety, of psychotherapy, or of anything else, and it is flushed by hostility and dread. Moreover, it is the only age we are likely to know. In response, many people in our literate culture have undertaken psychotherapy or some equivalent, seeking relief, release, redemption, and personal acceptability. But like efforts at philanthropy, psychotherapy has a very small voice amid the din of poverty and destruction surrounding us. Nevertheless, the questions it addresses, even implicitly, are the problems of human worth: Who are we, what should we care about, and does it matter?

Going to an expert is not at all a modern invention. In past ages, troubled people also took their problems to some established and sanctioned authority, seeking guidance, explanation, and forgiveness. There have always been experts ready to show why we are wrong and how to do things better, and each has his or her own remedy. Despite our suspension of doubt about experts, though, we are frequently forced to face and formulate problems in ways most congenial to ourselves. Advice surrounds us, and we are bombarded with examples of what to do. For most of the real and poignant problems that afflict us daily, however, we must go it alone, without much help from outsiders.

Moreover, underneath these problems that beg for ready and practical resolution are deeper universal questions that are common denominators of almost everything we do or try to decipher. These metaproblems are tacitly addressed in the course of psychodynamic psychotherapy, and implied by practically every other format within psychotherapy and counseling. Although I am not sure that there is a special format called existential psychotherapy, consideration of metaproblems gives life itself an existential twist (which is what it is supposed to do).

Three metaproblems that concern me are the *search for meaning, maintenance of morale,* and *negotiation with mortality.* They differ from more mundane problems by resistance to inquiry and mutual confrontation by therapist and patient. The existential confrontation also applies to the therapist, who must constantly examine his or her own vulnerability. Healing is bilateral. Therapists always need a better grasp of meaning, morale, and mortality as ultimate questions; if patients come to therapy for healing, the therapist also gets something out of the encounter.

Few therapists would doubt the value of understanding conflict, but many would query the necessity of monitoring personal vulnerability against the background of ultimate questions. I suppose that this is true of almost anyone reflecting upon the course and value of his or her own life. With courage and hope, however, this search can be successful in a provisional way. The mission of self-understanding or enlightenment is simply the cognitive side of freedom, because freedom is the ability to choose between options that facilitate one's search for the responsible self.

I contend that without at least implicit recognition of ultimate questions, psychotherapy would be a bare ritual for collecting fees. Metaproblems are not abstractions or philosophical problems seeking a hearing, but universal tasks. Looking for meaning is an obligation. Supporting and strengthening self-esteem is equivalent to nurturing morale. Ultimately death is not the enemy we seek to vanquish; if it is, then we must fail. But the question of dealing with our mortality in its several manifestations is a task that really matters. Actually, when confronting metaproblems, nowhere are we more nakedly exposed to our fallibility and finitude than when grappling with meaning, morale, and mortality. Perhaps that is why we dislike thinking too much about these ultimate questions.

Although I shall emphasize a more or less existential view, I make no effort to advocate or ally myself with a philosophy called "existentialism." First, I do not believe there is any consensus or body of theory by this name; there is only a heterogeneous group of writers, thinkers, and practitioners of one discipline or another who tend to concentrate on basic problems of human existence. Second, I do not advocate any special theory of mind, believing that practically all have merits and shortcomings. I try to keep my ideas close to the way they arise, namely, free of jargon, schematization, and moralization.

This in my opinion is also the way to do psychotherapy: without muddling things up by intrusive theorizing. In practice, a therapist operates on a fairly low level of theory, but with middle-level information that largely comes from the patient and then is tentatively generalized. The therapist, in order to penetrate ambiguity or self-serving rationality, will mostly ask questions just beyond those that a patient might ask himself or herself. Few patients are so candid as to surrender all efforts at denial, rationalization, self-justification, and adornment with good intentions; it would be pretty self-destructive to paint such a grim picture of themselves. Those patients who do describe themselves as totally at fault are probably more depressed than they realize. A therapist cannot spontaneously enlighten patients, nor uplift them from despondency; he can only help to assess and examine what is wrong and troubles them. This viewpoint is existential enough for my taste because it is both practical and fundamental, and, not least, helpful and hopeful.

Shakespeare's Hamlet took a more or less existential view when he informed Horatio about "more things in heaven and earth ... than are dreamt of in your philosophy" (Act I, Scene 5, line 165). Though being utterly rational is reasonable enough, there is much that defies definition and detection. No truth constitutes the whole of what we live, search, and die for. Science has much to be proud of, but we do not rely very much on scientific findings in running our everyday lives. We live by and with paradoxes, mysteries, metaphors, and unexamined directives of which, by and large, most of us are scarcely conscious.

As a practitioner, I devoutly searched for a more systematic and replicable method in psychoanalysis. I wanted to formulate problems at a higher level of abstraction, and even to measure degrees of conflict and emotionality. But my efforts at quantification only led to a cumbersome and distracting pseudo-objectivity in which I could count only the least relevant of many variables. Data gathering got in the way of a true and personal encounter.

An existential viewpoint, of course, will emphasize the value (indeed, the necessity) of self-searching. It is, moreover, a very practical strategy if the personal encounter yields relevant information. But I cannot (despite ample justification) advocate the bleaker kind of existential opinion that looks on life as a tragic vale of tears and ignores the validity of courage, hope, and authenticity. If such pessimism were warranted, what point would there be in seeking health, or in hanging onto life as we know and feel it as long as possible? I am familiar with the agonies and injustices that drain our existence. But paradoxically, even the skeptic's pilgrimage is fueled and sustained by belief in courage, hope, and authenticity.

No skeptical pilgrim can conscientiously urge any point of view that claims to be absolute. The idea that there is a supervalue that measures and adjudicates every other form of value is an example of an absolute claim. Values such as the ancients claimed—the good, true, and beautiful—would be fine, were it not for much doubt about perfection and scanty methods for defining and detecting what is good, true, and beautiful. Nevertheless, to profess no values whatsoever is a value in itself. Moreover, should such a creature exist who behaved as if he or she were free of values and value judgments, that person would be a robot, not a human who doubts, debates, suffers, and ponders the purpose in living. The robot will not care about agony, injustice, and evil, and would rejoice in nothing.

Personally, I prefer to believe that after creature safety and animal sustenance are secured, healthy autonomy, enlightened skepticism, freedom to choose, rationality that knows its place, and authenticity without arrogance are worthwhile values. To acknowledge that we cannot live without a sense of values is different from imagining a supervalue that would judge all other values. Were a supervalue to exist—and many people do espouse a fixed value judgment, such as white supremacy or death to infidels, that rejects any other viewpoint—such a supervalue would lead to fanaticism that ignores the diversity of humankind.

A supervalue is different from value judgments or deciding what is good or bad. We could not live without making such judgments, and these judgments are not as absolute as sometimes voiced. As a rule, value judgments according to some inner standards are held onto for dear life until (perhaps) the experience, wisdom, and culture of ensuing years wears them away. What replaces the dogmatism and determination of youth is an awareness that the universe is unlikely to be very interested in disclosing its basic truths to us. The fixed stars are not there for our benefit. That something is destined to end in nothingness is mystery no less ineffable than that we came to be in the first place (i.e., that nothing once became something).

We must believe, if only in paradox. If, like the Stoics of old, we venerate rationality, it shows a faith in reason that is firm and convincing only if intuition already approves of it. The true skeptical pilgrim therefore is searching for harmony in opposites, for a common denominator of meaning and purpose, for justification. If this can be grasped wholly, ultimate questions can be addressed. The combination of meaning, morale, and mortality may then validate our passion for living. This signifies that if we are to survive appropriately, then passion and principle must reign in harmony, and that we can at least conjecture about a connection between individuality and the totality of everything else.

Chapter 2

The Enigmas

I was a competent neurologist, and probably a pretty good physician, as well, when I began regular psychiatric training at the Massachusetts General Hospital. At that time, the psychiatric service was headed by its first chief, Stanley Cobb, an eminent neuropsychiatrist and neurologist who had been psychoanalyzed by Hanns Sachs, the first training analyst (who had recently moved to Boston from Berlin). Cobb staunchly believed in the neurological basis of psychiatry, although he acknowledged the ample role of psychodynamics and social psychiatry. Much of his research, however, was devoted to studies of the higher nuclei, tracts, and centers of the brain, where the so-called borderland between psychiatry and neurology was supposed to be located.

This was both a challenging and a very congenial approach. His associates, Jacob Finesinger and Erich Lindemann, also prominent psychiatrists, represented a broad vista in their understanding of neuroses and psychosomatic problems. What was particularly good was the department's eclectic orientation; the psychiatric service specialized in general hospital psychiatry, rather than in the custodial care and storehousing of chronic psychotic patients. We had much contact with other services and with medical professionals.

I had already encountered a good share of hospital patients with neurological problems who also had a variety of emotional symptoms that interfered with their comfortable functioning in the outside world. These disorders included progressive dementia (now generally regarded as Alzheimer's disease), central nervous system syphilis in all its baroque manifestations, seizures, personality problems, psychopathy, and so on. Many of the disorders were just nameless and had no recognized organic substrate according to the diagnostic testing of the day. To some extent, this was not altogether surprising. At an earlier period, I spent a year with Raymond Adams, studying neuropathology and doing a substantial number of autopsies at the Mallory Institute of Pathology in Boston. It was not unusual to examine the brain of someone who had been grossly psychotic, for example, and find nothing that distinguished that brain from any other. This, to be sure, was long before the advent of neurotransmitters and psychotropic medications, but I am not at all convinced that even today, new methods would clearly identify schizophrenic or alcoholic brains from other kinds. Syphilitic lesions could be found in some brains, but as a rule, there was a wide discrepancy between brain lesions and the degree of personality disturbance.

Sickness, Suffering, and Identity

Nevertheless, previous experience did not prepare me for the baffling experience of general hospital psychiatry and the kinds of patients whom I was called upon to see. Part of the drastic change came from being a psychiatrist, at least by title, and experiencing a different attitude in my medical and surgical colleagues. The other part was the result of consulting about patients who had no detectable or relevant physical abnormality to account for their symptoms, which included a high degree of suffering.

Among my medical and surgical colleagues, psychiatrists were always suspect. The latter dealt with problems that were outside of medicine itself; there were few tests and, in effect, little by way of pathology to rely upon. So psychiatrists, with or without previous medical training, were relegated to a position of polite indifference, if not the wariness one might reserve for impostors. The gap between high suffering and low comprehension characterized most of the patients I consulted about and treated. I use the term *treatment* advisedly, because aside from a sedative or two, or an occasional stimulant, it mostly consisted of psychotherapy—a discipline which, to a beginner, was amorphous, vague, and uncertain, despite efforts to impose a systematic approach. There were two large categories of suffering to deal with: One consisted of intractable pain that persisted to the point at which it took over the personality of the patient, whereas the other was simply a predominant symptom (associated with fears, depression, etc.) that interfered with a patient's total ability to cope with the world.

Up until that time, I had automatically assumed that certain kinds of distress were authentic, whereas others were not. Thus a sore throat was painful because the pharynx was inflamed, a spinal tumor caused pain because nerve roots were compressed, and a brain lesion might account for disturbed speech or paralysis; but these visible lesions had no analogue among the suffering I was witnessing. Indeed, the human and very personal cry that meant suffering could hardly be heard amid the barrage of testing that went on in hospitals. The gap between the mental and physical worlds remained exceedingly wide.

Measures of suffering were hard to find, and when estimated by clinicians, suffering was considered equivalent to pain, which was almost entirely subjective. Suffering became a pejorative expression. As a result, absence of lesions and suspicion about anything subjective promoted the idea that any suffering, without an analogue, was suspect and "excessive." Note that the term *excessive* already implies a negative judgment that the amount of suffering is unreal and probably something that the patient could do something about. So-called legitimate suffering might be dealt with and possibly relieved; the other kind was not only unmeasurable but difficult for patients to describe fully. Yet they hardly spoke of anything else. Compared with very sick medical and surgical patients, psychiatric patients suffered much more, with less to justify themselves. Their suffering was hard to pin down, let alone treat well.

For me, it was almost like starting all over again. I had little guidance from textbooks, and only slightly more from teachers. I felt as if my medical training and postgraduate work up to that point were as irrelevant as if I had spent my time studying almost anything else. Previously, there was an easy historical and phenomenological continuum between tradition and here-and-now clinical experience. If unusual things were found, I could look it up, or ask my elders and betters. They usually had an answer, which was often right. Now, although I was expected to know more than I did and to express opinions about a vast variety of events that typified patients' lives, I was perplexed by as well as inexperienced with the human problems that brought these patients to a point of despair.

Gradually I came to realize that it was social custom and protocol that decided how patients should behave, both in hospitals as patients and in the outside community as people. Hospital admission only heightened their despair, because it was equivalent to admitting openly that they could not cope. Furthermore, suffering was clearly an indication of not living harmoniously in the world to which they were supposed to have been accustomed. The schism between the self and the world outside had become unbearable. Moreover, even if the outside world and significant people in it seemed to accept the patient's disability, still the patient frequently tended to blame himself or herself for all their troubles.

It was also common for patients to feel antagonistic and suspicious about their world, and to blame misfortune on other people or on an intolerable situation. Combined with a variety of symptoms (e.g., anxiety, compulsions, depression), such patients were called "neurotic" for no good reason except that their nervous system was supposedly abnormal—although, according to the tenets of the time, nothing was wrong. It was not possible to say, "Of course, anyone would feel the way you do!" Neurotics were outside the elastic limits of normality, and their private suffering prevented much reconciliation with the outside world.

Just as patients with psychoneurosis—a term that simply combines the imponderables—find it difficult to tolerate the difference between their situation and the outside world of so-called normal people, I found it difficult to leave my earlier medical world and set myself up in the new world of psychiatry. People were different. This refers both to patients and to other psychiatrists, who talked a funny language and sometimes acted as if they knew what they were talking about. Psychiatry dealt with the human condition, with afflictions of the spirit and mind; but suffering was seldom addressed. In contrast, the medical world was factual and very pleasant. It had treatments that worked or did not work in a short time. My professional identity as a doctor had been secure. As a psychiatrist, I could scarcely disagree with those who found us strangely alienated from our respectable colleagues.

By becoming one of a loose confederation of clinicians who called themselves psychiatrists, I forfeited some of the prestige and respectability that went with being a physician. Psychiatry dealt with soft data, and those who lived with and among such data were considered just as soft, as well as very peculiar because the entire field was ephemeral, if not phony. Provisional recognition as a real specialist was usually withheld unless the physician gone wrong could find some other form of vindication, such as neurological competence. In the hospital itself, psychiatrists were kidded often, tolerated to a degree, and respected for very little. It was not very consoling to find myself inside, but feeling like an outsider most of the time. Among psychoanalytic colleagues, there was sometimes a curious arrogance that led many to believe that analysis had a secret message or that the analytic method was uniquely privileged by its ability to penetrate depths of unconscious life. This, too, was disconcerting.

Here was a dilemma without resolution: Suffering was incorrigible pain that seemingly took over a patient's personality and made it impossible to cope or thrive in any familiar sense. It both thwarted reality and became equivalent to it. But because there was no physical explanation, most physicians seemed to put the fact of suffering to one side, unless they had personally "suffered" at one time. At the least, I had an identity crisis. This took the shape of a moral dilemma between medical and scientific standards I had come to respect and revere in colleagues and the jargonized postures I sometimes encountered in my newfound psychoanalytic friends. I knew by this time that the suffering I had noted, like pain, was real enough and incapacitating to an ultimate degree. But like any doctor, I also know suffering could not be understood in another person by wholly taking that person's word for it. Phrases such as *mental* (or *emotional*) *disease* were more metaphoric than scientific, resembling the medieval distinctions between intellectual and vegetative souls. Quandaries proliferated. One enigma was followed by others, and very little valid information emerged except what patients told me.

I have already commented about how little psychiatry had to offer beleaguered patients—a little knowledge, medical competence, and wisdom, and if they were lucky, much patience and compassion. This also was a source of confusion, because some distressed patients who happened to unburden themselves and find that there were predominant problems troubling them that had not been suspected also seemed to feel much better. The improvement, coupled with a respectful doctor-patient relationship, continued far beyond the temporary benefits of mere catharsis. Total negativism about psychotherapy was therefore unwarranted. Moreover, this inadvertent outcome of therapy had at least as good a record as many medical treatments for more ordinary complaints.

Another enigma was that many psychiatric patients with physical diseases found that body symptoms were exquisitely sensitive to fluctuations of emotion. Though no specific causes were found, there was no doubt that suffering or "stress" kindled the fire of somatic events. Nevertheless, although these patients had no intellectual deficit, their unruly emotions were blamed on bad heredity, inadequate upbringing, conflicts with significant others, and so on. Disruptions of some sort were taken into account whenever somatic symptoms increased. Frequently, various unconscious feelings were also invoked; this usually meant that a consultant or therapist happened to surmise a great deal that no one else was aware of. It was easy to derive causative conjectures: All that was required was to develop an analogy, connect simultaneous events, or transfer a consequence into a cause. It was also easy, though, to blame patients for feeling as badly as they did, as if they were tacitly negligent about doing something to rectify themselves.

Although some patients failed to cope very well and had many intangible and distressing symptoms, they were often very compassionate, intelligent, and productive people who did constructive things and possessed many virtues. We took this for granted in medical and surgical patients, considering their strong points as irrelevant to the organic disease. Obviously, disease spares no one; good people get sick as often as others. But to some degree, neurotic patients were often thought to be at fault, as if in a mysterious but inexorable way, sickness and misfortune were self-inflicted. This punitive attitude persists, I am afraid. Some members of the healing professions (and certainly a large proportion of the public at large) still consider psychiatric symptoms as something that could easily be shed: Alcoholics need to stop drinking; depressed people should feel more optimistic; phobic patients ought to be determined to face down their fears; and so on. All this simply confirms the truth of an old maxim that the only pain that is intolerable is our own. Someone else's suffering or problems always seem far less significant.

An important distinction must be made between an *impersonal* disease, an *interpersonal* illness, and *intrapersonal* suffering. Many people can share a disease; there is nothing private about a medical diagnosis. Interpersonal illness, which most mental health workers recognize and search for, is whatever interferes with a patient's established place in their accustomed world. A common example is how grief or bereavement disrupts a familiar social field because a significant other has gone, disturbing the equilibrium. Suffering, however, is very private. Who can share a severe case of stage fright, although it is exceedingly common and known not to be fatal? Only a person who stutters knows the agony of not being able to speak or make his or her thoughts known just at the moment when talking is most urgent.

In terms of psychotherapy, symptoms (what a patient complains about) are intrapersonal. Disease is impersonal, because it is a categorical concept. Most interpretations, meanwhile, are about interpersonal difficulties called illnesses. If this distinction between disease, illness, and suffering is firmly considered, then perplexing problems about which factor is causal can be set aside. In Chapter 6, I will use these categories to compare different kinds of subjective and objective meaning. Those meanings in turn can be differentiated and used clinically. For example, cancer is an impersonal disease, but coughing and incessant smoking are interpersonal, because other people are also affected and patients tend to set themselves apart as addicts. Intrapersonal dimensions of sickness and smoking include disability and distress in facing mortality and trying vainly to relieve the pangs of withdrawal.

I have not made much of suffering in psychiatric patients simply because it is often extreme and hard to understand. Suffering is also a state of being that is primarily characterized by loss of meaning and vastly diminished self-esteem. Before psychotropic medication came along and made depression a somewhat impersonal disease, it was a somewhat contagious interpersonal illness. Depressed patients often made people around them depressed, and mental health workers especially tended to suffer diminished confidence, poor self-esteem, and dejection because so little could be done directly. It was not unusual for therapists to condemn as totally ineffectual whatever was done to help a depressed patient; and if depression could not be treated in either patient or doctor or both, then perhaps the whole field was fraudulent, a depressive generalization. Such a drastic condemnation arose both from lack of personal satisfaction and from absence of any compensation for ineffectual efforts. What might under better circumstances have been considered a sign of empathy became a source of intrapersonal suffering and interpersonal contagion. It is difficult to find authentication when efforts are both inadequate and unintelligible, as often is the case with depressed patients who can throw no light on the source of their misfortune.

Professional identity can be a shaky thing, sometimes reflecting itself in personal disrespect and suspicion everywhere. It may spill over into a condescending attitude toward other members of the profession. Disrespect (or even contempt) for one's vocation is an interpersonal illness, somewhat modulated by the impersonal phenomenon of burnout. What it signifies is that meaning is lost for the profession and for oneself; there is no excuse for life and conduct, according to this severe judgment. What it also signifies is a wide gap between disease, illness, and sickness that can be called suffering. The professional is no longer able to differentiate between profession, the vocation, the refractory nature, say, of depression, and shortcomings in himself or herself, as well as in the available means of helping others.

Selfhood: Caught in the Act

The advent of psychotropic medication has made psychiatrists more respectable to the medical community and perhaps more acceptable to themselves. But medication is not an answer to why psychiatrists would penalize themselves for finding exploration of the inner life so frustrating. Whether they can serve two masters—medication and the inner life—is still unanswered. Medication is fine in the right cases, but far from miraculous. Its effectiveness in ameliorating symptoms is not enough to overcome wholly the image of psychiatrist-as-outsider dealing with arcane or intangible matters.

Suffering is surely not a private province of sensitive psychiatrists worried about their image or the validity of the field. It is, by the same thinking, scarcely a personal symptom confined to patients. Suffering is a universal sign of vulnerability in a meaningless and frustrating world that puts demands on people without providing the means to fulfill expectations. The world is quick to banish and punish, using self-blame as retaliation for not doing better. For physicians, suffering without apparent reason undermines their identity.

If suffering is equivalent to a nebulous entity called "mental pain," then mental symptoms (whatever that term means) would be basically organic, because the brain is the organ of the mind. Such symptoms must be treated by organic methods; everything else related to how people feel, think, or conduct themselves would be nonmedical and incidental. Mentalisms and so-called psychic mechanisms are just presumptions without proof.

The organic view is that the mind is a by-product or epiphenomenon of being conscious. The same circular characterization would also be true in describing consciousness. Mental pain, therefore, is a diagnosis of exclusion, not a valid category. Suffering, however, is at least as real as the world itself and carries the authentication of the self experiencing itself. Thus, "mind" is whatever one is mindful of. The self and selfhood are directly experienced, caught in the act. It is a primordial encounter, such that without it, the stream of consciousness would be the dry bed that orthodox medicine treats it as being.

The primordial act of self-experience is how we regard the world, shorn of theory and preconception. It confirms the notion that suffering is not wholly a by-product of an aching body. In fact, self-experience authenticates a style and substance that are imprinted on illness and misfortune. For psychiatry and the inner life, the interpersonal and impersonal dimensions provide a matrix of meaning that goes beyond the elemental event of selfhood and establishes a relation between the inner self and the substance of things outside. Substance applied to the inner life may seem very thin and unsubstantial, but hypotheses and surmises about the mind are very real, too.

I do not wish to rehash ancient arguments and contemporary hypotheses about the mind/brain problem. I do underscore the point that the enigma called suffering, however, as well as much of the instance called sickness, share in catching the self in the act of experiencing its being. From this point, references to interpersonal and impersonal dimensions of disease and social disruption take root. Therapists generally spend much of their vocation in examining different kinds of selfhood. Therapy generally reflects this by efforts to change what is bad or harmful, and substituting what is good or beneficial. But in order to reach that point, meanings are ascribed before judgments about good and bad can be passed. Prior to that, however, being has its own existence in self-perception.

Vulnerability: Being without Meaning

Anyone is vulnerable to almost anything, regardless of status or position in life. We are healthy to the point where we become ill and dependent, and suffering to the degree that freedom is compromised and self-perception falls under a cloud. The reasons why certain people become ill, however, given similarity in their impersonal status, are as elusive as the enigma of suffering itself.

The precious core of empathy or the experience of selfhood gives rise to the proposition that we are all fellow sufferers, without exemption, and deserve each other's compassionate consideration. To do otherwise is to dehumanize. If suffering is sickness without a reason, then our vulnerability (or disposition to fall ill) is being without a meaning. What we believe, along with the kind of activity we specialize in, must remain secondary to comprehending the universality of being vulnerable.

Suppose a hospital staff did not have, as it seems to, an unlimited number of specialists, instead consisting only of cardiologists, orthopedists, or dentists (or perhaps accountants, clergy, or psychiatrists) without other fields being represented. It takes no great imagination to picture how perceptions of patients and concepts of sickness would vary. Each specialty would carry out its tests and examine patients with certain preconceptions in mind. Even the notion of suffering, if it were considered at all, might vary in its interpretation, according to the impersonal or interpersonal dimension. A pain in the chest could mean one thing to a cardiologist, another to an orthopedist, still another to a psychiatrist. Sickness is vulnerability made actual and given a meaning; this meaning is assigned by professionals who assess the difficulty according to their own context of meaning, or in a specialist's own image.

Professionals get paid for what they do and are trained to do. What they do is sanctioned by the society in which they practice. Their specialty, therefore, is given a meaning by society, which confers a certain status on its practitioners. Professionals thus do not practice in a social vacuum, but rather acquire meaning and qualification for doing what they do. I am sure that the practice of psychiatry and psychotherapy varies from one culture to the next, and that its practitioners accordingly are given different privileges and prestige. I would not be surprised if the practice of surgery were also socially determined, quite apart from who cuts whom and for what reasons.

Suffering is far more universal than any specialty would prefer. Religious interpretations of suffering, for example, are certainly apt to vary from psychiatric reasons to more organic postulates. Vulnerability, too, will follow in having different significance despite similarities in disposition to fall ill and to be fallible.

Vulnerability and suffering, which are originally perceptions of painful selfhood caught in the act, are established according to how various professionals describe them and themselves. Hospitals, for example, do not exist simply to take care of sick people, to do research, to teach medical students, or to give jobs to numerous health workers. They exist in order to give a meaning to sickness, a meaning that is validated by professionals practicing some specialty or other within its boundaries. Sickness in this sense can be considered physical, psychological, economic, political, and so on, depending on how the professionals define themselves and are defined (i.e., given a meaning) by the surrounding culture. It is not wholly wrong, from this viewpoint, to conclude that hospitals—like disease—exist in order to further the careers of doctors. But vulnerability, like suffering, would be there regardless of the methods, institutions, and manpower assigned to give it meaning.

As it exists at the present moment, psychotherapy deals with the self in its vulnerability to suffering. Its first task is to assign an appropriate meaning to the patient's state of suffering or vulnerability. Although this is decided by a therapist's training, experience, and familiar theories, the importance of a therapist's own selfhood in this process is far more critical than sponsors of one school of thought/practice or another would permit us to believe. The essential difference between practitioners is a product of their personality differences, strained through the filter of training and indoctrination. This implies that there are just as many methods of psychotherapy as there are psychotherapists, and perhaps even more, because patients differ so much. There is more, for example, to being a psychoanalyst than having a couch and chair and a set of the standard edition of Freud's works. Regardless of who is or is not "orthodox," psychoanalysts differ more than is usually appreciated, despite their relative uniformity in training. I suspect that the other kinds of psychotherapists are much more diffuse and heterogeneous than would be revealed by such designations as "cognitive therapy," "behavior therapy," "reality therapy," and so forth.

The phrase *personality differences*, which carries a slightly academic aroma, can be read as selfhood. I think that selfhood is how people define, package, and comport themselves in the world according to an inner assessment. Thus, in psychotherapy, the selfhood of the therapist reaches out to the selfhood of the patient in an effort to lend meaning. Some thinkers (e.g., Buber) have cast a religious glow over this encounter, but that is the privilege of specialists. Selfhood, in therapy at least, is an enabling experience: It enables the therapist to check on his or her self-perception and measure how this package presents itself in an existential encounter.

There are all too many publications that claim to make people feel or look better and to do something constructive on their own behalf. Self-help books are a contradiction because someone has to write them, thus causing readers to suffer the author's biases. Authors of such books enthusiastically affirm their information and results, which are usually not much less than stupendous.

I imagine that there is a strong demand for healers who minister to people in need or wanting to be better. And I do not minimize this need, because vulnerability is universal and suffering almost as widespread. Not less is the human yearning for someone who understands one's selfhood and its capacity to suffer.

The vulnerable self may not change, or if it does, the change may not be for the better. Clinical standards of what is right or wrong, correct or incorrect, or beneficial or harmful are very elastic, sometimes stretching ethical bounds. Clinical practices seem always to run far ahead of what is sanctioned by scientific consensus. Thus, practitioners are guided more by self-validation than by adherence to any other guideline. Sickness actualizes vulnerability, and healers may exploit the vulnerable self by imposing standards incompatible with freedom to live independently and enjoy the self-evident fullness of being alive. Among psychiatric patients, where self-esteem is impaired, few are confident about coping, and seldom know just what they are called upon to cope with. Selfhood is not, therefore, a very homogeneous pattern of predetermined types of appropriate behavior, but rather a cluster of mutually dissimilar self-attitudes that lead to doubting whether what one does is worth doing. When patients complain of not being themselves, they mean it. It is the self against the self, with one self scarcely recognizing the other.

The healthy self enjoys its existence, in contrast to the vulnerable self, which knows only its suffering and disability. The intact self is familiar with its own field of meaning, whereas the vulnerable self suffers without knowing which meaning, if any, to ascribe. In short, the vulnerable self, lacking authenticity, cannot fathom itself.

Therapists and patients are supposed to work at better self-definition, which in turn is supposed to give more meaning to vulnerability. When, for example, patients come to a therapist, their complaints may differ, but the plight is the same: excess of vulnerability, deficiency of coping capacity, abundance of suffering. The goal is also the same: Restore a sense of control, choice, and harmony. The preemptive problem is incompatible meanings or states of being. It is sometimes conflict between the life actually led and the unlived life of fantasy or illicit relationships. Double lives can exist without shame and secrecy. But whatever tears at the fabric of harmonious self-knowledge breeds self-deception, which cannot cope with vulnerability.

It is a true and innocuous fact that patients, as well as other people coming to an expert or authority of their choice, want desperately to feel better about themselves. They want to feel good in the sense of enjoyment, as well as in a moral sense, that what they do is worth doing and is approved by someone or something. Regardless of how nonconformist anyone takes himself or herself to be—and few consider themselves typical—there is some set of standards that justifies whatever beliefs and behavior they stand for. Psychotherapists, no less than politicians, are yoked to this demand. Self-judgment is an occupational requirement, which means that self-experience somehow conforms to the beliefs held most sacred.

Therapists are not usually rogues or rascals, but neither are they paragons of virtue or authenticity. They are never flawless and should not be strangers to adversity. Although society and individual patients have high expectations of therapists, even when the field is mocked, therapists must maintain comparative equilibrium, seldom deploring their own shortcomings. A therapist of quality, of course, knows that external poise and seeming authority can be deceptive, but nevertheless, heavy expectations can be balanced by self-knowledge of limitations and efforts to be better. Maintaining distance between self-knowledge and whatever the profession calls for or expects is not hypocritical. Maintaining just the right distance is possible, and when done effectively is equivalent to that virtue called maturity.

Self-recognition can be shocking, but it still must be checked by cultivating a tolerant perspective. Tolerance does not, of course, mean indifference; authenticity is still a goal. The capacity to suffer is not a virtue, only a human trait. Keeping an eye on vulnerability and potential misfortunes is an obligation that should not be confused with self-sufficiency, nor pushed to the point of pride in loneliness. It is wholly possible to become wrapped up in someone else's suffering and to acquire a kind of self-congratulatory glow as a result. It is also self-deception because no one, to my knowledge (which may be faulty), suffers in place of another. Rather, it is self-awareness of how tentative health or well-being must be, how contingent existence certainly is. Therapists, whom I identify as fellow sufferers needing and wanting to feel better about themselves, need to send out tracers for information about other people and to be alert for signals coming back. This is ordinarily called responsiveness. Mild depression, for example, can be turned into something useful, despite inner discomfort. Minor fluctuations in mood are not preambles to a catastrophe, and optimism is not an inverted signal of something dire about to happen. We would be less than human if we were not vulnerable and adrift in the search for meaning. But suffering is best dealt with when kept at a distance, using whatever insight and tolerance can be mustered to cope with the distress it signifies.

Two Kinds of Vulnerability

The importance of distance is simply to focus perspective and keep suffering from becoming too much a part of inner life. Self-monitoring helps do both of these things. Distance allows us to recognize that there are two kinds of vulnerability. The first is *actual* vulnerability, which is distress undergone right now. It indicates a painful emotion that is not clearly understood. The emotion's significance is vague because it has become a part of inner life, and threatens much more. As a result, actual suffering is usually found attached to hopelessness, as if it will continue indefinitely (because pain has no time sense). It is negative expectation that casts a dark shadow across the future. In fact, if only here-and-now actual distress could be separated from an ongoing propensity to expect no relief, then such suffering becomes more tolerable by acquiring a meaning. It is, after all, expectation of unceasing pain that makes going to hell so uninviting. One should even be wary of eternal bliss. Patients who are informed about what pain to expect, how long it will approximately last, and what means are available to mitigate pain actually do better, and require less medication, than patients who are not so prepared and do not keep suffering at a distance.

The other kind of vulnerability is *potential*, which constitutes a threat of suffering in a very singular way. Though patients are somewhat protected from actual vulnerability when told what to expect, potential vulnerability is clad in horrendous fantasies of intolerable distress. "Wait till your father comes home!" was a threat that presumably made unruly children quake in former times. The promise of punishment in the future hurts to the degree that a person feels unable to tolerate the expectation of pain, which often hurts more than the reality.

People who are inclined to be depressed do not regularly get angry; they blame themselves too much and fear their own guilt. So they commonly suppress an angry response, choosing to withdraw into wounded solitude. As a result, mildly depressed people are geared to the sadness of the world and suspect that altruism, for instance, is only a bribe for protecting self-interest. Potential vulnerability is also found among those who are clearly suspicious of other people's motives and, in pronounced cases, open to being called paranoid. As a rule, a paranoid disposition reflects vulnerability to rebuff, deceit, lying, cheating, or hypocrisy, usually from someone presumably trusted. The phrase *leaving oneself open* means open to a variety of insults or attacks, which adds up to a forecast of even more trouble to come. Paranoid people typically mimic strength imagined in others in order to cover up vulnerability, and to pretend more control than is truly there.

An excess of vulnerability usually means impaired self-esteem and negative self-judgment; as a result, its victims often get the worst of every deal or decision. The unquestioned statistic that there are many more victims in the world than victimizers (plentiful though they are) suggests that vulnerability is universal, and probably a leading characteristic of humankind despite pretensions and rationalizations.

One of the ultimate questions for and about mankind is to ask why there is suffering at all. How it is that the innocent or harmless person is so often made an arbitrary victim. Death or injury of so-called innocent bystanders is almost a daily occurrence. Children who perish in a school bus accident are another example that makes even the hardened skeptic wonder. Actual vulnerability is bound to be meaningless, but how can potential vulnerability, the propensity to suffer in special ways, be explained?

At another extreme, those who feel unreasonable guilt—though neither clear victims nor victimizers—suffer from absence of meaning, except that in some intangible way they seem to have violated a moral precept (often unspecified) or found themselves falling short of what is expected. If this is all that guilt signifies, however, then the guilty person really suffers from poverty of meaning, and therefore of the capacity to use guilt constructively and do something about it. To wallow in guilt or feel compressed by fears of disclosure is not coping, but rather experiencing the agony of self-rebuke. A very common observation is that those inclined to feel guilt for no apparent reason tend to withdraw so as to reduce exposure. Consequently, it is conceivable that very virtuous, even saintly people might refrain from situations that expose them to temptation, guilt, or rebuke. Over time, such restraint can become a positive character trait, even an embodiment of virtue and an example for others to follow.

To be conscious of potential vulnerability is typical of many people with so-called psychiatric difficulties, but it can also be a characteristic way of viewing the world and the sufferings of people. If sensitivity to potential vulnerability is kept at a distance, withdrawal and isolation are not always a regular outcome. It may be a position from which much good can come. Not all philanthropists are rich; many people are inconspicuous benefactors to others, with and without gifts of worldly material. A generous person might not give away all his or her goods and assets just because he or she realizes the abundance of poverty. But an early inclination to save up against potential vulnerability to starvation may gradually transform itself into a lifelong habit of helping unfortunate people. Such vulnerability becomes its own spur to action, justifying personal reasons for being.

Nevertheless, the vulnerable self is usually on the defensive against its proclivities to share misfortune. It is too busy dealing with problems that test, threaten, and terrify. Vigilance is in all directions; near misses are reminders of tragedies that can happen to anyone. Accidents that do not occur are just as threatening as the disease we might get. If potential vulnerability is magnified and brought closer, it takes over. In practical terms of what to do about anything, insistent concerns and potential disasters bombard the individual so much that the future is clouded with hopelessness.

Negative expectations on all occasions imply awareness of not being able to cope effectively with misfortunes or problems that do not occur. This indicates a split reminiscent of the enigmatic discrepancy found among psychiatric patients who lack a convincing reason for their suffering. Though perhaps pessimism is always justified to some extent, incapacity to cope might be true of some problems, but surely not all, and not at all true for those problems that have not happened except in the imagination. If we imagine problems too great to handle or suffering too severe to endure, then potential vulnerability has become actual suffering in the here and now. A common example is that of anticipatory grief, the suffering undergone by a potential survivor whose significant other has not yet died. Sometimes the shock of anticipation carries a conviction that the loss of a loved person will inflict a wound that will never heal. The potential survivor imagines only calamity, not the capacity to cope and to discover significant meaning in the future. In contrast, good copers who are in the position of anticipatory mourning are able to fractionate distress into a series of separate problems that can be dealt with individually, and they do not collapse into the perception of a hopeless life in a loveless world. It is the "what if" that is perilous, because it reflects potential suffering and is always amorphous. Besides, "what if" also quakes before a number of outcomes that are improbable and unlikely to happen.

The vulnerable self will always suffer as much from intangibility and ambiguity as from anxiety and ambivalence. One of its most reliable supports is to have a number of identifiable meanings available in order to render potential vulnerability into a series of problems that can be coped with. An anticipation of future disaster might be very real, but sometimes it signifies just a propensity for self-rebuke and punishment for unspecified misdeeds. In the world of practical, everyday risks (real and imagined), however, the chief antidote for vulnerability is the virtue called *courage*, which is not only a boon for the faint at heart but a necessity in facing uncertainty about coping well or in tolerating shortcomings.

How Does "Making Sense" Make Sense?

I soon found out that the best way to tolerate my anxiety about becoming a competent psychiatrist was to make sense out of what my patients reported. By careful surmise and ascribed meanings, I could add to my understanding of ways in which people suffer in order to relieve their (and my) distress. *Suffering*, perhaps, was too dramatic and intense a term to characterize most patients, but it clearly indicated the direction that their vulnerability took. Though my insight seldom played more than a minor role in helping a patient, it certainly benefitted me in trying to cope and achieve an optimal distance, which I soon learned was equivalent to "professional objectivity."

It is easy to talk about "making sense" of what patients discuss. But it is also very difficult when patients come in with baffling complaints that just seem to hang there, without a context to cling to. Questioning yielded very little information, so that the fledgling psychiatrist found himself somewhat impatient and perplexed. As a result I conjectured to myself, because I had not yet learned to wait for that optimal distance—between needing a microscope or a telescope—where a clean pair of spectacles, coupled with common sense, might do. In the absence of reliable information, my conjectures (even those called hypotheses) were at best enlightened nonsense.

Most patients suffered from low self-esteem, negative expectations, and so forth, but were not inclined to offer much that would explain what their vulnerability signified: There were recollections, criticisms and excuses, ambivalent feelings toward people close to them, and memories out of context. Making sense is not always identical with accuracy. But in some fashion, symptoms themselves (e.g., irrational fears and irresistible compulsions) are methods for dealing with conflicts and regaining some control and resiliency. Part of my training in those days, therefore, was to tolerate fallibility and to dispense with the urge to understand everything simultaneously.

What does making sense really mean? It is surely not the same as having insight, which means to understand accurately some hidden key to conflict. Psychodynamic psychiatry puts a high value on such insight, to the exclusion of almost everything else. In this precious sense, having insight is something like having perfect pitch, or such delicate perception that it is found only among people with a divine gift. For example, I found that interpretations proposed by more seasoned psychiatrists were challenged far less; this could be attributed to respect for experienced guesswork. But insight and just making sense, right or wrong, are different. Making sense is down-to-earth, and its major function is to endow ordinary experience with a general context of meaning. Insight is a far more sophisticated concept, applying to a specific context.

Making sense is such a primitive experience that it cannot be confined to what psychiatrists do, or whatever other professionals do in trying to convey information to another person. Furthermore, even now I cannot make much sense out of many heady abstractions, couched in terribly learned terminology, that are offered as clarifying explanations. What is needed is an attachment to life as I live it, either actually or potentially. Jargon makes no sense unless it has this attachment to an already existing body of knowledge or experience (in which case it becomes technical language that the initiated understand). The fact that many people sometimes mistake jargon and abstractions for profound observations is, I suppose, the reason it exists in the first place. Technical language is jargon until the context of meaning begins to make sense. In psychotherapy, technical language is apt to mean something, but until a patient is ready for it, the concepts it is supposed to convey are better left unsaid.

Making sense, therefore, is about listening and learning. What is said and observed may sound like nonsense at first, but it still, with time, constitutes a point of reference, a context in which other seemingly extraneous bits of intelligence take root. For example, the language of computers and information theory is incomprehensible to me. Therefore, computers make sense for me only in a very limited context, very far from their wide applications in science, astronomy, economics, and other areas. In dealing with some patients, I am just as baffled by what they say and complain about. If I were to conclude that they make no sense whatsoever, this would be equivalent to saying that they are crazy.

Learning consists of listening and, perhaps, asking intelligent and relevant questions before putting a jargonized terminology in its place. Making sense has to impinge upon my life, just as it must on yours. Otherwise, experience can have no meaning; both my life and yours will dangle aimlessly somewhere among unattached relevance and words without context. Making sense makes sense because it attaches something not understood to a body of information that I already have at least a primitive grasp of and need for. Making sense, therefore, means that something baffling is disclosed to me and makes a difference in what I subsequently do or think about.

Primitive experience that makes sense need not be very elaborate or sophisticated. If I bump my head, it is a brief shock, without much meaning except to say "ouch" and caution myself to be more careful. The immediacy is like getting wet or feeling warm, except that I localize the experience and feel annoyed about it. It precedes any other sentiment, such as "I really must do something about that shelf" or "Am I bleeding?" Making sense requires nothing further, although without further reflection, bumping my head would not lead to fixing the offending shelf. I propose that, elemental and mundane though such an experience is, this is how we begin thinking about the world and the foibles of its people. I must hasten to add, however, what should be obvious: Neither head bumping nor anything else occurs to a wholly innocent and uneducated person. There are already many contexts and meanings, simple and not organized well, that are ready to rush to the point of experience, just as white and red blood cells rush to a point of injury.

Most experiences are far more complicated than head bumps. There are many ways to feel suffering, or experience vulnerability, without making much sense of it at first. Making sense in a primitive way is almost reflexive; without much pondering, the reaction results in assigning clusters of meaning that usually deal with the future. Pessimism is an example of a primitive response to the world that has not yet arrived.

There are common examples of not making sense that nevertheless do not result in noticeably increased vulnerability or suffering. Politicians often make no sense in their public statements, and yet manage to get people's vote through appeals to emotion. Facts and previous behavior seem to make little difference in how the electorate votes. But this is not the same kind of nonsense that the primitive experience of making sense is supposed to counteract. I may not agree with what a politician says or does, but I know that he or she is speaking and is running for office. I may be bewildered by his or her thoughts, but they have some reference to my life as I live it. Conversely, those who are persuaded by his or her words respond because these emotional appeals tap into entrenched and established beliefs (i.e., context of meaning).

We are moved by passion far more often than by quiet reason. Although we commonly say that passion sways judgment, it is not correct to claim that passion makes no sense. To the degree that passion makes sense it does not cause suffering, unless followed by a stupid or heinous action. We may feel potentially vulnerable as a result of political disagreement, but only because a politician's message scares us into thinking what might happen were he or she elected.

Existentialists sometimes seem to be fond of such orotund phrases as "Ultimate Groundwork of Existence." One could find other examples of pompous phraseology in almost any other field. Does the phrase make sense, and if so, for whom? What kinds of action are apt to be taken? In the first place, capitalizing words unnecessarily suggests that the writer wants to identify something very profound and irreducible without any further explanation: Truth, Reality, the Unconscious, Tyranny, Faith, Deity, and so on. Many people talk as if their words are capitalized, like a call to arms or a waving flag that everyone is supposed to understand immediately. It is an *immediate appeal* that reflexively makes sense, with only a very thin shell of meaning. The meaning is basically a demand for belief. A phrase such as the "Ultimate Groundwork of Existence" is supposed to engage belief by making sense with an emotional punch. What it signifies is that it refers to nothing specific, but it is supposed to be the reference that other things refer to.

Making sense in the here and now does not necessarily mean making sense in a rational sense of careful definition and discrimination. I can, for example, read an article about art criticism that seems to be a series of murky and unrelated words. (Perhaps some reader of this book will feel the same way.) But I know that it is an article and that some expert who presumably knows a great deal about art wrote it. Even so, the article goes nowhere for me because I cannot take action on any of its ideas; they make no sense. The key question is, what difference does it make, especially to and about my life?

The ostensible difference is a practical matter. It is a springboard for elaboration of more precise and far-reaching meanings that may come in handy later on. I suppose that going from a very primitive experience of making sense to a cluster of more general ideas is what is meant by "thinking": We go from small nuclei of coherent meanings to larger abstractions that can be symbolized to make sense of many sorts of events and experiences. This simple notion is relevant and as true in the daily practice of psychotherapy as it is in trying to understand difficult notions that seem not to connect at all with ordinary life, such as $E = MC^2$.

It makes no sense to utter a skein of words such as *ultimate groundwork of existence* or *a priori transcendental synthetic unity of apperception* unless there is also a demonstrable connection to our backyard of practical meaning. A doctor first looks for where it hurts, connecting a location with our subjective state of pain, then tries to establish a relevant connection between this pain in a certain place and his or her preexisting body of information. Similarly, a psychotherapist also looks for where it hurts, as well as when it began to hurt, but calls it a point of suffering. Then he or she tries to uncover relevant problems (or, rather, meanings that paradoxically stand together) and show how this constitutes a problematic conflict. In both cases, the doctor and the therapist try to make sense in a way that makes a difference. As a rule, it is something out of the ordinary; call it a paradox, because the expected and unexpected exist together.

Suppose a patient comes to a therapist complaining of grief following the death of a close relative or spouse. This is a problem, not a paradox. The therapist will look for a conflict within the problem that seems to perpetuate the acute mourning. But suppose the patient is mourning for a near stranger, or someone in the public eye whom he or she has never met. I once had a patient who went through his mother's demise with scarcely a pause, never shedding a single tear and expressing no nostalgic recollections of what good or evil she represented during his life. I knew from our previous discussions that she had been neurasthenic, but that she was often very generous and seemed to be truly devoted to her family. Several months later, a prominent statesman died; my patient (who had never met the man) sobbed, lost his appetite for a while, slept poorly, and showed most of the common signs of acute grief.

Although it would not be enormously relevant to examine each of the possible hypotheses derived from this paradox, we would have to look into the likelihood that the well-known stranger mattered more to my patient than did his mother. Although absence of grief is not unusual, even for one's mother, it usually reflects absence of involvement in current life, or a death that entails so much negative baggage from earlier days that indifference is the result. Only the first was true for my patient, who retained a distant feeling for his mother akin to what one might feel for a favorite teacher from childhood. But my patient had read the statesman's books, listened to his speeches, and regarded this man as the kind of leader he himself might have been had his career taken a different turn. The fact that my patient was a businessman did not change the way in which he viewed the dead politician as a brother in spirit, a classic example of mourning the unled life. Had the statesman really been a completely unknown stranger, I would have to consider that mourning for him might have represented another death that was itself still unmourned.

Psychotherapy deals more than it realizes with making sense out of "perhaps"—the various possibilities that are never consummated, the contingencies that limit existence to the way it is rather than the way it might have been, and the crises that do not occur. All of these amount to a "what if" applied to understanding paradoxes and enigmas. What a psychotherapist looks for between the expected and unexpected is the common denominator that itself makes sense. Although common belief and practice hold that only kinfolk can legitimately be mourned for, life as lived clearly demonstrates that sometimes family members are less likely to be mourned (because there is more ambivalence) than a comparative stranger for whom there is much admiration and identification. A companion animal is often grieved for more than a remote relative or a sibling who has played little part in current life.

All these observations, I trust, will make sense because they evoke a bond of emotion attached to strong and persuasive beliefs already held. Although some psychoanalysts have been known to search for "exact interpretations" that make more than sense, it is illusory to expect exactitude in a field so diffuse and complex, and so interlaced with imprecise emotions. Real people do not feel or act with precision, and whatever makes sense and seems worth acting on is strongly dependent on unspecified conditions. Making sense is therefore approximate, not exact, and hardly subject to more than metaphorical understanding. Looking for a common denominator is a search into the hypothetical "perhaps." The enigmas in psychotherapy should not be confused with coming upon a secret combination that will open a locked safe and disclose a hidden treasure.

Not everything can be expected to make sense in the ways I have described. Not everything that patients talk about can be put into perspective; there are many episodes and observations that have no connection with suffering or life as it is lived. It is the enigma or paradox, however, that astonishes and demands attention. There is always an exception that refutes a general law, and there are hardly any—if any—universal laws in psychiatry or psychodynamics. Nevertheless, it is the exception that evokes a rule and elicits the broader understanding that therapists look for. When this understanding occurs, it is miles beyond primitive making sense; viewed comprehensively, it is like a pilgrimage that gathers meaning among diverse events. It is finally consummated by realizing a personal significance that endows life with value.

Three Virtues: Experience, Culture, and Wisdom

I have supposed that psychotherapy depends on life as lived. It has little to do with life as read about, or as conjured up in the imagination, except that the unled life may be a source of creativity, discontent, or still another view of contingency (i.e., "what if" or "perhaps"). Subjectivity uses the self to understand, and when we use personal reflection to understand, we are being subjective. Hence, whatever has meaning or makes sense has a meaning for me and is about me. This is a starting point that hardly ever is relinquished. Otherwise, I would be professing an objectivity about a non-me that could not exist. Except by specific denial or negation, I am caught within myself and what is mine. I need only note that in the case of scientific research, which is supposed to be wholly objective, subjectivity and self-interest are seldom absent and are just as seldom acknowledged.

In psychotherapy, which is far away from detached scientific research, you and I observe ourselves in action, as we are and as we would like to be. Part of the struggle is for veracity and away from deception or denial in all their forms. Honesty may be the best policy because it is so seldom used; other policies are easier to follow. Let us frankly acknowledge that it is hard to challenge what we strongly believe. In fact, any statement to the contrary must be viewed with suspicion. ("I am totally without prejudice," one man said complacently. "I don't even notice what color a man is when I meet him!" he added, without being asked.)

How we view the world and people in it depends on how we view ourselves—our motives, our experiences, and so on. Nevertheless, what is me and mine is not a wholly fixed position supported by a cluster of preconceptions, principles, and possessions. We automatically take a stand, embodying the spirit of relativism through a lens that seems standard and well calibrated only because we are used to it. Our beliefs spontaneously and selectively fluctuate in order to maintain themselves, much as a gyroscope spins to keep a steady course.

There are people who, by appointment, inspiration, or veneration, seem to have a wide latitude in how they evaluate what things really mean and which are worth paying attention to, or even living by. They are acknowledged to understand the world or some fraction within it; they are familiar with the conflicts and puzzlements that plague the rest of humanity. Perhaps they are our teachers, sages, gurus of different types, or delegated authorities who go beyond the narrower confines of their original specialty. These people are so esteemed because they possess the virtues of *experience, culture,* and *wisdom.* Whether endorsed by hordes of devout followers or simply admired as an unapproachable symbol, they stand above the crowd, sometimes as an honored elder, at other times merely as a prestigious personage.

I do not pretend that every prestigious person earns a reputation as an outstanding expert because of his or her own experience, culture, and wisdom. For example, being very rich and philanthropic will make anyone an expert on just about anything if he or she chooses to make a colossal contribution to a college. As a rule, however, educated and admired elders in a society are endowed with virtues that qualify them to speak in generalities and with much conviction. In addition to living a long time (so that their mistakes have been forgotten), these ancients represent traditional values in exemplary ways. They are peculiarly qualified and given the power to make pronouncements about their society, its problems, its history, and the reason why it is superior to all other societies.

Experience, culture, and wisdom are three well-known virtues that make sense of events and endow them with much significance. Sometimes, the society confers culture upon individuals because they represent the most honorific beliefs and creeds. I refer not to the appointed personage who simply holds a prominent office, or a celebrity in the public eye. Those who hold a special importance because of experience, culture, and wisdom get that way through their own merit and age. The three virtues are not unrelated, but they are by no means equivalent to one another.

Experience does not always mean that one has stayed long at a job and become an established expert at a single task. Besides, *experienced* may just be how we describe someone who makes the same mistake over and over but outlasts contemporaries; such a person will simply claim that the old ways are best. Experience usually means that a person has a skill amounting to a high value in the society. He or she has been tested under various challenging circumstances, so that what seem to be new problems for others may actually be quite old issues for him or her. More than having skill, however, experience means that the elder has thought about many other things for a long time and even has answers for some serious questions. In addition to having expertise about his or her own life-as-lived, they are given the right to comment on what you and I do.

But experience is not always a greater teacher, although we learn more effectively when we make our own mistakes. Seasoned veterans are not all experts, but it is hard to become an expert without faltering and then courageously persisting. Experience is not like a high appointive office that automatically brings high value to the person. It is a virtue that can be cultivated, but only through personal merit.

It is harder to pin down the concept of culture, just about as hard as defining art or beauty. As an approximation, however, a cultured individual has wide familiarity with the esteemed symbols of society, usually through broad education, and by cultivation of good manners as well. It is difficult to imagine a cultured person who is also a boor, although there are many learned boors who are highly experienced at what they do. In our society, skill at a valued job for a long time may mean experience, but not culture. It is also required that the cultured elder be fully familiar (or at least give that impression) with the arts, literature, and other artifacts or symbols of society at its best. A cultured and experienced expert gets promoted to that high station by seeming to know the most significant values for society.

A cultured individual need not be very skillful at anything, except perhaps in persuading people of his or her worth. In fact, having a skill, while important to experience, is not essential to culture. For example, a trained actor will become quite familiar with Shakespeare, Chekhov, and Stanislavsky, but he may not work regularly as an actor; unemployment is an occupational hazard. Sooner or later this actor gives up and, without using the hard-won skill, does something else. Nevertheless, he will still have deep knowledge of the theater, and perhaps of literature as well. He goes from limited acting experience (despite training) to culture by not using his skills. In a general sense, whatever is no longer useful remains as culture. Physicians of an age at which they no longer practice and do not keep up with current information still may deserve respect and regard, if only because they represent medicine at its best, not because their knowledge is obsolete. If prestigious enough, their medical culture is itself a merit.

Society honors many virtues, though of course it may not practice any of them very seriously. Of all honors, however, wisdom is almost always near the top. Caesar was a great general, but Socrates was the sage for the ages. Those whom people turn to in times of trouble are those reputed to be wise. It is curious that the sage may be neither skillful nor cultured. But he or she should have the attention of petitioners because of a reputation for understanding the foibles and peculiarities of mankind and knowing what kinds of questions seem ultimate. The true sage, in other words, will appreciate the ultimate in most problems, and he or she knows how people try to answer ultimate questions.

Granted, there are young sages and old fools. But experience, culture, and wisdom are virtues that burnish themselves with time. Moreover, with the passage of time, these virtues become better understood as *values* (i.e., criteria used to form judgments as to whether something is good or bad, etc.). Perhaps experience, culture, and wisdom are values that do not automatically diminish and that even may be distinctive to old age. If so, then wisdom may flourish while skills become stale and culture questionable.

Those who have all three virtues in abundance, however, may simply exemplify the obvious and the conventional. Psychotherapists can acquire a reputation in proportion to their longevity. I could praise the praiseworthy, celebrate celebrity, and otherwise follow the crowd in more ways than I like to admit. One of these ways is to regard certain well-known authorities as well-qualified, experienced, and as people apart from their profession, cultured and wise. This could be a mistake, and often is.

Appearances are often confused with substance, and what seems to be a combination of experience, culture, and wisdom may only be a certain age, somber bearing, facility with words, and penchant for uttering obscure and self-evident platitudes. Moreover, this combination of style and some substance goes a long way. Patients will frequently go to therapists because they are looking for just such a person. Merely believing in this embodiment of talent and virtue can be enough to make patients feel better able to cope.

The therapist has served as an example of excellence that fits into expectations. Admittedly therapists, just like other professionals, must be better than competent to be held up to admiration and acquiescence, and of course, no therapist matches up to this bigger than life idealization. It is an enormous burden to know so much, predict the future, and unerringly tell right from wrong; how to tell the authentic from the fictitious is an ultimate question. But because prospective patients are not likely to be referred to someone because of the latter's reputation for knowing ultimate questions, the synthesis of experience, culture, and wisdom—combined with the competence it implies—is a useful guide. Experience is necessary because a professional has to be very good at his or her job. Culture is important not only because a narrow intelligence applied to a profession or job is likely to indicate a narrow person, but because it implies better communication through flexibility and familiarity with various symbols and other cultures. Wisdom has to be its own justification. Someone who knows how variable human nature is, how arbitrary most standards are, how resilient people can be if given a chance, and yet how far a little help goes is probably quite wise.

The enigmas still cluster around suffering. Though we are bonded to the existence we have, it is difficult to know if we have any lasting significance, and whether what we strive for is worthwhile. Nevertheless, knowing the power of self-deception, the preponderance of style over substance, and the seductive lure of pride, skeptics are understandably wary of glib answers to ultimate questions. At the very least, experience, culture, and wisdom make sense by maintaining a perspective about ultimate questions. Absolutes are not to be trusted absolutely; permanence is but one transient phase in the long flux of emotions.

Although I began this chapter citing my early contact with the enigmas facing a young psychiatrist, I believe that maturation is very possible, and that primarily clinical puzzles are likely to change to ultimate questions that disclose our principles. Few problems are ever solved once and for all; if they are, then the next generation will have no knowledge about them or will routinely meet such problems in another form. Nevertheless, along with other professions, psychiatry's purpose is to contain vulnerability and give some meaning to suffering. Relief may be more effective than resolution, and a temporary solution is often good enough.

The mightiest monuments to mankind's glory are potential rubble. By keeping this in mind, it seems true that the authentic self, emerging for a time over the vulnerable self, must be dedicated to unraveling enigmas and finding what makes the most sense. The intelligent pilgrim will not find more than an uncertain quest. In keeping with the theme of compromise and perspective, the pilgrim must be reconciled to seeking vindication for past mistakes, when he or she did not cope well enough or failed in accordance with the best she or he was capable of. But because total victory over an opponent is seldom achieved, vindication is almost as good. Realizing this, even a skeptical pilgrim will find a certain selfless significance.

Chapter 3

The Skeptical Pilgrim

An Uncertain Pilgrimage

Experience, culture, and wisdom are supposed to endow certain extraordinarily mature people with the capacity to make sense out of problems and explain the complexities surrounding us. But because problems tend to persist—or at least transform themselves—regardless of various ingenious methods of dealing with them, there is always a demand for experts and sages who devise answers both for ordinary problems and ultimate questions. Among these answers sought are a reason for suffering, for the prevalence of evil, and for most of the things that beggar existence and belittle people who are merely trying to survive.

As an ordinary mortal steeped in wondering about what is and should be normal, I cannot imagine a world in which ordinary problems and ultimate questions have been dealt with conclusively. My imagination falls short of picturing a day of redemption, the arrival of a bona fide messiah, the dawn of reason on earth, or even a pill that will permanently inspire, tranquilize, or otherwise enchant the business of being alive. Utopian dreams of enhancing existence are implausible because the task of deciphering and ascribing meaning to what people do and stand for in the name of normality stretches out over eternity. Consequently, the job of neutralizing vulnerability requires that we look for something far more proximate than the promises implied by sages of all persuasions.

It is not always necessary to be a sage or some other kind of expert; vendors who offer respite and resolution for the rest of us are always available. Many professions seek to normalize suffering, if not abolish it altogether. And psychiatry is no less puzzled in facing ultimate questions and ordinary problems than other cerebral professions. The quandary, in one form or another, is how ordinary people should and do manage to deal with the ultimate questions that periodically make their presence manifest.

Amid the unlimited variety of people that pass by us every day, let alone the heterogeneity of mankind in its entirety, it is too much to conjure up a single prototype hero who might illuminate human nature and discover some unequivocal purpose for being alive. I can, however, picture a kind of antithesis to this unlikely hero. He is not an unfeeling brute, insensitive to the agonies of existence. Rather, he is a fellow who ponders ultimate questions but comes up with no answers. He regularly searches and finds a flaw in so-called explanations that are proposed. These flaws reduce such explanations not merely to bad theories, but to fanciful speculations. He is both a *skeptic* and a *pilgrim*, with all the uncertainty that goes with each.

The skeptical pilgrim finds that his journey is uncertain because it has no destination. Not being the usual pilgrim, who follows a leader for a lofty cause, he is a career outsider, looking for ways to harmonize opposites just as intently as he searches for exceptions to established truths. Most of the harmony and resolution is sought in his own nature, where vulnerability exists side by side with resiliency. And although I call him a skeptical pilgrim, he rejects every effort to call him anything. He refuses to be categorized, preferring a rather misty individuality that he cannot describe at all.

Evil and suffering are rampant. They make so little sense that the pilgrim cannot help rejecting the nostrums of piety or of quiet opposition to the experts. He has, however, good reason to doubt his skepticism, too. A true cynic knows that even cynicism will let you down. A true skeptic is never sure; he is willing to be convinced, but cannot believe that to seek is to find. What would he find? How could it be recognized? What is he looking for? If he found it, what would he do with it? By this time, his analytic efforts end in unfinished inquiry. His search is not just for what is reasonable and makes sense, but for what in the long run should establish some purpose, stability, and clarification.

A true skeptic knows, too, that searching for a purpose risks ending up with a plausible myth, a virtual reality that he is comfortable with and accepts. A true pilgrim accepts what he is told; unlike the skeptic, he is not worried about finding a lock without a key. Perhaps after all, the skeptic ruminates, life *is* a joke without a punch line. Maybe suffering is a collection of punch lines without a joke, or a joke that is on us.

Always an outsider, the skeptical pilgrim is not in flight from this generation, because he is entangled in its culture and idioms anyway. But he is wary of the hot issues that bedevil his generation and stands aside, afraid of getting burned. Not an activist, he seeks the coolness of quiet contemplation and the privacy of solitude. For him, virtues such as experience, culture, and wisdom are pleasant enough, and may even be reasonable enough. But experience could simply be making the same mistake over and over until someone gives you credit for knowing what you are persistently doing. Culture does not do anything except enjoy its own purposeless residue. And wisdom is only an affectation of some affluent oldsters who get prestige and acclamation for things that the young are reproached for. Indeed, experience, culture, and wisdom are probably all right, but they are souvenirs of travels, not indisputable badges of authority. What are credentials, anyway?

This pilgrim merely passes through, and he knows it. Very much aware of how transient reality is, he clings to its relativity. He exists because he cannot help it. He admires rationality, but by denying spirituality he also affirms it in himself and spends much time in reconciling these opposites. He is an oxymoron in many respects, but no fool. There is evidence that he first found paradoxes within himself but gradually turned skepticism into a character trait. He suffers from suspended judgment, however, not negativism. He hates despair as much as a physician hates suffering and a cleric hates sin. Hamlet's dubious lament, "to be or not to be," is not even a question but an unblinkable fact of life. What counts is to be something that makes a difference, not just to be.

My sexist language here has been referring to *he, him,* and *his,* but there are skeptical pilgrims of both sexes. The skeptical pilgrim is generally articulate and responsible; however, he (or she) is an upstairs version of the existential man described so unforgettably by Dostoyevsky and Kafka. But my skeptical pilgrim is unlikely to be put on trial for anything, let alone for nothing—except perhaps by his own slightly uneasy conscience.

For the skeptical pilgrim, it is essential to do something in order to justify the existence he cannot help. What he wants is an alchemy that transforms vulnerability into a triumph of the spirit. This will authenticate, because skepticism is a thin jacket on a winter day, although it is at better times, a mantle that warms his spirit and sharpens his mind.

Long ago, another skeptic, Pyrrho, said in effect that because certainty is impossible, the wise person ought to suspend judgment and accept the myths of the times, seeking tranquility rather than illusory truth. In still another paraphrase, Pyrrho might talk more directly: To get along, go along; don't make waves, you might drown. Relax, take it easy, avoid stress, and forget about eternal quests or ultimate questions. They'll be here still, after you've long gone. It's all right to seek the "real me," or whatever it happens to be called. But don't be a living sacrifice, especially for a cause that at best is obscure and at worst is a lie in itself. Keep your opinions to yourself. People don't listen, anyway. If they did, they probably wouldn't understand. And if they understood, it won't make any difference. They would argue with you, anyway, and that gets you both nowhere.

This is a true skeptic's creed, guaranteed to make a pilgrim out of practically anybody. But the skeptical pilgrim who forfeits a quest for significance, or gives up a quest to be something that matters and makes a difference, is already defeated. Furthermore, living in a frozen state of suspended judgment is as deceptive as claiming to be objective and fair at all times. It is more humane and gratifying to believe that something endures and has an enduring value.

In psychotherapy, the illusion of being objective at all times (at least during working hours) and able to suspend value judgments until we are good and ready is tempting. Perhaps it is possible for a short time. But as a permanent viewpoint, it becomes an excuse for denial and indifference. After all, it would be a poor therapist who did not, indirectly and tacitly, urge patients to follow a path that seems to be better than another path, especially if the former promises to be significant and to resolve difficulties.

Though the Heart Has Its Reasons . . .

The skeptical pilgrim is a creature composed of both faith and reason (otherwise called emotion and logic, instinct and rationality, or passions and principles). In this, he is just like lots of other people. He listens and responds to the message of Pascal's famous aphorism, "The heart has its reasons which reason knows nothing of . . . [and] we know the truth, not only by reason, but by the heart."

If sublimation is the putative process by which passions are turned into principles, what process is responsible for turning principles into passions? Say that a skeptical disposition develops by mistrusting those in authority, who have been too often wrong and unfeeling to justify their dogmatism. Suppose the future skeptic is persistently misled by rules that are supposed to be absolute and dependable. In the course of events he becomes more careful, subjecting popular beliefs and entrenched doctrines to careful scrutiny. Instead of automatically following the directives assigned by family and society, he comes to esteem intellectual inquiry as a high pursuit but shuns the easy conclusion. Is there a process like sublimation that accounts for skepticism and then transforms an intellectual attitude into a passionate principle? If so, then skepticism itself will come under scrutiny and be treated with no greater deference or dedication than any other point of view. Perhaps the ultimate question is, What is required in order to take something on faith? What is the psychology or purpose of faith, anyway?

Without quite knowing why, the skeptical pilgrim realizes, with a glow of understanding, that moods and metaphors are more apt to sway and persuade than mere logic and evidence. The heart is stirred by emotion, but chilled by an assault based on pure reason.

The head, too, has its passions, just as the heart has its reasons. Passions become principles, and principles turn into passions. Sometimes all it takes to turn a weak argument into a passionate crusade is plausibility and belief in the god-given invincibility of a strong leader. Blood has been spilled for causes soon forgotten, or seemingly so trivial as not to matter much. Irrational hatred plus racial stereotyping has tragically transformed many a citizen into a fanatical killer.

Legends, traditions, and keen metaphors have a tenacity that sticks to the mind; actual events and historical truths quickly fade away and are replaced by wishful revisionism. Both politicians and advertisers know this principle. They put it to work, playing on emotions and gullibility, as well as the wish to be happy, attractive, and not think or analyze too much, and to be on the right side of people who count.

There are many people who have self-destructive tendencies and are not controlled by guilt or shame. Without a constructive goal to work toward, they never settle into a rewarding groove. Often they take incredible risks and act recklessly. When questioned, they justify themselves by believing they are exceptions, born under a lucky star that will surely protect them and make things come out well in the end. They are often disappointed. There are many other people who consider themselves exceptions to some unspecified rule or directive or prohibition. Believing themselves more than ordinary, they conclude that ordinary laws do not apply. The range of exceptions seems to cover just about anyone, from the scofflaw to the celebrity dosing himself on cocaine in the faith that he or she has the ability to evade trouble. I have known people who truly deny that a medical risk applies to them and, as a result, are surprised when illness happens. Chronic cigarette smokers know about the cancer risk but smoke anyway, citing all the exceptions who live to a hearty and healthy old age, and others who die prematurely after leading a most abstemious life. The passion rules the head and becomes a principle for guiding their life. Sometimes it is called denial; at other times, optimism. It is hard to tell if passion is a principle, or if there really is a principle tacitly embraced. I once had a patient who sincerely believed that with a good pair of wings he could fly. One day he jumped from a sixth-floor window, injuring himself seriously but living. Later he recalled, "You know, Doctor, just before I started to fall, there was a moment when I could fly, even without wings!"

Patients will often claim belief in a so-called principle that really is a ruling metaphor (e.g., life is a gamble, a game, a blessing, a jungle) and act as if the metaphor were true. It is not mere impulse that is decisive for most people, but rather a favorite emotional position that generates an image of how life really is and ought to be—full of exceptions and lucky breaks or, conversely, infested by enemies and misfortunes that even good intentions and vigilance cannot thwart.

Psychotherapists ought to recognize that if patients do change their ways for the better, it is not necessarily because changing makes sense or would keep them healthy. Good reasons to change are seldom the cause for doing something constructive on one's own behalf. Despite assertions to the contrary, the quest for rationality and purpose in whatever we do cannot altogether be a search for an unequivocal boon or irrefutable syllogism, like medieval proofs for the existence of God. The quest for an unequivocal boon will only be found in a sense of harmony between what we do and the moral justification of the way things ought to be.

We could not live or talk to each other without metaphors and emotionality; anything more abstract or literal, for that matter, is an artifact. Meanwhile, we live between two worlds, drawing upon the past (which is often deceptive and skewed) and looking to the future (which is necessarily unclear and tentative). Psychotherapy follows in a parallel way: The past gives precedent for present complaints and future behavior, whereas the future tests the validity of what we conclude about the past. The skeptical pilgrim recognizes that most thinking is an afterthought, if that. His search for a reasonable justification for existing is driven not by a logical desire for a solid syllogism, but by an emotional yearning to find how things fit together. Heartfelt reasons and passionate beliefs will not only sustain people despite vulnerability, but even work together in forming a consensus about which strategies and values are best.

Good Theories, Bad Theories, and Acceptability

Although our viewpoint toward the world is largely a product of passions and principles, there is a coherence that is not attributable to mere fluctuations of emotion, mood, and irrationality. We have metaphors to lean on and a host of theories to justify and explain our positions, whether or not we have thought about them before. We constantly editorialize, even in the most casual contacts.

Perhaps using the term *theory* for our daily exercise of opinion is too formal and abstract. What I refer to is a ready-made cluster of conclusions that have been swimming around in our preconscious minds, waiting to be fished out and applied to almost any situation that might be problematic, whether personal, political, commercial, or familial. Something within us steers a conclusion to a body of preconceptions and half-facts. Without much qualification, our interpretation construes how the world makes sense and should operate. From this viewpoint facts are just low-level theories, because they have not been tested to any degree. Of course, we have many hypotheses about how and why things hang together, working for our practical benefit and moral enlightenment. We also have hypotheses about how and why things manage to conspire against us.

Our favorite theories combine everything that gives us exculpation and excuses but makes us feel good anyway. In psychotherapy, theories and hypotheses are profuse, although there are some therapists who confine themselves to whatever doctrines they have been taught. Mostly these hypotheses are expressed in general statements that draw upon the past ("Since you feel this way, I suppose you will continue to . . . just as before") and on the future ("If you pay attention to what happens whenever you find yourself in this situation, perhaps it might be different").

Hypotheses hold the world together. Theories combine just about everything that passes through the filter called experience; they make sense of the thoughts in our head and the perceptions of our senses. There are many bad theories, too, that subordinate and corrupt facts for fictions, besides taking metaphors quite literally. Because of bad theories, it ought to be useful to point out characteristics of a good theory. And because so much is proposed that is supposed to define what is true or good, criteria for a good theory deserve special consideration.

In psychotherapy, proof is in short supply. It is talked about soberly in discussions of evidence, but practiced less than regularly. Something that seems plausible or even likely is hardly a certainty, nor is its assertion necessarily a truth. It is only a working hypothesis. Moreover, the current popularity of a theory or school in psychiatry, psychotherapy, or casework is more an exercise in public relations than in demonstration of validity.

Quite apart from its validity, however, a good theory in psychotherapy—by which I mean an overall impression or formulation—has to feel right, even as we apply it to the problem at hand. It must feel valid and truthful to the therapist before it can be served up to the patient for either rejection, acceptance, or indifference. But it would be sheer arrogance or complacency to be so convinced of our insight that our theories make us feel right all the time.

The difference between a good theory and a bad theory in psychiatry and perhaps for human relations in general, is not wholly its explanatory value but whether the questionable theory is complete or left dangling as a plausibility. Outlined below are four characteristics or criteria for a good theory.

Generality

A good theory has to bring diverse observations and ideas together in a coherent form that overarches numerous events. The criterion that requires coherent generality is indispensable, although not enough to make a good theory out of mere expansiveness. A theory that is too narrow or refers only to a few subjects under special circumstances has no appeal. Generality is supposed to go beyond the facts and observations to a declaration about the whole. The declaration should make sense, and its opposite or negation should make sense as well.

There are all kinds of generalizations; we make them hourly, it often seems. But they come in different packages that depend on the domain in which the theory is supposed to operate. A few examples from psychotherapy include the effect of psychoanalysis depends on resolving the transference neurosis, patients who are overly cooperative have something to hide, therapists should always charge for missed appointments, and so on.

In psychotherapy, observations that are strictly limited to the present and to facts at hand are not hypotheses but paraphrases. Generality requires that the observation go beyond, either to the past or toward the future (including observations not yet made). The present mood only sets the tone for hypotheses about the cogent past or the prospective future. Good theories are supposed to sound right, too, but have enough allowances or strings attached to be wrong or to be falsified. Bad theories may be wrong for the right reasons; an incomplete theory also may be wrong for the right reasons, because it is subject neither to later negation nor to subsequent confirmation.

Specificity

Good theories must be anchored in specific cases or illustrative examples that confer a sense of confirmation. There are many good examples, however, of bad theories. Most of them get that way by including examples that confirm the theory but have to be turned inside out in order to fit comfortably. Many psychoanalytic theories are like this, either good, bad, or incomplete; the trouble is that it is hard to tell.

Falsifiability is necessary for scientific theories, but in psychodynamic theories often yes means no, one thing stands for its opposite, questions are redundant rather than revealing, interpretations can be reversed with impunity, and so on. It is easy to be dogmatic in psychodynamic theorizing, but hard to decide which are the best examples for illustrations, because the selection process may be flawed or dubious. If a therapist were conscientious enough simply to say, "I think that . . . ," "In my opinion . . . ," or "This is the way it seems to me . . . ," the moment would be open to cite examples, or even to elicit falsifying cases.

Most stereotypes about people, for example, are generalities in which falsifying examples are rigorously excluded. Occasionally I have been asked why "so many" Jews are psychiatrists, entertainment moguls, takeover specialists, or comedians; or why black people are hypersexual, unemployed, in jail, or anti-Semitic; and so forth. Because an example can found for any hypothesis, however objectionable on other grounds, many other examples can also be found that invalidate the implied generalizations. Though the questioners are not likely to change their minds, the biased questions can easily be refuted or undermined by citing "exceptions" to the generalizations.

Generalizations ought to be working hypotheses that actually work for a living—that is, justify themselves by specific examples that do not always discriminate in favor of the theory. It is conceivable that no theory in psychiatry is inconceivable. But there are many theories that have absolutely no supportive evidence and very thin examples on which to base themselves. The issue, however, is not a problem of the number or varieties of examples that can be brought to support a theory, but more specifically whether the theory has sufficient explanatory value to be applied in various situations. There is, for example, a psychodynamic theory that no one commits suicide without first wishing the death of someone else; this has been called "murder in the 180th degree." Though I do not choose to elaborate evidence for or against this theory, it would be enough simply to cite examples of suicide in which murderous impulses or ideas cannot be demonstrated. That some positive examples might be found, however, means only that the generalization is faulty and should be phrased in another way. An existential type of therapist would usually (and not always) keep generalities to a minimum, including this one.

Relevance

Just as specificity ties generality down to the here and now, relevance links both to the reality of the person to whom the insight applies. In short, making sense must make sense for me, for the life I lead and am accustomed to. Otherwise, there is a vacancy or irrelevance that prevents any understanding aside from abstract appreciation. The problem that the theory deals with must be real, not begged from someone else or borrowed from another kind of experience. By real, I mean that a theory will, through its sense of reality (which is somewhat emotional) and reality testing (which is more cerebral and perceptual), lead to a directive that will make a significant difference in how we handle things.

There are many examples of relevant interpretations in psychiatry. I trust that offices are full of them. But so are professional journals that regularly report insights and interpretations alleged to have high value, at least for the author and presumably for the patients who were observed and written about. For example, consider a therapist who says, "I've noticed that you always seem to look for and find a needy person to rescue, whether it is a woman you're devoted to or a younger colleague who wants your help.

You do so much for them without even being asked. It takes so much out of you until you begin to feel like their slave." The therapist could, of course, back up his comments with examples that make it reasonable and worth thinking about. His patient *is* very sympathetic to people who seem to require help, and he does them favor after favor. Soon they are in his debt and, not infrequently, begin to resent the implicit power he holds over them. Consequently they tend to draw back, wanting to free themselves from his grasp. Meanwhile, he has become their superior slave, looking for still further ways to do their bidding but paradoxically resenting it when he is called upon for help. Of course, he is even more baffled by their unwillingness to continue such a relationship.

The point is not whether this is an accurate interpretation, general and specific enough to bear watching. I use this example only because the interpretation, right or wrong, is relevant to the patient and his life. "Always" is, of course, a rhetorical device intended to get someone's attention, even though very few things are always or never. There are, moreover, many cases in which the observation about resenting the superior slave status would not hold. The interpretation would have been just as relevant if the therapist had said more cautiously, "You know, I have noticed that often . . . " Patients as often respond by citing something contrary, just to indicate that all this cannot be wholly or always true. But, to employ another generality, this is a better indication of ultimate agreement than immediate assent.

The criterion of relevance has to be revealing as well as real, bearing a clear relationship— right or wrong— to a patient's life. Whether a patient agrees or disagrees, the observation evokes a sense of disclosure that should be taken seriously. Although a therapist presumably has a number of illustrative instances showing that the patient acts and behaves in the manner described, these supporting observations need not be many; mere numbers are not impressive. Confrontations have to be pertinent, not necessarily forceful. Tact may be stronger.

Acceptability

Pertinence is probably just as persuasive as accuracy in proposing a theory or hypothesis. Moreover, theories in psychiatry have to begin with their impact on the patient, long before becoming a topic for general discussion and dispute among colleagues. Acceptability means that a patient hears the meaning intended, pauses, and seems willing to pursue it. When confronted, some patients say, "Well, I suppose that it is true, probably. I never thought of it that way before. It sounds right, but I'll have to think about it some more." Sadly, the therapist must realize that this patient will never think of it again. But he or she might, and if the therapist's comment seems revealing enough to be attached to other accepted theories, then it might gain acceptance for itself. It need not be absolutely true, but it does have to find an opening that allows the interpretation to enter a somewhat closed set of special attitudes.

Acceptability has a significant role in many disciplines that require both theorizing and examples. Kuhn (1970) has described the scientific paradigms that rule research until enough anomalies occur to challenge what had been previously accepted; another paradigm then takes over because it explains more and seems to account for the anomalies. In the scientific domain, acceptability is gradual, not an overnight sensation. But the paradigm is pertinent because it clarifies what puzzled previous investigators.

From another viewpoint, Tillich (1963) made extensive use of the concept of *kairos*, the opportune moment at which revelation becomes manifest and/or some crisis is averted. From an eschatological perspective, *kairos* refers to the eternal breaking through into the temporal, a concept not too far removed from that of pertinence and relevance. It is a kind of metaphysical moment in which truth *about* someone becomes truth *in* someone and thus makes much sense for living. I would like to think that acceptability of a hypothesis about someone requires a suitable paradigm or guiding metaphor that is useful and opportune enough to

reveal something significant to a patient and have it make a difference in future behavior.

The pertinent moment in psychotherapy, when acceptability
occurs, is seldom sudden. Actually it seems to be cumulative, and
the transformation is rarely very conspicuous. But acceptability
does, in fact, take place. Perhaps when a therapist sees that a
patient deals with problems using a different strategy than those
used before, and that it works out well, then the therapist has some
reason to conclude that his or her efforts have not been in vain and
that something has been accepted.

Acceptability presumably occurs at the opportune moment,
although when that is must remain speculative. When a therapist
talks to an patient's existential condition and finds that the patient
listens, and that what occurs makes unqualified sense— perhaps
then something constructive happens, but only perhaps. Some
theories or insights are never accepted, however, correct though
they may be. Others have to be worked over before they are
admissible. But the uncertainty of *kairos* and the difficulty in de-
termining the right metaphor, phraseology, or paradigm provide
ample reasons for a skeptic to reinforce his or her skepticism.

Another key moment takes place when a person actively
seeks therapy. He has finally concluded that coping alone has been
inadequate. Despite earlier resistance and reservations, half
believing that anyone who sees a psychiatrist is sick in the head,
he moves ahead with courage. It is a step undertaken with qualified relevance and acceptability. The patient is seldom if ever
aware that at this moment of acceptability, he has fulfilled all of the
criteria for a good theory. After all, most important decisions are
not sudden, but only seem so after a period of deliberation and
vacillation.

Failure to meet the criteria of generality, specificity, relevance,
and acceptability, however, does not mean that a theory is necessarily wrong, just incomplete. A body of beliefs is seldom rejected
because it has incorrect information, insufficient generality, or too
few applications. Bad theories sometimes have good reasons for

acceptability. For example, the so-called paranoid position, or a worldview based on mistrust and suspicion of others, may be socially unacceptable but very soothing to the unfortunate person whose view it is. It is much more comfortable to blame others and ascribe evil intentions to them than to blame one's own vulnerable self and to take responsibility for mistaken ideas. Self-esteem is very fragile for paranoid people, which is why they cling adamantly to sometimes preposterous beliefs.

Good theories are not always beneficial. Beliefs and hypotheses can rest on very firm grounds, still satisfy these four criteria, and seem complete; but no one is helped by them. Complete theories are what *investigators* aim for, but therapists seldom need to reach completion in any respect. Nevertheless, therapists are often unaware that just in the course of working with patients over many months, gradual structuring and assimilation of metaphors and paradigms do take place, piece by piece.

The somewhat sophisticated project of making theories is only an extension of the more primitive and reflexive act of making sense. It is necessary if anyone is to resolve the enigmas inherent to dealing with psychological problems. I have not described four criteria for a good theory in order to prescribe rules and procedures for conscientious therapists to follow; but in understanding the problems patients bring, we cannot escape some structuring of ideas and impressions, whether in generalizing, specifying, establishing relevance, or considering what determines acceptability. This happens in any encounter, from the long-range course of psychoanalysis to the briefest confrontation. Surely a complete theory is a rarity; most often, only one or another criterion can be firmly established in the absence of others. The outcome makes sense, but not as much as if all four were established comfortably.

The following vignette from a psychoanalysis will give an inkling of some of the technical problems inherent to making sense, working out a theory, presenting an interpretation, and establishing a groundwork for communication that is both pertinent and persuasive.

A middle-aged executive came into analysis at the urging of his family. They were worried about his irritability, incessant criticism, periodic depression, and outspoken bouts of despair in which he threatened suicide. During analysis, we had, with some difficulty, established that depression, self-criticism, and despair were brought about by profound self-doubt, perilously low self-esteem, much hostility to his family, and torrents of abuse and invective that he could not help but heap on them. His family members were exasperated. One of his strongest methods for getting relief, however, was to try and win over colleagues and coworkers, as if they could be appeased and be less critical.

Although he was often unjustifiably critical and scornful of his parents and immediate family, he was more sure that other people were potential enemies. They reportedly considered him a lucky fake who had been successful for unclear reasons, but would be exposed as a failure if the truth were known. Moreover, he had a belief that was near delusional: Other people's contempt could control his actions. There was a curious truth in this theory in that because he assumed that other people had contempt for him, he adjusted his behavior in ways that might win them over.

Whenever he spoke at meetings or conferences, he tended to feel exposed and vulnerable, always afraid that he might say something foolish or hostile. Consequently he went out of his way to be conciliatory, to compliment colleagues, and not to offend anyone. We had also recognized that the scorn and criticism he expected from others was redirected to his long-suffering family and parents, who put up with his tirades. Furthermore, he admitted that one strategy for protecting himself against hostile exposure was to agree unnecessarily with others, exaggerating their contributions. Strange as it seems, this highly competent man, acknowledged to be an authority in his field and in charge of an important division in a large company, generally felt like a weakling, especially when he buttered people up and gave them compliments for relatively incidental contributions. There was scarcely any limit to his self-derogation, nor any to his criticism of his parents and family, whom he insisted humiliated him on every possible occasion.

In one session, he once more reported going to an office meeting where he was afraid of being exposed. He withheld expressing an opinion until he was sure that he would not be considered stupid. Although he knew that his ideas were good, he felt perhaps others would disagree and humiliate him by their criticisms. Ordinarily he was so thorough in his homework and so competent that his ideas were accepted readily, although he took extra precautions about voicing comments in very diplomatic terms. During analysis he was typically silent, tactful, and cryptic in his few comments. He mulled things over before speaking and was always an acquiescent patient who seemed intimidated whenever I ventured an observation or question.

For the most part, this session was not much different than dozens of others; he was alert but reticent. Once again I pointed out how he usually tried to score points by agreeing with others, often being unnecessarily effusive. His main motive, I continued this time, was not that he thought so much of their ideas, but that he wanted them on his side. This did not just mean having allies. It meant that by laying the groundwork of approval, he could then take over in every respect, regardless of how the others felt or where their interests were. There was a side to him that wanted to dominate and be the leader of the colleagues he had flattered so indiscriminately. It was not altogether that he struggled to avoid offending them. He toadied, to be sure, but in subsequently going ahead, he offered further (and frequently accepted) ideas that sometimes refuted theirs and put himself in a stronger position. He became, in fact, a "superior and controlling slave."

This slight deviation in how I presented my understanding (or "theory") seemed to look at his active intent, rather than reiterate the fears that kept him cautiously silent on many occasions. Although my comments would not win any prizes for profundity, they did change the emphasis to a degree, opening up the likelihood that his self-criticism had much to do with wanting to dominate his family and his colleagues. Furthermore, it was plausible that his obsequious manner deceptively reversed his primary intentions. By initially flattering and cajoling people he was convinced were contemptuous and contemptible, he could diplomatically agree, then push them aside with his masterful presentations. He was a secret tyrant as well as a target.

I present this brief example from a difficult patient's analysis in order to show that although I had generality, specificity, and relevance on my side, I was not sure about acceptability. He would not risk offending me by disputing what I said; he was accustomed to agreeing with whatever almost anyone said. He understood what I claimed to have observed about him, including an active intention of controlling others. I had to be cautious, however, about a further hypothesis I had that he wanted to demolish others. This was based on investigating events surrounding his suicidal thinking.

Faithful to his custom, he agreed with me completely and without hesitation. And I completely mistrusted his response, knowing that he complied only to be ingratiating. But how could I test acceptability in case there was a faint possibility that my comments got through? The only feasible way was both very simple and very difficult: I had to wait for signs of changed behavior in analysis, at his work, and in his home. He could diminish the toady side of his character and present his views forcibly and unapologetically, in effect using the interpretation or "theory" I had conveyed.

This is a subordinate theory of acceptability called "watching and waiting," for lack of any other method of confirmation. It assumes that my interpretation had a definite effect, and that whatever change of behavior occurred would be directly related to my observations. I considered this unlikely, because it not only implicitly minimized whatever else went on in his life but assumed that he was open and at a point of *kairos* at the moment when I made my interpretation. My views were, at least in my opinion, pertinent and pointed, with much evidence to support them. Watching and waiting did, however, pay off somewhat as the patient gradually became more dissatisfied and found his compliance less and less automatic. He even tried being more straightforward and relented, to a degree, his fury toward his parents and family. In other words, he changed to a degree but never referred to my observations about his wanting to control and dominate others.

The theory that knowing more about one's behavior will promote a change for the better not only is basic to insight therapy but represents a belief that has very ancient roots in Socratic philosophy. It also draws upon a pious but naive notion that people will do the right thing, once they know what it is. This hypothesis is implicit in efforts to negotiate peace between enemies, but it applies equally to finding convincing grounds for declaring war. Every protagonist believes in the sanctity and rightness of his or her cause.

Although insight and understanding are worthwhile, they are not the gold standard. Their value shifts depending on other factors, still unknown, that help bring about acceptability and persuasion without coercion. Far more patients seem to have better insight into themselves after they feel better than in their darker moments of distress.

Vulnerability is not necessarily a good omen for acceptability. At moments of crisis, or shortly after the beginning of a conflictual episode, those who suffer might be ready to embrace almost any promising source of relief. Rationality does not always win the day; insight into oneself may not be the principal therapeutic agency. The opportune moment is indispensable, but it might not be as selective as we wish. The key idea, however, regardless of many unsettled issues, is that vulnerability may be ameliorated by bonding it to another fraction of meaning that enables the self to acquire more control and choice, and use vulnerability as motivation.

It should be noted, though, that lack of insight never helped anyone facing a real problem. Good coping must depend on adequate assessment and identification of central problems before judging what the best strategies would be. It is not just a matter of skepticism and equivocation over unsettled issues, however, but a reasonable truth that acknowledges the imprecisions and suppositions of therapy. Therapy is primarily supposed to relieve suffering, not just strive for complete theories. Moreover, we cannot depend on the hope that vulnerable people will realize what is wrong, spontaneously gather meaning unto themselves, and do what is best for their own welfare.

With only those contributions that therapists conscientiously prefer and provide, psychotherapy is not able to achieve much more. Total transformations of personality, with complete relief of distress and perfect understanding of everything else, are impossible, and would be very frightening if they were possible. After all, a theory may clarify a problem, or at least account for its own incompleteness. And one reason for the incompleteness of most theories in psychiatry is because there are so many meanings that can be attributed to so much. Meanings are seldom exhausted; only therapists and patients get tired. There is always something more to be added, especially if a body of beliefs is to be taken seriously.

Conversely, if it seems that a theory is totally complete, it is apt to be trivial. For example, I have heard colleagues report telling patients, "The reason you are anxious is that you're afraid of what might happen." This is not only unrevealing but redundant. If I point out to a patient, "You are not apt to worry when things go well and you are feeling good about the future," this is equally redundant and quite stupid. As a rule, people do not worry when things go well (although there are some chronic worriers who do, fearing that their good luck will abruptly come to an end). They do not expect the other shoe to drop, because the first shoe has not fallen yet. It is very easy to validate a self-evident proposition. That is no consolation to a therapist of quality who still wants to understand better and does not confuse understanding with acceptability, nor acceptability with recovery.

Existential Vulnerability: Meaning without Being

I have already proposed that actual vulnerability is acute distress, and that it is synonymous with suffering, being without meaning. Another proposition is that any suffering is intensified by lack of meaning. As a result, the suffering patient, for example, has nothing to base an assessment on, and therefore has few meanings to use in trying to cope with the significant problem. But there is another variety of vulnerability: a disposition to see the world in a peculiarly idiosyncratic way that, in itself, interferes with effective coping. This disposition plus actual and potential vulnerability typifies the vulnerable self in the travail of just being alive, trying to survive in an irrational world.

Both ordinary vulnerability (i.e., suffering) and what I call *existential vulnerability* are brought about by a split between meaning and being. Suffering itself is being without meaning; existential vulnerability is meaning without being. Although ordinary suffering is at least made more severe by lack of meaning, existential vulnerability has much more meaning to deal with than it can use, but it is cut off from the corrective function of being in the world. In the absence of a worldview that is completely general, specific, relevant, and acceptable, existential vulnerability is apt to present highly unusual external manifestations. Peculiar personalities and odd characters are but two common examples. But almost anyone seeking guidance may be thwarted by their own vulnerable self and its fixed, antipathic attitude toward the world.

Existential vulnerability is generally characterized by a perception that the world is hostile, evil, and certainly doomed to destruction by its own malice. It is rather ambiguous in that there is a serious question whether this attitude actually refers to the world at large or to the vulnerable self. In self-experience, however, the vulnerable self is sure that it lacks the resources, personal resiliency, or even enough courage to cope with and confront ordinary problems.

My patient who tried pleasing everyone whom he considered a potential enemy demonstrated the impenetrability of his worldview. His vulnerable self was alienated from his resiliency to cope and from his competence to deal with ordinary daily work. His resilient self allowed him to contend with an inimical world filled with hostility and contempt by trying, covertly, to dominate others. But there was still an incongruency between this irrational world and his solid belief that he was doomed to ingratiate himself or else heap scorn on his family. The detachment of meaning from being prevented him from truly appreciating his wish to dominate and destroy others. Instead, by assiduously pleasing others he could at least temporarily ward off what he was most afraid of.

If a successful strategy, such as ingratiation, helps only in countering a fictitious cause, it scarcely has much meaning in reserve for true being and authenticity. Ingratiation, for example, worked only when my patient believed others were ready to attack and thus bring about his humiliation. This is an outcome that hardly promotes resiliency but does fortify a negative attitude toward the world and certain fixed ideas about it. My patient was very successful in the manufacturing business, but he was also successful in manufacturing a world in which constant vulnerability seemed to reign.

His attitude was characteristic of existential vulnerability. The world had a place for potential distress but there was no place in his world for feeling the fullness of being alive, for coping well, or for enjoying reliable and resilient self-esteem. To cite another example: If a person is fearful of any stranger coming down the street, she is likely to give up walking on that street or to begin carrying a gun or some other weapon. In either event she remains very vulnerable to strangers, an existential plight that cuts her off from living in a truly ambiguous world where strangers may or may not be threats. The vulnerable self is ready and able to deal only with the manufactured world in which all strangers mean harm; it makes no distinction between casual passersby and the truly menacing. Generality abounds in *always* and *never*; hence the vulnerable self can point to various examples to justify its beliefs, because examples that seem to prove a point are never far away.

In truth, just by being alive, we are all victims and victors in a variety of situations. It is also true that in more situations than we like to admit, we have been victimizers. Vulnerability is a life-and-death propensity that belongs to the so-called human condition, which I prefer to call the "human conditional," which means "It all depends." Resiliency and courage are there to be developed; otherwise, neurotic types of exaggerated or inhibited behavior using inappropriate coping strategies may prevail. If a person protects his rights in the absence of a real threat, he is often called vigilant and prudent. His disposition to protect himself may only be a policy, however, and not a firm existential expectation that he will be attacked by almost anyone in some fashion.

The key difference between vigilance and constant worry that the world waits for a chance to do us in is a difference in worldview and in existential vulnerability. Such vulnerability belongs to our character of far-reaching mistrust and deep expectation of harm, balanced by resiliency (i.e., the latent capacity to cope). To some degree we construct the world we construe.

Two prominent examples of existential vulnerability are frequently met with in clinical work. They are called *resistance* and *transference,* which have more in common than suspected. Resistance has been noted and complained about since the early days of psychoanalysis. It refers to a tendency for patients to be obstinate, indifferent, negativistic, uncooperative, and very opinionated, contrary to their analyst's expectations. Resistance throws many obstacles in the way of progress, according to conventional wisdom. Such behavior is frowned on and deplored by the therapist, who tries hard to get his patient to respond in a more positive fashion.

At the other end of the spectrum is transference, which is hope or belief that the therapist will make up for all the deprivations and frustrations that a patient has undergone in the past. The therapist is given idealized powers beyond reality to confer these absent blessings, and in return, the patient is willing to do just about anything needed to force the therapist to comply.

Although resistance and transference seem to be opposites, both are manifestations of a vulnerable self and its characteristic tendency to dissociate meaning and being. Resistance is predominantly a style that preserves a typical attitude toward the world, the therapist, and the threat of change in therapy: "I am not comfortable being what I am, but even if I am nothing, I have nothing else, and want to stay as I am!" On a milder scale, resistance can mean, "Let me alone. This is the way I want to experience myself and be seen." Such a patient may in fact want to change or to cooperate, but the vulnerable self cannot take a chance on intrusion, and so therapeutic efforts are resisted.

Resistance and transference are the Scylla and Charybdis of therapy. In facing these two faces of one phenomenon, the therapist must contend and cope with actual, potential, and existential vulnerability. He or she is neither the demigod who rectifies all that went wrong earlier nor the enemy who tears away defenses and leaves even greater wounds in the resistant patient.

The Self-Enclosed Personality

We are all creatures of our times, prisoners of our prejudices, captives of our consciences, and so on, but we dwell in a world partially created by our presuppositions, yearnings, and presumptions. We are self-enclosed, and our enclosures can be sanctuaries or fortresses, depending on whether resiliency or vulnerability is uppermost at the time. The skeptical pilgrim is honest and candid enough to know when he denies his own vulnerability, and to recognize his own peculiar self-enclosed personality. If he were a patient, his self-enclosed personality would certainly favor a high degree of resistance and transference problems for the therapist.

Most of us, I assume, would like to be understood and to understand others. This also means that we like to put a label on how people habitually package and present themselves. But it also means that every person, whatever his or her outward manifestations, has a number of relevant hidden meanings that no one can get at. Understanding others in their incompleteness, therefore, can only mean that we appreciate their *good intentions*, which are implied. Otherwise, their bad intentions would be only too obvious, and as a result I would choose not to try and understand them any further. It is quite a paradox: Bad intentions are obvious, whereas good intentions are there but have to be looked for. What kind of existential vulnerability—meaning without being—does this represent? It is false that to know people is to love them; perhaps we could hate them for similar reasons. But to know people *better* is a goal of understanding which meanings are most relevant to the being that we find acceptable, or perhaps unacceptable.

If we appreciate someone's good intentions, and despite a poor outcome can still give them credit for doing the very best they could, we are then able to have a more rounded perspective about the external manifestations of the personality that person presents to the world. Existential vulnerability requires that we find those selected meanings that appear to be relevant that would contribute to the person's authentic balance of good and bad. Unfortunately most of us—even in clinical circles, where compassion is supposed to thrive—notice only the negative or pathological side of a personality, divorced from its strength, good intentions, and acceptability. Consequently, in attaching various meanings to the way people actually present themselves, enigmatic behavior finds itself severely suspect or deeply deplored, because only negative intentions are accepted.

Axis II in various editions of the *Diagnostic and Statistical Manual of Mental Disorders* refers to personality types who are classified, it seems, according to their existential vulnerability and general style of coping. Different styles and worldviews are named by adjectives such as *paranoid, histrionic, narcissistic, antisocial, borderline, avoidant, dependent,* and *compulsive.* What this means is that under unspecified but obviously obtrusive and deplorable circumstances, each of these representative patients is expected to behave in typically negative ways. We do not understand such behavior, but we assume that its motives are negative. Good intentions (or what psychiatrists call ego strengths) are positive coping characteristics that we like, but are seldom taken into account in arriving at a personality diagnosis. As a rule, then, the patient is at fault for having faults, even without having a reliable method for ascribing good meanings to whatever they do. Ego strengths and other positive characteristics will be more fully described in Chapter 7. Nevertheless it is not fair, and it is certainly incomplete, to describe personality types as if their less admirable traits predominate. Existential vulnerability does not necessarily consider the split between meaning and being in self-enclosed personalities as a sign of inner evil to be deplored and ignored.

A very common coping strategy is called *denial*, which refers to the repudiation of a significant portion of whatever meanings are contained within a social field. The motive for this tendency is to keep matters at a stage of status quo, if not substantially better. The gap between meaning and manifest being is very obvious. Denial appears in many forms, coupled with such positive traits as optimism and courage, or with such negative qualities as avoidance, distancing, reversal of affect, and delusions.

Without undertaking a more complete discussion of denial (which has been done before in other places), the relevant point here is that the strategy of denying may be the mortar holding the self-enclosure of a personality together. It enables the individual to present a united front of opposing traits, offering to the world an image that is wholly admirable and acceptable, at least to the individual concerned.

Few people catch themselves in the overt act of denying and do something to correct the mistakes and diversions it creates. Denial can be dangerous, because it tends to become a character trait and to distort one's image of the world. Denial's primary motive is to keep the self-enclosed personality shining with unaccustomed health and vigor. For instance, the "good old days" were probably never as good as the person remembers, because examples of the "bad old days" are seldom mentioned, and then only to minimize them. Furthermore, ascribing good intentions and wholly positive traits to one person while withholding them from another may be an example of selective denial followed by fabrication; it manufactures distinctively good and bad people. In either case, good or bad fabrications do not correspond to a real person or an authentic world, because in a real world only a mixture of good or evil acts occurs. It is, however, a clear sign of splitting and stereotyping all people into two categories. This does little to promote insight into the human conditional of "it all depends."

No one survives on a diet of constant candor. But the chronic denier lives within a self-enclosure of false (good or bad) recollections and romanticized visions of the future. Even vulnerability must be disguised. Hope is fresh, despite disappointments, because it is seldom brought into the open and scrutinized pragmatically. "Someday I'll . . . " is a promise that must be deferred indefinitely. Habits of a lifetime seldom change, especially by the mere act of wishing them to. Denial tends to make up a reality without significant problems, instead of coping with the vexing mixture that it is. The vulnerable self is therefore unguarded; manifest meanings are false, the real being is concealed; and the positive image is counterfeit.

Whether denial is a form of alienation or not, it undoubtedly is a way of keeping a safe distance from unwanted inevitability and risk—that is, until the risk, unexpected and prone to be especially severe, descends. It is not safe distance, really, but a scotomatized distance that is ill prepared for misfortunes. Unmistakably, there are many people suffering from various kinds of alienation. Their vulnerable self is constantly exposed; the best they achieve is a humiliating second-class citizenship that mocks authenticity. Indigenous peoples exploited by invaders often find themselves strangers even to their own traditions, and they become anonymous outsiders, feeling unworthy, unwilling, and unable to fit in with foreign expectations and values forced on them. They are usually left to get sick and waste away through neglect, alcoholism, suicide, or sheer inertia. Vulnerability, existential and actual, is their way of life.

Another common example of alienation is found among efficient and conscientious professionals who exhaust themselves trying to cope with inexhaustible problems. Professional burnout tends to occur when satisfaction in work diminishes. Appreciation by others goes down, too, and institutional demands increase without adequate compensation or recognition. Self-esteem fades, and distance from resuscitating rewards increases.

Still another example of alienation (or existential vulnerability, where meaning and being are no longer joined) happens to certain people in the so-called midlife crisis. This popular diagnosis reflects deep distancing from present reality and expectations that are now gone. The formerly fresh and hopeful reality becomes mechanical, stale, and fulsome. But this can happen at any age; for example, I imagine that certain older people are particularly vulnerable to having no meaning for their being. They may forfeit individuality, having found no avenue for operating as a person who matters and makes a difference. They live on scraps from the table of life. Surely it is only practical to reduce visionary expectations and to provide for as much as autonomy as possible. But in all candor, the spiritual and actual impoverishments of old age contribute mightily to existential vulnerability. Social withdrawal is but another instance of self-enclosure for safety's sake. This is the estrangement that existentalists are keenly poised to decry.

Vulnerability is truly typical of whatever common threads there are in the latticework of humankind. It takes many forms; the mean-spirited, contentious, biased, rude, resentful, self-righteous, and self-inflated— all of these and more become the negative Axis II personalities of clinical psychiatry, although few ever permit themselves to acknowledge their own vulnerability. Milder cases are just cranks with short tempers and loud voices; more severe cases are sour and disillusioned. Disgruntled to an extreme but without admitting to overt suffering, their vulnerability seems at times only to be solidified by the villainy and evil they see in others, and therefore enjoy.

The skeptical pilgrim cannot escape experiencing and coping with a wide range of problems to which his own considerable vulnerability exposes him. But these problems will change to a degree, according (but not proportionate) to the effort he puts into opening his self-enclosed personality. This, too, is one of the aims of psychotherapy, or whatever equivalent is apt to liberate people from spiritual servitude and bring meaning and being together in the generous proportion each deserves.

Chapter 4

The Courage to Cope

Final solutions to the vexing and persistent problems of human nature are seemingly elusive. Similar problems are addressed in every generation with much variation in form, relevance, and expression but at best only temporary easement. Whether progress itself permanently changes the nature of human problems or merely transports them to another stage is questionable. Problems of disease, poverty, pain, warfare, violence, and crime are temporarily abated by social, medical, and political innovations, but not by much. Considerations such as these cause the skeptical pilgrim to hesitate before rejoicing in small, temporary gains. Other pilgrims, not at all so skeptical, do not seem to be bothered by the paradoxes of existence and by the endurance of ultimate questions. They are sustained by faith and enjoy deep credulity about ultimate reasons, meager rewards, and questionable resolutions. But skeptics need more than the testimony and fellowship of faithful believers in order to thrive.

A Curious Virtue Called Courage

Because there is no certain promise that final ends will ever be reached, or that decisive answers to ultimate questions will be found and abolish all doubts, we can scarcely question that it takes courage to be a skeptical pilgrim. It would be far easier (and socially very desirable) to join wholeheartedly with the many who believe in what is or seems to be in store, and who hope fervently that at the end everything will become not only clear but pretty close to blissful.

Meanwhile, the enigmas of existence continue, and it is hard to find them willing to give up their secrets. At moments of ease and satisfaction, when all things seem possible and happiness reigns, the courage to cope with whatever might present itself in the future has to be considered a fundamental virtue. Dealing with practical problems, instead of assuming that whatever hazards exist are trivial, requires giving up the denial that distorts and splits meaning from being, and which ignores the unexpected crises that are never very far away.

Courage itself is a curious concept. Though acknowledged to be a virtue because it resembles bravery, it has seldom been thoroughly investigated, especially by psychologists. For the most part, clinicians have considered only the negative side of courage: the absence of fear, or the pathological consequences of lacking courage. This includes doubt, despair, avoidance, anxiety, guilt, and so on. But what is true of courage is also true of such other positive virtues as hope, generosity, altruism, loyalty, and compassion. It is not the nature of hope that gets attention, but despair. It is not compassion but cruelty that gets analyzed, not generosity but penury, not equanimity but anxiety and fear. Investigators have generally been concerned mainly with what goes wrong and who is the perpetrator of misfortune and misery. Like tabloids, vice gets featured; virtues do not unless they are turned inside out to show that they are vices in disguise. Examples of the latter include reaction formation (where, out of evil, something good becomes entrenched) and counterphobias (the fear of being afraid that leads sometimes to actions synonymous with high risk and courage).

Nevertheless, regardless of their origin, we admire courage and admonish cowardice as if they were opposites. As in a dull sermon that praises the virtue of being virtuous and damns the evil of being bad, neither the nature of courage nor that of cowardice is thoroughly explained.

Courage always contains an element of risk, but risk is not always courageous. Risk and recklessness are close companions. When smokers face the risk of lung cancer and emphysema and continue to smoke, their behavior is seldom admired and almost never called courageous. Courage has to represent the highest values to which society owes loyalty. For example, patriots are called courageous because they demonstrate in an exemplary way the courage to cope with threats facing their country. But we do not offer terrorists the same praise, because they throw away their lives for causes and values that many of us do not admire. In short, courageous acts have to entail risk for an approved social value. Without a reigning value, the risky act is simply foolhardy.

Historians are still not sure whether General George Armstrong Custer was a brave and authentic hero or an ambitious grandstander who died, not for his country, but for his vanity. It all depends on how one views the reasons for the Battle of the Little Big Horn. Mountain climbers risk their lives and limbs participating in a sport that not everyone finds equally praiseworthy; are they courageous or foolhardy? Even death for a good cause, however, is not always courageous. People can be innocent bystanders who are shot or hit by a speeding car. Their deaths merely but tragically indicate that it is sometimes risky to walk on the street. They did not die for a noble cause. A soldier who is killed by friendly fire is not heroic but merely a victim, although he fought for a good cause under hazardous circumstances. He may also have been courageous, but not because he was killed.

Even hardened skeptics admire a courageous act, provided that they agree with its value. It makes them feel good and provides a confirmation about the importance of values and ideals they believe in and would like to emulate. Thus the heroic side of the courage to cope has several requirements: risk, high value, inspiring emulations, and making people feel good about one person's coping with adversity and mastering insecurity.

Courageous acts—those that cope with significant problems

challenging highly established values—also justify and exemplify the highest standards of which society is capable, regardless of risk. I have mentioned that such acts are worthy of emulation, except that few people are actually capable of duplicating a courageous act without also confronting the risk and equivocation about which values are best. Jobs that are risky (belonging to the military in wartime, police work, etc.) have good causes backing them, but people do not flock to apply. Courage to cope with pressing problems, despite risk, may still be worthy of imitation. But it does not seem to be enough. Until recently, soldiers were drafted, and police work still is considered a somewhat blue-collar career. Just being put in jeopardy apparently is not enough to be called courageous.

The Rationality of Courage

Risk in representing a worthy cause, though, is necessary for truly courageous acts. Indeed, those who become heroes provide a rationality in that the very act of living courageously seems superlatively worthwhile. Compared with courage, other estimable virtues (honesty, learning, prudence, etc.) seem pallid by comparison. Perhaps it is because other virtues require little risk, although an equal amount of skill for a good cause. Even so, we might wish to emulate someone who plays good tennis or is expert in figuring out income tax without help. Neither constitutes a risky challenge, although the values they represent might be very high.

Any virtue is worthy, but it changes over time just as values change. It may be admired by one group, but not by another. Technical skill is usually admired by those valuing self-reliance and competence in using tools. In an age of technical obsolescence, however, self-reliance is usually confined to knowing who to call in the yellow pages. Chastity was once prized so highly that it was not only a virtue (usually for a woman), but a sign of courage to die defending one's honor. Nowadays, chastity is hardly honored at all, and in some circles is viewed suspiciously. There is another element to virtue or courage, however, in that it does not always consist of meeting a challenge. Virtues may be good examples for social policy, to be respected and worth emulating especially when there are no laws in place to enforce such actions. In other words, soldiers and police are expected to act courageously because that is their job. Honesty is a sign of integrity, but also a caution about being caught stealing.

Seeing virtues as unwritten social policy would account for their temporary value and likelihood to change along with the society. Some skeptics, however, claim that virtue is a very dubious concept because it changes easily and conveniently (e.g., some virtues are middle-class values that the poor cannot afford and the rich do not need). Virtue is good as long as it claims to represent what society would like to believe it stands for. But courage seems to be in a class by itself, never quite going out of style because it makes risk seem sensible and worthwhile. Being and meaning come together in courage, and are admirable in so doing.

Though courage is usually associated with physical bravery under fire or in similar circumstances, it is not confined to this kind of danger. The anxiety of the risk could be implied, not declared outright. For example, the legendary suffering undergone by a starving artist might deserve admiration and even represent to society the importance of artistic values. There is risk of failure, and of falling ill and wasting much time if talent development and recognition are slow. Thus it takes physical courage and much conviction to be an artist, especially if one is unsure about the level of skill required.

Courage also insists upon a degree of pain. Giving generously to charity, for instance, is virtuous, but to be courageous the act should also hurt (as in "Give till it hurts"). Without pain, the gift is only a potential tax deduction, which in its way is still an excellent social policy, closely related to paying taxes in the first place. But the key characteristic of giving very generously to good causes (or struggling to be an artist) is not primarily physical courage. The goal in charity for others and cultivating artistic skills is self-fulfillment through a way of life that others might admire, although many might withhold wholehearted approval. If either way of life is physically hazardous, it is only indirectly.

Telling the boss that a fellow worker is stealing funds might be a good example of honesty and courage, a fine social policy not covered by specific laws. But to others, this is snitching, which is not at all noble. In fact, the thief might be stealing money to feed hungry and homeless people. And considering the risk of discovery, arrest, and disgrace, the thief could deserve to be called more courageous than the whistle-blower. It depends on who does the judging.

There are forms of courage that involve little physical risk except for those risks contingent on just being alive and vulnerable. These other types of courage risk scorn and ostracism. For example, standing up for an unpopular but noble cause, or advocating an action that violates social policy but obeys conscience, might show much *moral courage*. This form of courage goes against conventional beliefs and moral standards that many people, perhaps a majority, support. It might however, be admired by a respectful minority or by a few virtuous folk whose good opinion the moral rebel wants.

Physical and moral courage, therefore, have similar criteria. Both represent exemplary standards held by members of society, although the exact number of supporters is subject to variation and change. In a sense, where there are no laws or principles involved, courageous acts may be acts of social duty or policy not sanctioned by established rules and regulations. There is risk, of course, but not always of the same kind. In any case, risk must include a sense of anxiety to keep from just being headstrong or heedless.

In a curious way, those who carry out exemplary acts of courage and social duty, even for an unpopular cause, do so out of a sense of authenticity, not vulnerability. The vulnerable self suffers, but seldom to justify a cause (other than something highly personal). For example, a cancer patient who suffers intractable pain is pathetically vulnerable, but not for a noble cause that represents social duty or policy. Those who are said to think that pain is somehow liberating and redemptive, in my opinion, are referring to someone else's pain, not their own. To be courageous truly means a will to cope, despite threat and suffering, for a noble cause.

The Courage to Be

Paul Tillich (1886–1952), one of the most influential thinkers of our era, put courage right at the center of human activity and conduct. For Tillich, courage is an act of self-affirmation despite anxiety. Without it, we are vulnerable to the deepest form of threat, which is nonbeing. *The Courage to Be* (1952) represents an effort to deal decisively with ultimate questions (e.g., finitude, death, nonbeing, or guilt) or whatever helps overcome an otherwise meaningless existence. Tillich did not single out physical courage as a requirement for restoring meaning to being. He confined himself to the courage to be courageous in an existential sense. Although he provided no details as to how this could be done, he did indicate that courage is required whenever a person grapples with fundamental existential problems through ultimate questions.

In classical times, the Stoics balanced courage against rationality, so that a true Stoic could, for example, meet death without fear, having lived a life of reason. For Stoics, the purpose of life was to deal directly and courageously with problems, supported by a lifetime of dedication to philosophical inquiries. Tillich was strongly influenced by this position, especially by the idea that courage meant self-affirmation despite difficulties and dread.

Even a cursory review of Tillich's prolific writing leads inevitably to a conclusion that he must have known skeptical pilgrims, as well as more conventional believers. Perhaps Tillich was a skeptical pilgrim himself; he had many of the characteristics that I have singled out. Nevertheless, in and through his theological language, he showed how profoundly he was aware of the difficulties in self-affirmation. It was not self-affirmation for any particular gain, but for its own sake. Self-affirmation, self-realization, and authenticity all seem to mean the same; consequently, I do not find it difficult to adapt some of Tillich's ideas about the courage to be to my own impressions about the courage to cope. Moreover, some of the aims in self-affirmation are analogous to those sought in psychotherapy and in mental health standards. Self-esteem, sanity, congenial social policy, and a strong sense of responsibility are pursued courageously. But none of these aims and standards means very much without an appreciation of finitude, fallibility, guilt, and other ultimate questions.

Tillich's thinking brings out still another form of courage. As with that of physical risk and moral dilemmas, this type of courage calls upon the vulnerable self (my term) to deal forthrightly with finitude, fallibility, and what might be termed *existential foolishness*, often called absurdity. In an existential sense this courage is pragmatic, because without it ultimate extinction of the self is guaranteed. Vulnerability in an existential sense is equivalent to being doomed.

I cannot undertake a searching summation of Tillich's viewpoint. It is beyond my scholarship and purpose, which is to follow the courage to be into its clinical and practical applications, called the courage to cope. I shall knowingly paraphrase a bit, condense and abbreviate much, perhaps distort a little, but I will try to provide an understanding of how these theological and existential concepts fit into the notion of the vulnerable self in its confrontation with ultimate questions. According to Tillich (1952), there are three major forms of existential anxiety: fate and death, emptiness and meaninglessness, and guilt and condemnation. He makes clear that these represent existential anxiety, not an abnormal state of mind. I expect to translate these ideas into a recognizable series of clinical conditions—not diseases, but forms of suffering related to the vulnerable self. Furthermore, the courage to cope is a prerequisite in mastering anxiety in either its existential or psychopathological form.

Fate and Death

Fate and death are concerns about the nature of survival. In a specific existential sense, survival anxiety centers on the brevity of life, its contingent and uncertain nature, and the certainty of death. Death anxiety overshadows everything else that causes anxiety, and it gives everything else its ultimate seriousness. Fate, Tillich says, is the rule of contingency, a fascinating phrase that means that anything can happen because there is no well-defined causal determination, nor is there absolute meaning and purpose in what we do. Nevertheless, fear of death is an absolute, a living reference point. It makes us pause and wonder about the worth of such matters as self-affirmation or the courage to be anything at all.

Emptiness and Meaninglessness

Emptiness and meaninglessness in Tillich's view also provoke anxiety, this time about loss of an ultimate concern, which is the meaning that gives meaning to all meanings. Although Tillich was concerned about a spiritual center in man, I am not. I usually forget to think about spirituality, except when I find someone who is spiritually bankrupt. But if making sense makes sense, as I believe it does, then making sense contributes to whatever is meant by a purpose in life. Tillich's anxiety, which takes the form of emptiness and meaninglessness, will inevitably signify living without courage to be. Nonbeing that results from lacking courage to be signifies alienation and apathy about achieving self-realization. Tillich maintained that doubt is a condition of all spiritual life, a claim that a skeptical pilgrim might find supportive. Tillich means that doubt alienates individuals from their spiritual center. It is not, however, part of the skepticism that a pilgrim might cherish; for the skeptic, doubt is a sign of health.

Guilt and Condemnation

Guilt and condemnation are vexing terms that inevitably resonate with the vulnerable self. Because of its difficulty coping with the contingencies of existence, as well as with its own fallibility and failures, the vulnerable self (a term I am encouraged to believe Tillich might understand and accept) falls far short of authenticity or genuine responsibility. It is rebuked and condemned for self-betrayal, as if the self had a hand in failing to achieve the best he or she was capable of. Guilt, which is close to shame, represents a moral viewpoint. It also implies demoralization, a clinical condition resulting from repeated failure to fulfill directives and resist violating prohibitions. As a result, the existential term *estrangement* is appropriate because the vulnerable self stands ambiguously between good and evil, devoid of hope and courage. In psychological terms, the vulnerable self is lost in its quest for personal responsibility because it has failed to match up to expectations and coped poorly with prospects for betterment.

I do not believe that Tillich would advocate moral self-righteousness, which not only condemns but pretends to have the right answers. Freedom to choose has to mean something other than being free to be at loose ends. Motion without a purpose is as deplorable as purpose without motion. Freedom to choose has to heed the freedom to lose. But some others are so caught up in self-congratulatory certitude that they scorn those who falter, or who cannot or will not live up to their very high standards. Whatever strength these moral misers get from orthodox affiliations, their moral superiority is an evil virtue; like the joy in gossiping, moral superiority is another spectator sport. The courage to cope does have confidence in its own capacity, but not certitude—only fortitude to find joy in excellence.

Existential Courage in Psychotherapy

Conflict, a force that pits wishes against fears, also violates custom and standards that we have been taught to uphold and respect. There is a psychopathology of guilt and a psychopathology that feels no guilt, only condemnation. In psychotherapy (one of the many avenues that troubled people take to find relief from the ambiguity of suffering), faults can be enormously magnified, often in inverse proportion to the actual offenses and failures that are blamed for a downfall.

It is exceedingly difficult for even the best-motivated patients to face shortcomings and to confront anxiety, guilt, and emptiness. Who is not willing to deny, or to excuse, or to plead his or her case instead of putting aside pride and carefully contained narcissism to courageously cope with key conflicts? Our self-image, especially in instances of low self-esteem, is often complicated by a strong belief in being right and responsible all the time. There is at least a conviction that this is a desirable and perfect end that "good" people regularly achieve.

The courage to cope is not at all the virtue of heroes; the virtue that makes it possible is not the courage of saints. People who are in psychotherapy simply are, at most, striving to become the best they can. At the very least, they want some relief and resolution of whatever agonizes their existence. This, too, may include an unrecognized wish to live up to potential. In order for them to do so, psychotherapy should encourage autonomy so that a patient learns to cope better and develop skill in self-affirmation.

The courage required in psychotherapy is neither physical nor moral, but the *courage to become*. Existential courage, therefore, signifies what the vulnerable self must accomplish in overcoming difficulties. In the privacy of the self, such courage finds no glory. But it does entail a willingness to pursue and confront ultimate questions of fallibility (the negative conditions of existence), finitude (the boundless limitations of being alive), and the final certainty of death.

At its best, or most encouraging, psychotherapy is a project in self-affirmation, not an endless circle of complaints and good intentions. Although few if any psychotherapies directly deal with such portentous topics as fate and death, emptiness and meaninglessness, or guilt and condemnation, all of which are sources of existential anxiety, most patients (and a good many therapists) are constantly bombarded with existential threats from every direction. Yet such considerations are implicit and therefore require courage.

Even at this moment, three forms of existential anxiety are being tested, from issues about (1) survival to (2) competence in coping to a strong sense of (3) responsibility. The existential meaning of *survival* is more than the question of withstanding illness and injury to get through the day intact. Survival means to triumph symbolically and literally over the contingencies of fate and the certainty of death. Our life span is limited by nature, but symbolically it is feasible to survive with significance—to have a purpose, and to matter in some respect. In a sense, as some investigators and philosophers claim, our biological destiny is to die and disappear without a trace. This is true enough, but what sense does it make if we only turn out to be or become something that will eventually disintegrate? Granted, survival takes a strong constitution, much luck, agility, and immunity in abundance, and at the far end, there is nothingness. Courage is obligatory, and it must be sharpened enough to survive the bleak fact of obliteration.

Considering the odds, it is a lost cause, yet the existential attitude (which Tillich called the courage to be, and I, as a therapist, must interpret as the courage to cope) tries to put a plausible and acceptable meaning on this fateful discontinuity. Self-affirmation is as good a meaning as any that have been suggested, and it is much more feasible than yearning for another incarnation in which we either make the same mistakes all over again or, possibly, have the opportunity to make different mistakes and see how it comes out. Self-affirmation in psychotherapy needs courage to accept indistinct goals. But self-affirmation helps overcome the weaknesses of the vulnerable self through an alliance that confronts ultimate questions, which have no ultimate goals.

The second form of existential anxiety concerns *competence to cope,* along with the courage to develop the skills and strategies necessary to do the job well. But this kind of competence is not just learning to be good at what you do (the ordinary meaning of skill), but doing what you do in order to be good and not to fall readily into emptiness or futility.

Responsibility means a strategic effort to live up to potential by examining possibilities. It strikes a deal with reality by struggling to formulate, and to be formed by ideals melded to practicalities. The opposite of conscientious self-affirmation, which means the same as responsibility, is guilt and condemnation, which is equivalent to self-betrayal.

A skeptic is wholly justified in wondering if deep within these abstract pronouncements are only meager platitudes that make minimal sense. Self-affirmation, for example, may mean militant self-observation, which it does. But self-observation in psychotherapy is not an easy skill to develop; it can cause vast unease, suffering, shame, or other demeaning feelings. Competent observation, however, is what we think about what we experience, in contrast to what we do without thinking much about. Self-disclosure can be frightening, so it needs a substantial degree of courage.

Psychotherapy usually contends with guilt and shame, especially in the absence of due cause. But existential guilt and shame differ from neurotic guilt or baseless shame. The ego ideal that responsibility reaches out for may be unattainable, and so is designed to bring about failure and condemnation. For example, some people dream impossible dreams in order to tolerate a painful present, or to erase events that emphasize their inadequacy. They often come to therapists asking to be made happy. This in itself is an illusion, assuring failure, and is not a goal. Nevertheless, they say, "If only . . . then I would certainly be happy!" The existential situation is such that elusive or illusory emotions called happiness are simply romantic diversions, destined at best to be short-lived. The courage to cope cannot accept happiness as a reasonably permanent objective, but neither is unhappiness a permanent condition. To accept this concept is in itself somewhat self-healing, if not altogether therapeutic.

Survival, competence, and responsibility do overlap, but each constitutes a separate level of anxiety. Their differences are demonstrated by differences between *must, can* or *could,* and *should,* which are often confused. Survival depends on what I must do to survive. Competence means what I can or could do in order to cope adequately. Responsibility is what I should do to affirm myself, according to the best in and for me; this is also called an ego ideal.

The vulnerable self declares, for example, "I *must* go to Harvard," as if it were a life-and-death problem. A more relaxed person might say, "I *could* go to Harvard," meaning that he or she has the competence to do so, or, "I *can* go to Harvard," to suggest that he or she has already been accepted at the school. To declare, however, that "I *should* go to Harvard" implies a directive stemming from an obligation to attend, as well as a conflict about doing so.

Existential anxiety lurks in all three of these statements, ranging from life and death (at least symbolically) to the question of qualifications and to moral and social expectations. An alert psychotherapist would have to disentangle these different anxieties through understanding the different meanings that each statement or attitude conveys. The meaning that equates going to Harvard with actual survival differs from the declarations about competence and choice, and both differ from signifying a failure of conscience resulting from failing to live up to the standard that others want and expect.

The core concept depends on distinguishing between choice and necessity, which is always critical in psychotherapy. The courage to resolve such ambiguity of meaning is just as important in psychotherapy as the courage to deal with anxiety or ambivalence in other connections. Furthermore, if courage can confront and contend with ambiguity (i.e., choice between meanings, or accepting the necessity of one meaning over another), patients are then enabled to confront much more in psychotherapy, particularly the conflicts and self-defeats that cause so much anguish.

If such attribution of "courage" seems very tepid in comparison with such grand virtues as bravery on the battlefield or fortitude in standing up for a principle, it is still courageous to deal directly with the anxiety, shame, guilt, or other risks inherent to dealing with conflict. Self-appraisal is an uncomfortable, even humiliating task that most people would rather not do, but it is necessary when examining what causes trouble. There are few who do not see themselves as always standing up for all the values usually approved and admired (intelligence, reason, dedication, decisiveness, etc.); if they do not, then there are always ample excuses. Perhaps modesty, another popular virtue, modulates the more extreme assertions of virtue and value. Because of conflict and low self-esteem, however, people entering psychotherapy seldom see themselves as possessing these virtues. As a result the vulnerable self is most prominent, almost to the exclusion of ego strengths and authenticity (which are usually ignored, anyway, except during resistance). Nevertheless, it takes courage to move ahead in the task of therapy; otherwise, restoration of normality would not be so difficult. Denial, rationalization, resistance, defensiveness on all fronts, and narcissistic enchantment get in the way.

On Being Bad

Countertransference, in simple terms, is how a therapist feels about transference; that is, about a patient arriving in need and expecting restoration of what has been deprived or lost. At the center of countertransference are emotional needs and conflicts distinct to the therapist that are almost certain to creep into clinical judgments. Many so-called clinical judgments turn out to be moral judgments disguised as practical decisions about what is correct or incorrect at a particular juncture in therapy—that is, "it is good to do that," or "bad to feel or think that."

Therapists who praise themselves for having a "nonjudgmental" attitude are not confronting their own ambiguities and ambivalences. Too often, they are taking part in a hypocritical farce. From a patient's standpoint, disclosures of wrongdoing, weakness, deviance, or plain incapacity to cope or to know what to cope with are reasons enough to feel bad in a moral sense. The courage to become is still embryonic. When a patient judges himself or herself to be unpardonably guilty, it is a clear sign of depression. But coming into therapy at all and admitting insurmountable problems is enough to make many people feel gravely inadequate, if not incurably flawed. The vulnerable self is always a victim who feels intolerable and shameful when compared with others. The therapist who ignores countertransference and fails to examine himself or herself is surely "resisting" therapy, especially if he or she lacks compassion for and appreciation of the patient's will to change.

Even the diagnosis signifies how a therapist regards a patient's abnormality. It often reflects how acceptable and unacceptable a patient's behavior, thoughts, or problems are to the therapist, who has a personal set of normative standards ingrained in his or her mind. In fact, symptoms are medical analogies drawn on the basis of what a patient is or is not considered capable of doing, and as noted, clinical judgments sometimes are disguised moral judgments made by a very fallible therapist who measures the patient against his or her own presumed normality.

Who does the measuring? What standards are applied? Which form of normality is approved? It has been said that sexual perversion may be defined as what a therapist would not do himself or herself; otherwise, everything falls within the range of normality and acceptability. The same flexible standards of good and bad may apply to the practices of parenting, marriage, business relations, leisure activities, religious affiliation, and so forth, which are largely matters of opinion. Regardless of how broadminded any therapist professes to be, he or she cannot help but define certain kinds of thought and behavior as good or bad. As a result, the courage to cope usually is affected by judgments about being outside the realm of acceptability. This makes prognosis somewhat personal and conditional, often to an egregious degree.

Ordinarily, therapists suppress approval or disapproval of someone who happens not to believe as they do. There is a double standard in therapy itself that requires unlimited candor and disclosure from a patient, regardless of embarrassment, and yet an impersonal distancing on the part of the therapist. I do not object to this double standard, because it might help prevent the more painful examples of sticky transference and countertransference alliances. Therapists are not friends, although they are friendly; they are not confidants, although they are ready to accept confidential information. The sole difficulty of the double standard, aside from offending our sense of democracy, is that therapists are also supposed to feel relatively judgment free (i.e., to realize themselves clearly enough to know what they pretend not to feel).

Moral stances are neither good nor bad in therapy. But such judgments of good and bad should not be disguised, and should be traced to their roots in the silences of a therapist's heart. My "shoulds" in the previous sentence are, of course, moral judgments, too. Therapists are only human, after all, and they are not required to revamp their moral standards—only to be aware of them. If such beliefs then interfere with the acceptability of what patients do or stand for, a therapist is directed to refrain from imposing them. This, too, is a moral stance, urged upon therapists who are by nature or indoctrination tempted to use moral judgments as a regular instrument of work.

There are many ways of hiding moral judgments. Psychotherapy itself can be considered an exercise in strategic self-appraisal and self-correction for both therapist and patient. The vulnerable self assumes many deceptive guises; including a righteous wish to be a healer; to guide others into proper channels; to be a shining example of virtue, courage, or principle; or to advise, even to laugh at, in a benevolent fashion. Social support, which is generally approved, is in fact an alliance intended to normalize erroneous or ineffective, even objectionable, behavior. But it may become a power ploy that implicitly requires strict adherence to what the therapist or person providing such support demands. Almost any interpretation or insight has echoes of a judgment— usually one of disapproval, however mild, but sometimes quite tart. If a therapist cannot refrain from a private moral judgment about a patient's extramarital affairs, for example, the secret disapproval will come out in what the therapist chooses to interpret.

Forbearance is a virtue that is imperative in psychotherapy, because it is necessary to believe that nothing is absolutely evil, even if we cannot wholeheartedly sanction it. These days, for example, many people are more tolerant than they once were of single mothers raising children out of wedlock and on public assistance. Just a few years ago, the same situation would have been frowned on or considered sinful. Today, while appreciating extenuating circumstances, middle-class society still might deplore a mother who supplements welfare checks by earnings from prostitution and drug dealing. Good and bad judgments are not a matter of choice.

Therapists, too, need courage to resolve conflicts between what is and what they think ought to be. There is no obligation to like everyone, nor is it a mandatory social policy to please everybody under all circumstances. Fawning is generally speaking, a sign of social insecurity that needs tending to lest another judgment ("I want to be considered a nice person") be transformed into unwarranted criticism of someone else.

If therapists are to survive, be competent, and practice responsibly, they need courage enough for honest self-examination and to cope adequately enough to correct shortcomings. Complacency can be an occupational hazard; it is certainly an enemy when combined with reluctance to self-correct. And no therapist can truly profess not to have boundaries beyond which he or she makes negative (or even suspiciously positive) judgments. Boredom, dislike, amusement, admiration, envy, and the like are signs of implicit moral judgments getting in the way and neutralizing morale.

Respect and Regard

The central imperative for being a therapist of quality is respect and regard in both directions. Empathy, which is greatly prized, is not much more than respect and regard for a patient's irrationality. This imperative will not imply approval or disapproval, but it does eliminate both unjustified scorn and undue admiration.

Boundaries exist here, too. Not every therapist and not every patient can work out difficulties with giving and getting respect and regard. I could not, for example, have high respect and regard for people whose behavior repels me. Conversely, those who despise and hate me as a matter of personal bias and principle would find no occasion for respecting me, let alone having any regard.

Respect and regard are priorities before anyone can be considered courageous. Heroes, after all, exemplify our principles, whereas those who go to their death for alien principles are simply fanatics. Most of us, for example, would put Dietrich Bonhoeffer high on any list of heroes. He put his life on the line for convictions and principles that any civilized society is supposed to live by, and died in a Nazi prison. In contrast, Martin Heidegger, the noted existential philosopher of the same era, would not be considered particularly courageous in the way he apparently embraced Nazi doctrines. His advocates, however, would revise their criteria for heroism and find a place for Heidegger because of his eminence.

Rhetorically speaking, I might embrace the devil on occasion, although he has never shown much interest in bargaining for my soul. But I could not conscientiously or productively treat a Nazi, or a former Nazi, or a member of a hate group in this country. I find it difficult to empathize with certain other groups whose principles grossly violate mine until I establish a range of respect and regard within which mutual work can proceed. I did have a couple of patients who were former soldiers in the Wehrmacht, as well as a few militant anti-Semites. They managed to tolerate me after a while, at least as well as other patients do. We worked out respect and regard despite our differences, including a better understanding of the contingencies of their existence. Nevertheless, the question of courage never came up. I was able to put aside personal anxiety with a certain effort and found much relief that times had changed, that the war was over, and that our positions were not reversed.

Respect and regard are, of course, value judgments that the good outweighs the bad and that risk of any variety is minimal. Existential courage respects fallibility and faults as inevitable contingencies, not sources of absolute evil. In the therapeutic encounter, respect and regard are possible if the participants see themselves playing complementary roles (as opposed to good guys and bad guys). Skepticism could not exist unless it were possible to entertain opposing viewpoints and consider what it might be like to be that person we now find so strange or objectionable.

Why, then, does psychiatry still emphasize the pathological qualities of patients and practically ignore their strengths and virtues? If therapists of quality show respect and regard for a wide range of conduct, what makes it difficult to appreciate or perceive desirable traits? These questions become even more pressing if we fully acknowledge that most psychiatric patients suffer from shaky self-regard, and that most psychotherapeutic efforts are designed to develop better self-esteem. I can only conclude that to some degree patients are faulted for having faults, as well as for some of their good points. Some years ago, a group of psychiatric residents were sitting around a table discussing new admissions and the progress of older patients. One of these patients was a middle-aged man who was obsessed with the size of his penis and traced all of his inadequacies to that source. In fact, he was so absurd that without realizing his error, he consistently called his organ a "pencil," not a penis. Several of the young psychiatrists began to banter about pencils and penises in ridiculing the patient who was absent. The senior doctor stopped them sharply. He reminded them that the man they mocked was a fellow-sufferer who felt pain, was not to be laughed at, and despite his whimsical convictions, deserved respect and regard. If they curtailed their amusement long enough, perhaps they could appreciate his suffering and helplessness; then actual respect and regard might come about. They had to see beyond the pathological to the existential, putting aside the ridiculous and seeing this human being in his loneliness. Their task was to search for strengths and whatever virtues could be culled from such an unpromising situation: The good in him had to outweigh the bad.

Good and Bad Copers

If coping requires courage, then should good copers be considered more courageous than those who fail to cope? Do courageous people cope better than others, or does their success tend to make them more courageous? Is coping a learned skill, and if so, can courage also be taught and acquired? Are good copers those who practice better strategies, or do they just cope effectively by choosing problems they already do well with? Is courage simply a by-product of energy, initiative, and ingenuity? Do courageous people take risks, despite anxiety, as a character trait and come out ahead regularly? How do good copers and bad copers get that way? What are their other personality traits?

These are all pretty weighty questions, and I am sure that no one has the audacity to claim the correct answers. Each question can be considered a plausible hypothesis about people who cope, however, or at least they are subject to having appropriate and testable hypotheses made up about them. Otherwise, such signal concepts as the courage to cope, to be, or to become are only pious and portentous abstractions, without a lot of meaning.

I have already emphasized how courage, whenever it is found, always commands respect and regard. Conversely, holding someone in high regard (as we might with an esteemed teacher, doctor, or leader) usually implies that we expect them to behave courageously should a proper occasion arise; otherwise, we would be deeply disappointed. To find, for example, that a respected and beloved father is little more than hot air when it comes to courage, physical or moral, is an event that is remembered for a long time. Sigmund Freud wrote about his own disappointment with his father, as have many other men of lesser eminence who expected courage in exchange for their admiration.

Ordinarily, lack of manifest courage is taken to be cowardice, which may be an unfair and pejorative judgment. But some people seem to lack physical courage while exemplifying high moral courage; the reverse is at least as common. It is far more important in understanding the vulnerable self to realize that those who do not cope well, and seem cowardly under certain conditions, are not despicable but simply unfortunate enough to face selected problems with excessive anxiety and a sense of overwhelming risk.

Good copers are usually expected to succeed and expect themselves to succeed in whatever they undertake. Noncopers with multiple problems are thought to get that way by coping so poorly that they get in trouble regularly; when problems snowball into great masses, control is lost and coping fails completely. By contrast, good copers do not shrink from problems, and by tackling them successively and with dispatch, they are likely to deal very effectively with whatever else is put in their way.

How does coping affect respect and regard? Is a poor coper who fails at a task respected as little or as much as those who always seem to have easy problems to cope with? Or do we withhold the label of courage from copers until they regularly master difficult and dangerous confrontations? It is likely that bad copers avoid certain problems not from prudence, but because anxiety is so difficult to control. Good copers might not hesitate for the same reason. In neither case, however, is lack of courage necessarily a significant fault. It might be foolhardy to undertake an action doomed to catastrophe.

The difference between good coping and bad coping primarily depends on skill and choice of available strategies to use; it also includes willingness to act despite anxiety, which is courageous. However, it is not a simple matter of who has or does not have sufficient courage to cope.

In almost any phase of human activity, success breeds more success. While we learn from mistakes, we need to be encouraged and have some successes before we can continue learning from mistakes. After all, encouragement means to take heart and be heartened, despite difficulties.

Good copers may not be good people; those seeking power and perverse influence may successfully use effective but undesirable strategies to reach their goal. In contrast, bad copers may fail, despite impeccable strategies and much courage, physical and moral. They may continue to fail, and still be thought of as courageous, since persistence and determination despite obstacles are admirable, under certain conditions. We cannot be sure that the best copers are the most courageous, but we do tend to admire successes and give them much credit, although they may not need as much courage as a poor coper.

Because we admire those who cope well and have other positive traits, it is not surprising that psychotherapists, like many teachers or employers, prefer clients who are agreeable and share the values and virtues they approve of. Such clients are therefore likely to succeed, where a less attractive person might fail. Much is expected of them, because much is given. Such patients, therefore, by self-selection and therapist validation are called promising. As a rule, therapists like patients from a similar cultural background, or at least one to which the therapist might aspire. These patients share certain values and are preferred because they are verbal, attractive, educated, somewhat introspective middle-class liberals who have respectable jobs at which they generally succeed. Because they generally do well, there is no reason to expect that they will not continue to do well with a little help from the psychotherapist. The therapeutic help is necessary because even such admirable and promising patients come with low self-esteem and a record of recent failures; therapy is expected to correct such deficits. To fail would make the therapist a poor coper who might well also lack the courage to cope.

In general terms, good patients are those who seldom complain, never blame, ask for little, are not very sick, and are exceedingly appreciative. And, of course, they pay bills on time and are never late, but are understanding when the therapist has to cancel an appointment. Even when therapy fails or the results are less than expected, the therapist is never made to feel incompetent or guilty. Respect and regard consistently go in both directions. Courage is seldom in question because it is never tested, or because the values both stand for are enough.

Superman, for instance, could never be expected to need therapy. His larger-than-life accomplishments in coping with very high risk show him to be an ideal person, earning our respect and regard, and he can never have a poor opinion of himself for very long. But even at high risk, is Superman courageous when he copes so smoothly and triumphantly? In my opinion he is not, because with his skills and strategies that work out so unfailingly, he does not have to be. There is risk in what he tackles, but no genuine anxiety. I cannot imagine a fearful Superman, however baffled he might seem at times. There is no need for the triumph of will over anxiety that is the hallmark of courage. Although he leaps high buildings as the rest of us climb stairs, neither his leaps nor our climbing is an example of ultimate coping or high courage.

In contrast, Walter Mitty, the ultimate wimp, imagines himself in a variety of precarious plights where he overcomes odds, defies risk, and copes supremely well. Obviously, he would like to be a supercoper, as he imagines Superman to be. But Walter Mitty's accomplishments stop in his head. He is not courageous, nor does he have to be. Walter is a good coper only in imaginary situations.

Between these two extremes of the supercoper who never fails and the amiable wimp who never needs to cope, who among us is likely to have courage? Good copers are courageous enough to face physical, moral, and pragmatic problems despite fears about having enough skills and appropriate strategies for coming through, and they succeed more often than not. Although a successful outcome, consistently reached, is *not* the only difference, it is a very significant difference between a good coper and a bad coper.

What Do Good Copers Do?

1. Good copers are usually *optimistic* about succeeding. Though optimism may be partially the result of denial, good copers are well aware of risks, and they prepare to take steps to minimize the risk involved and thus reduce anxiety. They are confident, but neither foolhardy nor neglectful of potential consequences.
2. Good copers are *skillful* and fairly *methodical*. They do not dwell too long on details or what might go wrong, nor are they stalled because of remote consequences.
3. Good copers are very *practical*, but with values sufficiently high to live up to. One such value is not to address impossible issues; instead, they will work at more immediate tasks with a better chance of solution or relief.
4. Good copers are *flexible* and *resourceful*. They are willing to change tactics and objectives when necessary, and they do not limit themselves to a rigid program that might not work out to their advantage.
5. Good copers expect to come through, having made *informed decisions* about what to do and how to do it. They visualize consequences, trying to adjust for each possibility, and when needed they use reliable information. They do not depend on unsolicited advice.
6. Good copers are good at what they do as a rule, and not easily rattled regardless of risk. Few people are prepared for any threatening situation, and fewer still always ready to do the right thing, whatever that may be. Nevertheless, good copers usually perform competently, if not always successfully. In addition to having skill, they are generally quite composed in evaluating what they are called on to do.
7. There is no true composure, however, without a balance of *vigilance*, prudence, and appropriate emotionality. Good copers may be distant and intellectual, but only in predica-

ments where these traits are helpful. Emotional extremes that warp judgment are kept to a harmless few, and they are short-lived.

8. Good copers have *self-respect*. They deplore rash behavior as much as they reject prolonged equivocation. In undertaking tasks, they have tactics for keeping risk and dread at a manageable minimum. This gives them a distinct edge in coming out ahead.

Optimism has a definite advantage; if they feel pessimism, good copers keep it in check. Risk reduction is a problem to be dealt with, not avoided. This makes it easier to be a good coper.

Although good copers are usually optimistic and self-confident, I know none who attribute their success to feeling immune to failure or to living under a lucky star. Too many people, I believe, rely upon a strong conviction that the heavens will look after them and prevent harm. This reveals a dangerous naïveté comparable to believing that nothing evil happens to the pure in heart. That there are many dangerous situations which anyone can fail at, and be vulnerable to, is beyond any reasonable doubt. Serene (not resentful) resignation may be the only strategy for these occasions.

I believe that coping well with the problems presented to us is at the center of our quest for resolution of ultimate questions. But I cannot prescribe a sure formula that will make anyone a better coper, except to note that both courage and coping, including the courage to cope, can be cultivated and adapted to our own peculiar and unique circumstances or character. The following items (also referred to above) are goals to be pursued and practiced: rehearsing strategies, using reliable information, learning from errors, cultivating ingenuity, drawing sustenance from success, and gaining support from others we respect and regard.

This exceedingly brief and optimistic sketch of what good copers do is relevant to what psychotherapists of quality want to accomplish for themselves and for those coming to them because of vulnerability. But patients, like others, are not wholly vulnerable, and good copers are not regularly flooded with abundant assets that work well. Vulnerability belongs to the human condition, and we must—in the triple sense of survival, competence, and responsibility—learn to know it and use it as well as possible for our own benefit.

What Do Bad Copers Do?

Bad copers are not always bad people, nor are good copers invariably good people who operate exclusively for noble motives. Bad copers just fail at what they do more often. Something goes wrong; maybe they aim too high, take on inappropriate tasks, or get discouraged before they exhaust plausible alternatives. Or they may not think through consequences, or pay enough attention to obstacles in the way. They may expect the outcome to be easier, or impossibly difficult. Their intentions may be good, but poorly matched with inadequate skills and experience.

Poor copers may be thorough, but dwell on the likelihood of bad outcomes and ignore the intermediate steps required before a final goal. Or they may just be bunglers who feel themselves incapable of or unqualified for just about anything that requires training, persistence, and a sense of plausible success. And we should not omit the people who fail at some things and forever after fret and complain, as if their unfulfilled promise or aspirations were a mark of distinction. One woman preferred a rather low-level job doing routine work in a large office to taking an examination for a promotion. She was competent enough to have passed the tests easily (although, understandably, she had an unimpressive résumé). Her reason for not taking the examination was that she might fail; her self-esteem was low anyway, and failure would only confirm her incompetence. She was not a good coper and had little courage, but she was a success at tactical failure.

I do not believe that bad copers can be identified by clinical inspection or psychological testing, although I am surely not an expert or authority on the variety of tests that are available. If no such tests exist, there is certainly a place for them.

1. Bad copers tend to give up easily, but they have high regard for their own past failures. They believe that faults are failures and failures are faults, and neither can be changed; not doing well is destiny.

2. Bad copers could cite many examples of self-fulfilling prophecies of failure, but denial may be so strong, instead, that they come across with an unnatural opinionated arrogance.

3. Bad copers inherently believe that nothing ever works out, and are strong adherents of Murphy's Law.

4. Bad copers ask advice but, consistent with their character, often fail to use adequate information and advice. However, bad copers may also find poor sources of information and advice.

5. Bad copers may have high academic degrees and much relevant experience, but strangely find themselves unprepared for the tasks they attempt.

6. Bad copers are addicts to hopelessness, carefully couched in plausible rationalizations. Setbacks turn into denial, as if the goals were not very desirable in the first place (this is commonly known as sour grapes).

7. Bad copers do not lend themselves easily to correction or to trying out new strategies. Their relative inflexibility is often mistaken for stodginess or insensitivity, which it is not.

8. Bad copers are as emotional and intellectual as anyone else, but they fail to use these qualities for their own advantage. Composure is not an outstanding trait, however, perhaps because vigilance and anxiety interfere with a good assessment of problems to be faced.

9. Bad copers fail to differentiate clearly the ambiguities of faults, setbacks, and a hypothesized destiny that accepts only failure.

10. Finally, bad copers seem to sow defeat, anticipating the worst, retreating from challenge, or mistakenly attempting tasks with built-in failure. Courage may be there, but everything else seems to conspire against them.

Do bad copers suffer from too much anxiety, or from too little? How much anxiety or dread is just right? The vulnerable self is almost defined by overt and excessive anxiety and suffering, and therefore is apt to be plagued by bad coping. But pessimism may skew judgment, even of the foibles and failures of society. This can be fatal, despite or because of so much pride in deploring existence.

Bad copers do occasionally succeed, but often through no effort of their own. Impulsive people, for example, are seldom good copers because they lack varied coping skills and adequate preassessment of problems facing them. In psychotherapy, where the distinction between good and bad coping is usually very important, outcomes may differ, nevertheless, in ways unrelated to the outside coping skill of patients. Some patients succeed or fail in spite of themselves, and the explanations given for success or failure are seldom the correct ones. Self-deception is usually strong, or there may be accidental factors that turn out well even for the person who copes poorly.

Years ago, a middle-aged man consulted me about an extramarital affair he was having; he was very dissatisfied about his prolonged equivocation about what to do. He was in love with his friend, but fond of his loyal wife and did not want to lose the love of his two adolescent children. He wished to break off the affair, but hesitated for fear of public scandal and exposure. What he really wanted was for his wife to get a divorce, which would allow him to escape guilt and exposure. The quandary found him squarely situated in the middle: He was reluctant to undertake any step that could implicate him, and he steered away from coping with the problem.

Consulting a psychiatrist was part of a pattern of wanting to have things done for him, in this case the divorce, without sticking his neck out. He was anxious, but disinclined to take any action on his own behalf. Certainly my task was not to advise him for or against a divorce; I could only and very feebly inquire into his fears of exposure and the reasons why openness was so objectionable. I do not know how fate decided his case for him, because he was obviously dissatisfied with my therapeutic stance. It clearly showed that whereas conscience does not make cowards of us all, fear paralyzes some and energizes others.

Another man once told me that fear made him a coward. This was not the redundancy it seemed, because there are others who use fear to take on difficult and dangerous tasks in order not to be considered a weakling or a coward. But for this man there were strong elements of counterphobia, too: His high expectations led to taking on exceedingly difficult jobs and making them even more difficult by imposing built-in restrictions on success. Failure was almost predictable, after a "good try." His basic conviction was that cowards always failed and that failures were cowards, but he was a coward who did not shrink from hard jobs.

A poor coper is not necessarily a constitutional failure, nor is he or she necessarily a coward. Psychodynamics being what they are, this man was not a dismal failure. He only failed to select jobs he could regularly succeed at; he did a good job working at difficult assignments with unrealistic expectations. Fortunately, his superiors admired his fortitude, because others would not even try such jobs. He was convinced about cowardice (a distinctly inappropriate slander); consequently, his toughest job was self-vindication.

The Befitting

According to a well-worn maxim, the outcome of psychotherapy depends on the chemistry or "fit" between therapist and patient. As with most maxims, the case for this idea is oversimplified, but there are few other criteria that make prediction reliable in psychotherapy. In estimating how well any patient might do in therapy, my criterion of respect and regard in both directions is somewhat easier to use, because it has to do with expectations. Good copers are often content with a limited outcome, whereas bad copers usually consider any limit further proof of their inadequacy. Therefore, modest improvement for the latter is equivalent to no improvement at all. Good copers correct themselves; bad copers surrender themselves.

Psychotherapy is not only not an exact science, but scarcely a science at all. Logic does not always win the day, and few people are persuaded by it. This is just as well, because life is not a good receptacle for syllogisms, either. Actually, facts and theories conflict so often that life can be a nonsyllogism, with unlimited contingencies and qualifications that make most judgments somewhat tentative. There are many unrecognized points of view and enough sneaky consequences to skew anyone's predictions. Nevertheless, we must cope if we can, knowing that solutions are temporary and accommodation is precarious. Though we have many faults and fallibilities to flesh out our vulnerability, the basic fear is not failure but extinction, with loss of meaning. In the long run, this means dying without a trace, beyond anonymity.

For generations beyond numbering, mankind has tried to dilute this fear with myths and dogmas designed to refute or repel the existential fact that somethingness will surely turn into nothingness. Existentialists are prone to making bleak predictions, often in the magical belief that the gloomier a prediction, the better the chances of its not coming true. Psychotherapy has a more optimistic version of this gloomy existential fact, which is hard to dispute. The compromise version is that despite the vulnerability of man and an uncertain and threatening world, there can be tolerable acceptance and adaptation rather than gloom and doom. Man is not a mere fabrication made up to serve his own illusions, but a finite thing searching for authenticity, and is entitled to respect and regard.

Because there is no consensus about any ultimate outcome—only gloomy guesses and pious hopes—perhaps a befitting harmony between man and the world could be a source of transcendence in everyday life. If we use vulnerability *combined* with the courage to cope, perhaps the aim of self-realization will affirm somethingness. To be befitting means "Here I am, at one with an acceptable plight"; pressing problems, once threatening, have been reduced to a befitting moment.

These sentiments might sound strange to a skeptical pilgrim who vacillates, as always, between acceptance and doubt. But to be befitting does not require some resplendent epiphany between an inspired self and a gracious universe; that is carrying a sense of purpose too far. But *befitting* can describe something as mundane as a task well done, with its inherent satisfaction.

I once asked a man who was dying in a hospital of advanced cancer what in his life he remembered with the most pride. Without hesitating, he recalled his years as a restaurant chef. During World War II, when coffee was scarce, he was proud that he continued to make the best coffee in Boston. It was not easy; he could have stinted and served a diluted substitute, but he did not. His very prompt answer suggested that he had been thinking about just such matters: what he had done with his life, and what gave him his good memories. This moment, filled with sadness at passing and pleasure in a proud recollection, was to me befitting, and I could not let it go without wondering whether, despite his mortality, somethingness was still there.

A librarian, about 55 years old, once consulted me about her increasing difficulty in controlling anger, especially when it was aroused by lack of appreciation. She was a childless widow whose family consisted of an aged and sickly mother and two older brothers, with the latter living some distance from her. In fact, she saw them all infrequently, except when some emergency came up. The current problem that brought her to me was that the mother faced a serious operation and expected my patient to take a leave of absence and care for her during a long convalescence. This expectation ignited familiar resentment, because her brothers always seemed exempt from such obligations. It was an old issue, dating back many years; her mother evidently put semi-invalidism to work in getting her way, and my patient felt like an indentured servant who was helpless to voice resentment, find compromise, or work out something else besides submission. She had made most of the decisions about her mother's care in the years since her father had died. However, she resented the responsibility, but felt guilty whenever she demurred only slightly.

I saw this woman only three times, but in that time I had to formulate the presenting problem, assess the reasons she felt so guilty, understand more about her smoldering resentment, and suggest other ways to cope with her mother. In asking more about her brothers, I discovered that they were not as difficult and distant as she initially alleged. They offered to help frequently—only, she said, because she neared collapse from fatigue and was forced to seek assistance. Nevertheless, they did help, and they followed through until the crisis subsided.

Consequently the meaning of her complaints changed, and so did my questions. I began to wonder why she had to be near collapse before calling for help, and what prevented her from sharing some of the burden with her brothers far earlier. There is a difference between these questions. In regard to the first question, she had depicted herself as an overly conscientious victim exploited by an unappreciative and indifferent family. I now knew this was not true. The second question was designed to challenge her helplessness by implying that she could have called on her brothers much earlier and avoided an angry confrontation, with tears and recriminations.

I learned that she was most angry not when flatly imposed upon or when assistance was refused (as it never was), but when she was forced to realize that she needed help. Until fatigue set in, she hung onto all the work and responsibility she could. All matters were under her control; her power and importance were unchallenged, though bought at a price. She volunteered help in situations unrelated to her family, soon becoming overloaded with responsibilities. She then would feel unappreciated and resent it strongly. Not without pride, she said to me, "I never want to let anyone down." I was tempted to add that she offered to take over even when she was unsure how much help was needed. Never-

theless, she felt guilty when she only gave part of herself to someone ostensibly in need, and thus initiated what she later would
think was an exploitation.

I did not allow our few sessions to drift into other realms, past
or present. But I did ask, since there was more than enough guilt
in her, why hadn't she shared some of it with her brothers? Instead, she kept all the responsibility for herself; she demanded her
own distance until fatigue made it impossible to go it alone any
further. I thought she had let her brothers down by keeping all the
work to herself. What made her so selfish?

The very idea that she could be guilty and selfish about not
letting her brothers help made her laugh. She was more accustomed to being the solicitous and self-sacrificing servant, not the
central power, wholly in control even of her fatigue. The main
purpose in not calling on her brothers was to perpetuate the fiction
that she needed no help and was entirely capable of carrying any
burden alone. Apparently her brothers believed that all was well,
and so they did not volunteer.

My upside-down interpretation, suggesting that perhaps the
woman's brothers were only waiting for her to surrender a little
of the control she had kept for herself, challenged her complacency. I asked her to call on them earlier and see just how reluctant
they were. If they refused or hesitated, she had the satisfaction of
proving me wrong, and once again she could revert to being the
dutiful but resentful daughter. Much to her surprise, the brothers
not only agreed to pitch in during the forthcoming convalescence
but arranged to hire help, so that she would not have to ask for a
leave of absence. A plan was set up that she could veto or approve,
but it was not necessary for her to carry the burden alone. By this
time, my patient understood that her guilt had come not from
resenting exploitation but from an unacknowledged wish to have
everything under her control. This, in fact, was a strategy she had
picked up at her mother's knee and bedside: the tyranny of the
helpless and the power of desperate tears. Her theme had been "I
can take care of everything!"

It was enough to see her these few times. She might have

refused to continue, because I sensed there was much more to be revealed and that this very private woman would resent too much disclosure. In fact, she had deceived herself for many years, avoiding the truth of her wish to be indispensable and of central importance, especially if another person was helpless. To her credit, she was willing to experiment with other strategies and to find a very gratifying (if perplexing) result. After so many years, there was a befitting accommodation between her expectations and the response of her brothers. It was, without exaggeration, an occasion of self-realization, when authenticity overcame vulnerability.

The term *self-realization*, which I have used often but hesitatingly, has a deplorable ring of pop psychology. It is a new jargon word; but any good coper will feel a befitting correspondence between outside facts and the inside capacity to deal with them. When success elevates self-esteem, the befitting consists of harmony and propriety, and with it comes self-realization.

It has been said that the existential viewpoint makes a distinction between hope and optimism, a very fine difference that not everyone readily understands. I am not sure about the distinction, but hope does imply that the current problem can be coped with, which does not necessarily mean that it will be obliterated. Hope for a miraculous cure of terminal illness sustains some people, but it rarely saves them. Hope for coping well would then apply only to things within reason and expectations. Optimism, which is largely a character trait, goes beyond present problems to a remote future when almost any positive expectation might be fulfilled. The unfortunate contingency, however, is that this faith in the healing powers of the future might prevent a person from taking feasible action in the present, even though visionary and remote expectations are unlikely or questionable. Optimism should know its limitations; the future is too misty and unclaimed to superimpose highly unlikely miracles. Hope, however, is confidence in being able to survive despite setbacks. The vulnerable self is seldom without residues of courage, and therefore has elements of hope.

The courage to cope is not the designated property of good

copers. But it is the good copers who seem to take appropriate action and affirm themselves. The match between what they believe and act upon in confrontations with the world and its proximal problems may be befitting, and feel good that way. If freedom to choose and act is used wisely, then the vulnerable self can make use of the courage to cope by first accepting its faults and fallibility and then working with those faults to devise strategies that might work more effectively, with more suitable proximal problems.

Chapter 5

Skepticism in Psychotherapy

If a pilgrim—perhaps a bit skeptical—were to wander into the field of human interaction known as psychotherapy, he or she would be understandably bewildered by the profusion of schools and methods that exist in order to serve people in some form of psychological distress. Methods and theories confidently and unconditionally oppose one another, and each method cites cured cases and devalues the results of the others. Consensus is rare; disputes are common even among practitioners of the same persuasion. Irrefutable facts are few. Principles are widely scattered generalities, laboriously dissected to the point of tedium without producing much more enlightenment than at the start. Proof in a scientific sense is unheard of, and may not be possible. Reiteration and reputation take the place of validation. But this hardly prevents anyone from advocating and advertising their own form of practice, or from citing their own successes without genuine comparison with any other method or viewpoint.

Psychotherapists have been compared to indigenous practitioners of all sorts, including so-called witch doctors. There are actually several analogous principles in the practices of all forms of psychotherapy, but few methods are practiced according to a stripped-down version based only on common characteristics. There are many idiosyncratic formats that are special only to the person practicing in that fashion. As a result, therapists are generally reluctant to give up their familiar way of treating patients, or educating clients, simply because a more popular type of therapy has come along and claims to have a theoretical understanding far better than preceding viewpoints.

I expect that any conscientious therapist would like to find a better and more flexible method of dealing with patients. Preferably, it should be based on what he or she already does, but help to do it better. That psychotherapy helps some distressed people is beyond doubt, but questions about who benefits from doing what remain. It is not my chosen job to review the statistics about psychotherapy, but rather to look at the fervent belief that any patient willing to try might feel (or be) better afterward. In the present climate of psychotropic remedies, psychotherapy has an honorific position; serious questions about what forms of psychotherapy are best for some or all patients are not in the forefront of psychiatric research.

Radical empiricism and positivism about psychiatric theory are not philosophically popular. A skeptic would have ample grounds for being dubious about the more dogmatic claims that abound. In making sense and rendering clearer meanings for much that is said and written, he or she will be required to translate jargon and dialects into plain language. He or she will also keep in mind that what is preached from books or lecture platforms may not exactly correspond to what is practiced in fact. A skeptical pilgrim who accepts such a job has few points of reference that are stable and noncontroversial. In a way, therefore, his or her pilgrimage will not be a scientific venture so much as an excursion into different versions of truth.

Psychotherapy for Skeptics

Let us assume that the skeptical pilgrim is not altogether naive about psychotherapy, but also is not attached to any special set of doctrines. Consequently, he or she realizes that asking obvious questions is only open and fair. Among these questions are the following: What is psychotherapy? What does it do? What works and works best? How should psychotherapy be done, by whom, and for whom? Such questions may not be phrased very elegantly, but the basic meaning is there: What is psychotherapy all about?

These may not even be the right questions. Generations of inquirers, therapists, and others of like curiosity have asked similar questions without convincing results. From my perspective I have no convincing data to show that an existential viewpoint in and about psychotherapy—by its emphasis on metaproblems, making sense, and ultimate questions—will actually help more patients cope with their problems than other viewpoints could claim. I believe that an existential viewpoint such as I have proposed thus far, however, must ask different questions about psychotherapy, and could be valuable with a gathering of concepts relevant to life as lived. Claims about validity and claims about therapy are different. For example, patients have been cured and not cured by all sorts of legerdemain, verbal dexterity, doctrinal zeal, and technical performances. But questions about validity persist, including a very specific question—how is validity validated? The search for personal authenticity by the patient has to be squared with authenticity in the therapist. Because I put emphasis on the vulnerable self, which both the therapist and patient have, the meaning of authenticity assumes significance greater than that of what is ambiguously called validity.

Highly institutionalized, culturally sanctioned, and traditional methods for reaching out and ruling, informing and instructing, and educating and consoling distressed and disadvantaged people have gone on for ages. As long as there have been people who are hurt or confused, and who live within a society that values and esteems certain kinds of conduct, doctoring will be acceptable. In our era, it seems, practically any reasonable (or slightly unreasonable) method of psychotherapy is legitimate. There is no state religion or standard ministering to the perplexed and distressed among us. The very legitimacy of various types of doctoring is declared to make them potentially helpful, but their common themes are few. One of them is to endorse strategies that make sense in different ways because they are based on different philosophic positions. These strategies, practiced in abundance, are professed to be beneficial in the long run. Testimonials about effectiveness are easy to come by, and few practitioners would be skeptical about claims in their favor.

Most therapists require the participation and cooperation of the patient in need. This is surely not the same as coercion or even conspiracy to do something against the will. Therapy is *for* the will, or choice, or however such a notion is conceived. Another theme consistent with the form of doctoring called psychotherapy is that its practitioners are considered qualified to deal with a variety of specialized problems.

Psychotherapy is difficult to define. A general statement that it influences distressed or disadvantaged people by psychological means is hardly a good definition for professional doctoring of this sort. If true, the definition applies to anyone who influences another person. Politicians, preachers, parents, teachers, attorneys, actors, and an unlimited number of others influence people who are often very distressed. Influencing people to feel better, change, or ask for help in a special way as part of one's job is not altogether psychotherapy.

Professional psychotherapy is a somewhat recent phenomenon within the ancient practice of doctoring, and the medicalization of psychotherapy is a product of this century and our culture. Now the pendulum has swung back, and there are many nonmedical practitioners who charge fees for helping people, making them technically professional. They call themselves by assorted titled (educators, teachers, leaders, facilitators, etc.). The term *mental health professionals* is somewhat less inclusive, yet retains the connotation of medical doctoring.

I find it only fair not to persist in attempting a pure and precise definition of psychotherapy, and especially of who is qualified to practice it. Not only would a specialized definition not be very persuasive, but it would reflect my own bias and unavoidably omit a number of very gifted and conscientious practitioners who lack conventional credentials. Vague definition of a field, ambiguous credentials, and lack of consensus, however, do nothing to certify who is qualified to do what. Although nothing specifically leaves the door open for unscrupulous promoters, they are not hindered either. Psychotherapy is a jungle, but it is presided over by cultural approval. No one can condemn the field entirely; too many conscientious practitioners have tried to serve a beneficial goal for us to dismiss them invidiously. The skeptical pilgrim, in fairness (determined by his or her own standards), makes a distinction between the jungle of discordant voices, each one outshouting and outboasting the other, and the diligent professionals toiling to clear the jungle.

The existential viewpoint has a strong central role for what is commonly called *subjectivity*. Many observers and investigators have noted that the personality of the practitioner, and whatever goes with it, has a decisive influence on what happens during therapy. (By personality, chemistry, or individual style, I mean whatever promotes a befitting result.) When we ask what works best for whom in psychotherapy, it is also essential to ask who does whatever works best for them. Differences between practitioners are more critical than the differences between schools and what they teach. Moreover, in the absence of critical facts and closer study, it is presumptively true that whatever differences there are between various viewpoints in psychotherapy will arise more from the personality and preferences of the individual practitioner than from theoretical superstructures. The basic foundations are laid down in personal experience and smoothed out by professional training.

If this point is seriously considered, the case for enlightened subjectivity in psychotherapy is strengthened. Enlightened subjectivity is so flexible, however, that as a result, various forms and formats within the practice of psychotherapy seem to be rooted not in science at all, but in semievangelical missions that acquire credibility on regional and political grounds—and, of course, on highly personal viewpoints.

I do not decry this, nor should the skeptical pilgrim, if he or she wants to make sense. Anything else would not be responsive to the special needs of the community and local culture. Just as we know people differ in so many ways in different regions of the world, it would not be surprising to discover that their problems and quandaries differ. As a result, psychotherapy would differ too, and be called by appropriate categorical terms. I imagine that the enlightened subjectivity of the professional will itself vary enormously from culture to culture, place to place, and person to person.

Trends and contemporary issues are always with us, and there are always new experts claiming more new triumphs than new facts to back them up. Variations on old themes have a familiar ring. Like dragon's teeth that spring up quickly and multiply, yet also like a mayfly completing its life cycle in a single day, so goes the evanescence of innovations in psychotherapy.

Fewer patients, it seems, achieve the remarkable results reported by practitioners in the earlier years of this century. Perhaps there were fewer psychiatric practitioners to check, or possibly these were exceptional cases and unusually gifted practitioners. I recall from my very early years in psychoanalysis hearing about the successful cases who found total relief of symptoms as the result of a few sage interpretations. It is still true that psychotherapy helps, but not nearly enough; its effectiveness is selective, as well as limited for certain kinds of patients. Even at the gloomiest and most cynical, however, any fair-minded and knowledgeable person would hesitate before declaring that psychotherapy is an empty vocation of little value. I have known several very harsh critics of psychotherapy and psychiatry; only a very few are uninformed enough to damn psychotherapy categorically and claim that it is merely a hoax perpetrated on the gullible by the unscrupulous.

Still, what does work? In making sense out of what psychotherapy aims to do, there is a curious dilemma. Subjectivity and intuition are regarded as highly valuable, if not indispensable, but enlightened subjectivity may not be enough to make psychotherapy do whatever it does. Even if we professionals were sure about the most essential factors in psychotherapy, however, this remarkable discovery would not be equivalent to knowing what makes patients feel better, or identifying which patients benefit most.

Like many other seasoned psychiatrists, I have had my share of moments when surmises based on strong intuition turned out well. These are good moments, quite harmonious and consistent with what I have called befitting. But I have had other bright intuitions that were totally wrong, and corrected myself on many occasions in an effort to home in on just what patients meant. Intuition and enlightened subjectivity may be tributes to the mind's remarkable capacity to generate insight, but I do not confuse these rare moments with extrasensory perception. Nor do these instances of remarkable insight add up to having any therapeutic value in and by themselves.

Motivation may be strong, but although it helps, it is also not enough. There are too many powerfully motivated patients and practitioners who are well matched, but for whom progress is marginal at best. Who, then, is at fault—the patient or the practitioner? Usually, each accuses the other person. But blaming the victim is not very informative, nor is blaming the therapist very productive in the absence of good information. Egregious instances provide no problem, but these are comparatively infrequent and constitute questions of ethics, not results. Sometimes patients do surprisingly well under very inauspicious circumstances; even weeds will sprout flowers occasionally. No one can predict confidently who will do well and who will fail in psychotherapy, except when the cases are so obvious that hardly anyone would wonder. I find it hard to use the concept of false positives and false negatives in assessing results, because some difficult patients come through and some very good patients (in the sense previously described) do poorly.

Cynics, of course, can deplore just about anything except their own judgment, and point to failures all around. It is said, however, that nature abhors a vacuum, and many would-be therapists offer services and promise success with scanty attention to qualifications. Psychotherapy is an ambiguous field in which the ambitious thrive, without control or correction, until something demanding public attention happens. Monitoring colleagues in psychotherapy or psychiatry is an onerous task, done either not at all or arbitrarily and inconsistently. Boosting one colleague over another is somewhat arbitrary, too, because it is rarely based on results. More often, it is because we like the person or because recommending them makes for effective public relations.

Strupp and Blackwood (1975), in an influential and authoritative textbook, recommend a healthy skepticism for anyone who looks into different schools of psychotherapy. They, too, question the grounds of argument between rival therapists and their claims. The central theme of their discussion is to remind the profession and public that organized efforts to heal or offer relief have been around for a long time. Moreover, these efforts are framed within the cultural values and social aspirations of the particular society in which they are established.

I have already pointed out that the existential viewpoint accepts this reminder of cultural relativism. Consequently, in psychotherapy we are obliged to look for significant cultural beliefs, symbols, and practices that therapists and patients live with and consider absolute. Culture commands our values and sets standards; we are the product of our upbringing and of whoever molded our character. We differ among ourselves, even more than is implied by our accents and speech.

Every society has its own myths and creeds in which it staunchly believes with scarcely a question. Most of these beliefs, values, axioms—call them by any other preferred name—are enforceable, if not directly by punishment, then by other kinds of censure or reward. There is scarcely an exception; culture, too, is enforced by imperatives, customs, and prohibitions. It puts a stamp on just about everything, including standards for behavior and criteria for what makes sense. To go against these implicit or explicit decrees requires a vigorous thrust of rebellion or, in the more subtle atmosphere of psychotherapy, a tangible quantity of courage.

Society decides what people should want and need. Television commercials understand this well, and public relations has a good deal to say about what is considered desirable to live well and be successful and sought after. These expectations also enter into the expectations of psychotherapy, and are not matters of health at all. For distressed and vulnerable people, what is wanted, needed, and expected are *normalization* and *acceptability*.

A skeptical pilgrim with a touch of history realizes that the things society and its populace want, need, expect, and forbid are not immutable. Problems of one generation become irrelevant for the next, and may not be recalled at all by the generation after that. Principles and their factual foundations are subject to this same historical erosion. Because psychotherapy mirrors society, it is understandable, given a very heterogeneous society, that patients' complaints widely differ, and that psychotherapy will take many forms that correspond to unsatisfied needs and wants. For example, certain groups (usually the highly educated and articulate segments of society) gravitate to therapists who emphasize the verbal, and who expect insight to be most effective. Other segments (e.g., blue-collar or no-collar patients) may find talking a boring distraction from what really distresses them. Taking a pill or getting an injection is a must for certain people in order to feel well taken care of. Healers must do something tangible, accompanied by something verbal, perhaps, that reinforces the power of the manifest act. Sometimes this something is an adept and pertinent comment or assessment; at other times the manifest act consists of ointments, incantations, specific rituals, or directives. Disclosure is usually a general requirement, too, although the content of confession is apt to vary from rote formula to detailed, anguished, individual catharsis.

A recent example of how therapy blends into the dominant culture and reflects its values is end-of-the-century psychoanalysis. Psychoanalysis began to emigrate from Europe in the early 1930s, mostly because of religious persecution and political upheavals. At midcentury, classical psychoanalysts dominated the field of psychiatry; there were few outstanding psychiatrists who had not had classical training.

In its original imported form, classical psychoanalysis reflected an authoritarian society: The analyst had a silent but powerful role, speaking rarely but without much fear of contradiction. When the patient and analyst did not agree, the burden was on the patient, who was readily cornered by interpretations of resistance, narcissism, envy, a wish to turn the tables on his or her parents, and so forth. Analytic patients were required to lie down and purge their minds without hesitation, precondition, or censorship. The analyst was impassive, sitting silent and inscrutable behind the couch except when offering sage interpretations or asking very infrequent questions. When the analysis ended was up to the doctor, who also decided how well the patient had done over the course of treatment.

If this brief description now seems somewhat harsh and atypical, it is because psychoanalysis gradually underwent democratization in coming to the United States. Coercion now is seldom explicit, and patients participate more in major decisions about themselves, including about what is wrong. Although the original European psychoanalysts reflected the authoritarian societies that, ironically, they were obliged to flee, the unequal relation between physician and patient was stereotypical almost up until our day. The doctor was generally regarded as several levels above ordinary humans, and it was considered unseemly or offensive to question his (and it was mostly *his*) pronouncements. Only with the rise of consumer advocacy programs, including civil rights movements, did this attitude tend to change. Today second opinions and patients' rights are almost taken for granted. Doctors are not only open to question but vulnerable to lawsuits, even for comparatively trivial reasons. Psychotherapy has also changed from a didactic stance to a more collaborative venture.

At the present time, psychotherapy is bound by economic strictures, and decisions about treatment are usually decided by a third person acting as a representative for the insurance system of payment. As a result of such parties' careful monitoring, briefer psychotherapy has come to the fore. It is not only short-term but well packaged for the marketplace. Patients are consumers, not suffering supplicants. Negotiation between near equals more accurately describes the doctor-patient relationship, with just the right balance of democracy and elitism to generate enough respect for both parties. Long-term therapy seems doomed, even though it takes a long time to change anyone's mind. Short-term therapy is therefore not expected to have the profound effect that earlier practitioners claimed for psychoanalysis. A pluralistic culture produces a wide variety of values and expectations. Ego ideals differ, and not even skeptics are exempted, because skepticism also has its own format and agenda that the collective culture determines.

Regardless of its name, format, method, locale, or philosophy, psychotherapy has four major aims: *normalcy, success, approval,* and *fulfillment.* It is not the diagnosis that drives people to therapy, but their own dissatisfaction. These four aims are values that signify optimal socialization. It is always good to feel better, to think right, and to be appreciated and approved by the relevant group we are immersed in, even when we rebel against it. The value of psychotherapy stems from this consideration.

Beyond Morale

Not even a hard-shelled skeptic would quarrel with these four aims. The happy confluence of strategies, aims, and outcomes such as these should certainly consummate in what is befitting, along with strong morale. It must also have a lot to do with self-realization. Alas, appropriate methods for reaching and enjoying such values are considerably more questionable; indeed, such methods are themselves ultimate questions that we spend our life pondering and practicing.

If nature were kind, fair, and just, then society would surely emulate it. As Cannon (1936) first described it, the wisdom of the body seems to be limited to animal survival, with little to do in furthering personal competence, social responsibility, and strong morale. In this respect, the wisdom of the body is secondary to the stupidity, mistakes, and mischief of the mind.

Meanwhile, the four aims of normalcy, success, approval, and fulfillment are sufficiently strong to decide what psychotherapy ought to encourage. Although it is clear that these aims are general enough to fit almost any society in any era, their impact and implications seem particularly relevant to a free and democratic society. In an ideal democratic society there is no genuine freedom without genuine choice, and this includes willingness to fulfill obligations. It is freedom to be autonomous and to value individuality within the sanctions, values, and responsibility set up by society and its traditions. Respect and regard for others, as well as for oneself, tempers the range of freedom by assigning responsibility.

Practitioners and therapists of quality are not only delegated to sponsor these ideals, but dedicated implicitly to encouraging appropriate behavior for a democratic and generally nonauthoritarian society. The skeptic might draw back in alarm, recoiling from the idea that a therapist who is supposed to be dedicated only to relieving distress and dissatisfaction would impose his or her values and call them goals of treatment. Therapists of quality and other representatives of authenticity, however, are just as dubious as the skeptic. It is paradoxical, at least, to advocate freedom at the front door while dragging a set of prescribed responsibilities in through the back.

Conformity is a treacherous vice or a hypocritical virtue; it bribes where it promises to liberate. Nevertheless, there are configurations of attitude and conscience that are so deeply ingrained in culture that conduct based on them can pass through any door, unnoticed or unwelcomed. For example, practitioners (whether therapists or physicians) are brought up to revere concepts of strictly scientific standards and logical principles in their work. But these are not absolute decrees set down to be worshipped. They are relativistic ideals, straight from a nineteenth-century point of view known as rationalism. Yet within its limitations, rationality is to be respected because, in a sense, it guarantees freedom based on itself. Those who follow its precepts have confidence in being able to select goals consistent with such freedom; their morale is therefore strong. But the ultimate question, never to be taken for granted, is the relation of morale to conformity and conventionality.

Morale is as neglected a topic as courage. Both have much to do with self-realization. Lack of morale is like lack of courage; they are synonyms for vulnerability and suffering. Jerome Frank (1963) in his classical studies, emphasized that the principal reason anyone seeks healing, instruction, or enlightenment is *demoralization.* Demoralization keeps people from coping well and creates distress and suffering in them because they cannot thrive without the sanction of themselves and society. Demoralized people experience the opposite of normalcy, success, approval, and fulfillment. Instead, they are ground down by failure, frustration, deviance, sickness, and impoverishment, usually of the spirit. Demoralization is fundamental suffering of the worst sort, because hope and the capacity to cope have gone. When demoralized people seek healing, or whatever else, it is actually a search for deliverance into healthy well-being.

But there are degrees of demoralization; it does not signify total collapse any more than suffering is completely intolerable, or every crisis is of calamitous proportions. People can be distressed for any number of reasons, and be injured in various ways besides violence. A person might stumble over a stone or be hurt by a cruel and callous remark; there is no need to be struck by lightning or a falling tree to know hurt and pain. Temporary incapacity is not chronic invalidism without hope. Nevertheless, acute distress is what most health professionals understand. Among our patients, there are many who are pretty successful, having already reached a reasonable approximation of the four values. Though their demoralization seems rather mild, it is still substantial enough to cause dismay, often verging on despair. To keep up morale, patients need respect and regard more than speculations about why they feel as they do, even though respect and regard simply ameliorate, to a degree, anguish and cannot by themselves regenerate morale. For example, most people, especially those in a quandary, acknowledge that being listened to with respect and regard does more than being talked to, however sagaciously, about their faults and fallibilities.

The skeptical pilgrim has also learned that alliance with a special person who is competent and has access to information of relevance is invariably helpful, and he or she sometimes is tempted to stop at that. By itself, truth does not set anyone free, or at least free enough to develop stronger morale. The approval or sanction of a benevolent authority seems more effective. The salient quality of a therapist should be that of benevolent authority, representing the four aims he or she is supposed to sponsor. But therapy must transcend morale; morale is only the self-esteem required to thrust forward into the unknown, which is a dusky domain needing courage.

On Being a Therapist of Quality

What does a skeptical pilgrim look for in the event of needing a therapist? Naturally, to sustain morale, he or she needs a benevolent authority (not always so benign) who is filled with accurate information that is not only relevant but readily accessible. The therapist is, of course, competent and skillful, must listen well, and generate an atmosphere of respect and regard that the skeptical pilgrim can recognize and reciprocate. This kind of professional I call a *therapist of quality*. His or her character and credentials, which are additional qualifications, are highly desirable in any profession. Thus, *therapist* is only a special designation; such a person would represent a somewhat idealized version of any professional of quality. Professionals of quality would preside at moments of crisis, not merely to do what they are good at (for this is not a performance) but to answer a human need. They care to a degree matching their competence, caring enough about a patient's values to heed them well. They know that values are needs.

Competence needs no justification, but a gifted boor or qualified hack does not fit everyone's taste, even if his or her technical skills are desperately needed (and therefore tolerated). Beyond competence are *credentials* and *character,* already mentioned, *compassion,* and *credibility.* Technical skill has its worth, even in the hands of boors and hacks, but the wise patient knows just how far to tolerate and trust such people. Credibility is therefore highly important because outside of our particular sphere of expertise, most of us are gullible, paranoid, or both. We fear being reduced to an existential zero.

Character means a capacity to trust and be trusted, basically, and is linked to compassion. A therapist of quality clearly knows the difference between authentic compassion and pity. For him or her, there are some people best described as "pitiful poor souls," but never in psychotherapy. Patients are expected to muster strengths, striving to cope and using whatever courage is available. This is not true of a poor soul, with an empty closet of hope. Compassion is a respectful virtue.

The issue of a living will for those who cannot make informed decisions about themselves is deservedly debated. Who shall decide for very sick patients who are living without much quality, dependent on instruments, and devoid of competence? Ultimate questions about life and death then become intermingled with issues of care, compassion, character, and credibility. Who knows enough, and who should be disqualified?

Committees of qualified experts are scarcely better able to answer ultimate questions than anyone else. I would look for a professional of quality who embodies character, compassion, competence, credibility, and credentials, perhaps in that order. I do not deplore credentials, of course, but suitable credentials depend on the task at hand, and there are few professionals with credentials enough to solve ultimate questions without additional help from the other traits.

Without sturdy morale, not even professionals of quality can endure extended dismay and dilemmas. They need to be relieved of pressure to perform superlatively and, in the privacy of self-examination, come to terms with unsuspected limits and faults. This must include an enlightened self-exploration of beliefs, values, and needs that, unless recognized, may hinder regeneration of morale. No one is a stranger to demoralization.

Flight from Fallibility

Erich Fromm investigated how some people who fear freedom flee from it. Therapists of quality do not flee from their own fallibility or freedom, nor should they barter being acceptable for loss of autonomy. Those who fail to recognize that freedom has its limits, however, are destined to surrender it.

Freedom is worth fearing, because it puts everyone to a test and (despite indications otherwise) cannot be taken for granted. Moreover, authority is there to intimidate and, in exchange for security and acceptance, will require people to conform with conventional expectations. Freedom to choose may be lost, and successive losses gradually erode authenticity and autonomy.

Along with impaired self-esteem, patients often fear freedom to choose, and they may even avoid looking at alternative ways to cope dispassionately. Fear of freedom comes about not only because one fears defying authority and expectation, but because of a risk of failure in being too autonomous, which would only add another insult to self-esteem. Freedom to fail is, indeed, a curious exercise. There is little skill involved in failure, but much anxiety. Freedom to fail, however, which is inherent in the character of therapist and patient alike, is not the same as coping with fallibility, with which it is confused.

Fallibility includes risk of failing, of course, but recognition of limits indicates an openness about risk that is not devastating. Fallibility is consistent with courage and responsibility, although it is closest to vulnerability. If courage means the triumph of will over anxiety, then fallibility is willingness to be wrong; it is therefore almost a strength that the vulnerable self must acknowledge and use. The price of being free to choose also gives us the right to be wrong. Those who cannot risk being wrong can hardly use freedom well, and surely, then, will lack essential courage. Intellectual integrity, for example, means to be willing to acknowledge error or the inability to understand better. Limits to freedom and courage do exist, and those who believe in absolute freedom are as deluded as those who believe in the unlimited potential of man to achieve. Infallibility is as likely as immortality or self-levitation.

It is another conventional paradox in therapy that self-engrossment combines with difficulty in admitting limits. Moreover, therapists who fail to recognize their own fallibility will yield to an occupational hazard called "playing God." This entitles them to rescue everyone, cure one and all—and risk demoralization when they fail to do so. There are good-hearted, yet arrogant therapists who respond to their patients' idealizations and try to restore what these patients lack, for example, by trying to be an ideal parent. The sense of fallibility is often a protection against victimization, and an assurance that freedom knows its limits. It is not unusual for notions about unlimited power to masquerade as compassion and therapeutic zeal. It takes courage, sometimes, to refuse the role of absolute authority. Courage to be fallible and limited, however, is surely protection against the temptation to play an unsuitable role of absolute freedom. Naturally, everyone could stand much improvement, but idealization of the therapist is not the way to achieve it. The skeptical pilgrim should see through pretense. Those who become intoxicated with the authority or power expected of them by needy patients suffer from delusions of eminence that are no more than robes without an emperor.

The Coinage of Therapy: Care, Concern, and Support

The flight from fallibility, like the road to hell, is paved with good intentions, as well as with complacent arrogance about therapy. Most of us know that a quack in medicine is someone who promises more than can be delivered and who gladly accepts such expectations. The therapist of quality helps morale in other ways, not with false promises or by playing the role of master practitioner, but by generous care, concern, and support, which are truly the coinage of therapy.

There is an ancient truism that although money is prized by everyone, it has no value unless it is spent. Care, concern, and support in therapy need to be expended in order to have value; they do not exist in the abstract except when we see how patients and therapists suffer from their absence. It is likely that without such coinage, therapy is bankrupt. And though care, concern, and support are often found together, each is capable of operating alone, just as nickels, dimes, and quarters can be spent separately. For example, there is a sharp difference between intensive care in busy hospitals and concern for individuals and their private suffering. Parents can care about their children without sharing their concerns.

The problem of offering intelligent support needs special attention. It is often recommended, but can mean almost anything (or, for that matter, almost nothing at all). There is a clear difference, for example, between support and reassurance. I suspect that in open reassurance, the therapist gets more from it than the patient. But support is distinctive in being bilateral, which means both therapist and patient get something positive out of it. Regardless of how support takes place, the goals are normalization and acceptability, which are good guidelines for coping well. Giving a patient something tangible (e.g., lending or giving money to help out over a short period) may be beyond the limits of psychotherapy, but not when it is done by delegated agents of support, such as caseworkers in a community agency. Not a few psychotherapists do what amounts to the same thing by reducing fees or allowing patients to pile up debt over several months, something that a business would not ordinarily do. Even free treatment for therapeutic reasons, rare these days, has its own advocates. Before insurance was available, it was an act of *noblesse oblige* for members of a hospital staff to treat patients for nothing. But it was not wholly for nothing, because both patient and therapist got something out of such generosity and support.

In other instances, support is more subtle and less tangible than offering financial assistance, even to the point of seeming to deny support at all. For example, psychoanalysts are not supposed to be supportive in transactions with patients. They will abstain from outward evidence of support by seemingly allowing patients to struggle alone. But what seems to be lack of compassion, caring, or concern is deceptive. There is more support given in psychoanalysis than some purists or critics admit. Permitting a disconsolate patient to struggle alone, for instance, could be construed as an act of confidence in that patient's capacity to cope independently. Neutrality itself may signify that the analyst is there, at least, and that the patient is not wholly alone. I have no way of generalizing about the motivation of every analyst who maintains an Olympian distance, preferring to interpret instead of intervening at difficult junctures. I expect, however, that most therapists of quality would clearly intervene if their patients significantly acted out in extremely illegal or very compromising and self-destructive ways.

Support is far from global; it must be selective. It is needed just as holding up a building at places where weakness and vulnerability are unmistakable is vital to the overall structure. Support normalizes or makes possible acceptable conduct consistent with independent and autonomous action, and compliance with standards. Ideally, the purpose of support is the ability to get along without it.

The Gist of Therapy: Counseling

Most therapists would not concede that they counsel as much as treat, nor would they acknowledge that support is a predominant portion of what they do. The skeptical pilgrim, though, still in search of indispensable ingredients, could scarcely deny that support and counseling *combine* to offer most of what therapy (or any other form of relieving distress or restoring confidence) purports to do. Long before the modern era of scientific treatments, doctors treated most illnesses with care, concern, support, and counseling while patiently waiting for the healing powers of nature to take effect. Doctors were, and still are, fallible; using these nonspecific but selective factors is a classic example of how to make good use of fallibility and limits, without pairing with failure and capitulation.

Counseling can be a form of authentic support, because its avowed purpose is normalization and acceptability. Not all support means or includes counseling, but psychotherapy, regardless of its form, does have its roots in generic counseling whose aim is facilitating change for the better. Information, guidance, encouragement, and (in some cases) toleration all have supportive effects. But counseling about specific problems also seems inevitable, because it requires communication that is reciprocal and bimodal. Clichés in the form of cheap advice and gratuitous encouragement may deaden the importance of counseling and support, just as the acquisition of "understanding" has been popularized beyond usefulness. If we characterize communication as the art of being understood, however, then the bilateral purpose of counseling is clear. We must both understand and be understood, a difficult task in either direction; otherwise, communication is irrelevant to critical issues.

Psychotherapy's basic aim, aside from helping people in distress cope better, is to make sense in both directions. And if this makes sense, the therapist and patient will reap a mutual understanding that bears a sense of consequence, not triviality. Even silence says much more at times than words that fail to capture the essence of what one wishes to communicate. Communication is a difficult art, and even artists have a hard time communicating what they do. Consequently, most people resort to and rely on being categorical; specificity is more complex and personal, a flaw in many kinds of psychotherapy. The command "Be specific!" may sound rude, but it is actually no more than a serious request for making sense and making a difference in what we communicate.

Today, counseling and counselors are both widespread and devalued. Criteria of excellence found in some therapists of quality are sadly missing in many counselors. Melding what counseling means with how best to encourage, support, and offer beneficial intervention are seldom addressed, and, as a result, the skeptic drifts away into the indifference typical of the true cynic.

An Existential Predicament

If counseling could be reduced to a bare nugget of specificity, then it might be defined as a transaction designed to provide compassionate communication and informed social support. All that is left would be the problems, strategies, and predicaments that govern the substance of therapeutic work itself. This, though, is a mighty remainder to contend with. One starts by identifying pressure points of potential suffering:

1. Health and well-being
2. Family responsibility
3. Marital and sexual roles and relations
4. Job and money
5. Community expectations
6. Cultural and religious dilemmas
7. Self-image and quest for approval
8. Existential issues.

Behind this categorical list are a number of relevant questions that lead more precisely into individual difficulties of how patients cope and hope to resolve what troubles them. For example, what illness or impediment is serious enough to matter, damage health, or to compromise an autonomous way of life? If there is a responsible family, what leading problems declare themselves? How has the patient faltered in fulfilling any role, either personally or in the community? What satisfactions and frustrations occur in the workplace, at the job, or at home? In any respect, how does the patient consider himself or herself (e.g., a failure, deviant, alien, impoverished, bereft)? Who are the key people, and what are the customary signs and sources of support? What kinds of loss and bereavement have occurred that are relevant to current suffering and sorrow?

This list of potential pressure points helps a therapist assess just how his or her patient has identified and dealt with problems in general. No problem exists without being attached to other problems and pressures that might not have erupted by themselves into a situation of suffering. Consequently, the singular situation that has developed and caused a person to seek aid is a plight of vulnerability, a predicament that causes concern about survival, competence, or responsibility, the ingredients of existential anxiety.

Therapy starts at that hypothetical moment in the here and now that is drawn from the limitless past and uncertain future. The existential predicament fills up the moment with its presence. The vulnerable self, brooding on its existence, and a therapist of quality share the encounter. This is a kind of encapsulated existence that contains and contends with ambiguity, ambivalence, and anxiety.

A Philosophical Aside

At this point, before abstractions drift away into impractical generalities, I must draw back. Patients seldom present themselves with philosophical suffering or as aching from metaphysical concerns. Nevertheless, an existential viewpoint must insist that there are ultimate questions most reflective people care about, whether knowingly or not. And because ultimate questions so seldom enter into conscious, everyday concerns, they defy articulation and seem unnaturally remote. A first encounter in psychotherapy, however, will reveal that both therapist and patient are often adrift in a sea of mutual bafflement. Their frailty and fallibility are very apparent, but potentially useful. Vulnerability is no secret, although almost everyone tries to conceal it (and patients, for their part, would not consult anyone who is obviously vulnerable and impaired).

The vulnerable self is a perilous structure that struggles to make sense and to be a steadying influence. Consciousness is both the vehicle and object of interest, but in practice, it is either hopelessly obtuse or not very precise in targeting trouble. Communication, especially its aim of being bilateral, is often in trouble. Meanings are vague and variable, and methods for getting from me and mine to you and yours are incomplete and undependable. Consequently, an existential predicament is not only a concern about values in living or dying, but a collection of private moods so personal that you and I must take our words as approximations resembling each other. We share symbols, just as we share reality, as if we could be wholly objective. A therapist might as well admit that his or her unspoken words are "In my opinion, I believe that . . . "

Consciousness is the embodiment of subjectivity, and objectivity becomes real when the self becomes conscious of something other than itself. In other words, I need symbols and signs even to know what is me and mine, let alone you and yours. I need to bolt my world to yours, because the barrier is only semipermeable. After all, what is taken to be real is a fusion of what is and what is not (but might be). It is not enough simply to claim "I exist" or "I doubt" or "I feel something or something else." Who really cares, unless there is an object to care about? Even the absence of something to care about is a negativity that makes a significant difference. I need the befitting adherence of a circumstance to which my consciousness is attached.

It is a temptation to wander into a fulsome discourse about the nature of mankind, a topic dear to an existentialist's heart. Relation between opposites has always attracted philosophic attention: the one and many, body and mind, tradition and innovation, heredity and environment, and so on are integrated antitheses considered basic to an existence with meaning.

An existential predicament may be a life-and-death matter, but it does not necessarily involve risk to life and limb; it may simply be a complementarity of opposites leading to conflict. On one level, for example, risk to being may mean actual survival, but on another level, it could mean risk to being significant. Wishes and fears complement each other, or are in direct and incompatible opposition. This is no more than the gist of regular observations that can be made about what we do or contemplate doing. For example, humans periodically seek both power and security (a possible incompatibility) by destroying themselves. As someone said, peace is a temporary and untenable pause between wars. Whatever decides mankind's preference for destruction, despite its irrationality and waste, is certainly qualified to be an ultimate question. Freedom and servitude are ancient enough to symbolize opposition to resolution of this conflict between destruction and security. Can we have one without the other? This is as true for wars going on within the vulnerable self, striving for authenticity and away from servitude, as it is for those between nations.

If we wait for consensus on these ultimate questions, we would only agree about the nature of waiting. Neither a skeptical pilgrim nor a psychotherapist has any answers, except that the best we are capable of may not be good enough. The temptation to seek refuge in pat formulas or remote doctrines that rely on supernatural mysteries is strong, but such solutions basically rely on not making sense.

By now, an existential predicament should be understood as far more comprehensive than what patients complain about to therapists. It is a confluence of conflicts that, making no sense together, threatens existence. Few conflicts are resolved for very long by quiet, rational discussion; fewer still are resolved by warfare. We look for indefinite regulation, not total relief. Time does not heal as much as it ceases to heed. In negotiating with conflict, it is not unusual to wait for irrelevance to set in, much as we wait for a boiling pot to cool. In itself, therefore, an existential predicament is not a philosophical question; there is too much anguish in it. But at its center is the special meaning given to it by an individual who is then cast into conflict with the meanings assigned by everyone else.

An existential perspective about the nature of a predicament should strike deep into passions and reasons alike. It should evoke fundamental questions about the dilemma of so many obligations in living, then being obligated to die with the quest for significance sticking to our memory. Besides this immediate concern, however, the phrase *existential perspective* calls for further explanation. It is also bound to raise questions about the philosophy known as existentialism, or its first cousin, phenomenology.

In the years during and just after World War II, much was made of a worldview that pointed with grave dismay at the fate of society, regardless of which side won. Traditional values were observed crumbling (one generation always views earlier values as crumbling, never intact, just as the following generation after that swings back with pendulum-like regularity). Power was in the wrong hands, and security was nonexistent. Established institutions were condemned as being concerned about nothing but materialistic self-perpetuation. Giving support to those in need was meager; it was much more common to support those not needing it, but wanting more power. Thinkers (and, I suppose, many others) were discouraged in the here and now, and very gloomy about the future. The entrenched authorities on which one might depend were the enemy, not an ally.

Concepts of alienation, anomie, destruction of culture, and genocide came into common parlance. But although this viewpoint, which recognized and advocated unqualified pessimism, was identified with the philosophic position of existentialism, the linkage was incorrect. Existentialism and phenomenology were largely academic in tone and very distant from the world at large. A great many artists, philosophers, and novelists, however, did base their work on the bloody reality of wartime and the postwar era. Out of this came further suspicion about familiar authorities, including governments; anti-intellectualism and antimaterialism followed. Getting along and getting ahead seemed to typify many aspirations, but there were others who seemed simply to relinquish any effort toward self-realization and to turn back toward more passive and mystical philosophies. Who we are and where we are going were out of date as ultimate questions and the question of what is befitting to be was scarcely articulated. Yet psychotherapy, in some form or other, seemed to gain in popularity, and psychiatrists gathered more prestige than ever before. I suppose this phenomenon could be called "looking for answers." But what were the questions?

Existentialism, or its equivalent way of thinking, neither started nor ended with World War II and its aftermath. Discouragement about the fate of mankind, despair about progress, anguish about power in the wrong hands, and related worries have been concerns perhaps as long as history has been recorded. I cannot imagine a stage of humanity that, in thinking about itself, did not find good reasons for despair. Nevertheless, I found that what I construed to be an existential viewpoint was rather congenial to my own thinking in that it rejected high-order hypotheses that defied comprehension and did not seem to speculate about the supernatural. There were exceptions, of course, but I already knew that I could never expect consensus. Though some philosophers might get caught up in radical empiricism, or no theories at all, and uphold cover-to-cover materialism as the sole value underlying human efforts, I did not believe that materialism and pragmatism had that much in common. In fact, I thought that the existential viewpoint never did get carried away by materialistic values, nor did William James, whose work in philosophy and psychology left a most significant imprint. Even so, I could not understand how so many concepts came into conflict so often, and I assiduously struggled against the notion of a supernatural purpose behind persistent evidence of order, system, and regularity.

Despite many contradictions and indications of man's utter insignificance, there remains a cluster of concepts related to a special role for the individual, who always seems to be striving for something, perhaps even for self-affirmation and a sense of responsibility that could fit with a sense of reality for the world. If responsibility and realization could become real, then custom certainly would take over, creating guilt and values in its own image. Contemplation of life as experienced by real people tends to abolish the false dichotomy between the vulnerable self and the world, whose orderly indifference seemed irrefutable. This existential viewpoint has a strong bond with the philosophical issues implied by postwar psychiatry and psychoanalysis. Questions about authenticity and reality itself leads to probing what is meant by reality sense (a feeling that something is real and true, both positive and negative) and reality testing (an unspecified set of instructions that ties something deeply emotional to something capable of being thought about). If there had been a consensus about existentialism or phenomenology, it might have contributed a bit to the regular practice of psychotherapy or psychoanalysis. But I found none, except for a resonance with what I felt to be authentic and worth thinking about. Anyone who appreciates what an existential predicament is like could call himself or herself an existentialist, and why not? It is clearly no distinction to do so, and it requires no explanation. In fact, any self-designation is an artifact except as a convenient category to share with others. Anyone who tries to come to terms with his or her own singular existence is entitled, therefore, to whatever modest accommodation of nomenclature comes his or her way.

Anti-intellectualism pervades our society, a natural consequence of mistrusting institutions that formalize and ritualize themselves in search of authenticity. Credentials and nomenclature are not diplomas, however, nor are they mere pieces of paper. The Bill of Rights is a document that changes life as lived, here and now, in this century, but it did not originate here and now by any means. Character and credibility deserve to be respected, too, regardless of disillusion and hypocrisy. In the recent past, however, anti-intellectualism combined with elitism and the so-called counterculture to form "experimentalism," just to give a vague movement a label. The term meant roughly to do what feels right, even if it is wrong. The movement found apparent support in semimystical therapies and viewpoints that required very little effort of thought or discipline of body except by the devotees, mostly foreign, who originally practiced it.

Despite my skepticism, I must recognize that anti-intellectualism and its related consequences did reach for an authenticity that education failed to embellish; but there are other consequences that have not yet become irrelevant. Deploring society and its institutions for shortcomings is as easy as scoring mankind for being what it is. Drugs do the job of reaching emotional highs better than doctrines or rituals for self-enhancement. Viewing mankind in its global disappointment tends to be an excuse for individual surrender; such surrender means despair without revolt. It is easy to be pessimistic, but sometimes downright cynicism cannot be counted on. For example, if wisdom is confused with pessimism, experience with the rites of experientalism, and culture with dilettantism, then our plight is truly tragic, and our doom inescapable. The slogan would be that nothing means very much, anyway, so what does it matter?

Perhaps it does not. If so, however, therapy would be a vain pursuit, with no particular purpose but reconciliation with despair. Authenticity would be a misleading ambiguity, concocted to indicate some sort of compromise between freedom and conformity that sweetens our fate without our really tasting it. But does autonomy signify total independence from regulation? Does it equate flaunting cultural norms with making uncoerced choices? In therapy, a frequent concern is whether distressed patients will feel any better, or regain any self-esteem, by talking about autonomy and authenticity. Of course, talking about anything is likely not to do much unless it stirs one to action. Perhaps autonomy and authenticity mean whatever we decide, including freedom with responsibility *and* freedom to act without purpose or obligation.

Such are the roots of conflict. Unless we heed consequences, however, coping by just hoping for a better resolution of conflict is an empty promise, which I have tried to disdain. It would scarcely justify a more optimistic slant to an existential viewpoint. A therapist of quality might represent hope for more sustaining values, as an example, and thus put a ceiling on skepticism. Its alternative is either dour cynicism or faint dogmatism. Neither seems very practical, because regardless of doom and gloom, people continue to live in the present, very perplexed and without tangible evidence of future improvement. Suffering, I am afraid, is here to stay. Although it is possible to abolish counseling or psychotherapy aside from a gesture or two, and to cover up suffering with statistics, the special contribution of humane values and enlightened awareness is also difficult to eradicate. That we are still very much concerned about individuality—without much encouragement—means something to be respected, even though authenticity and autonomy are admittedly feeble bulwarks against relentless tides of anonymity.

Psychotherapists of quality must be assumed to be serious about their vocation. We should not expect their existence to be sufficient guarantee, however, that psychotherapy will endure in its present cultural form. Opportunities always exist for opportunists, and this does not imply that therapists of quality have nothing better to do; there are plenty of theories for everyone. But faith in humane values and the intrinsic worth of the individual lend themselves to optimistic theories that have a hard time finding much support in any fair assessment of the world.

No psychotherapy is an end in itself, self-sufficient and exempt from inquiry. At best it is a way station, and this is what an existential view represents. If courage, care, and morale can be mobilized during the course of therapy, however, then such negative states as despair, suffering, and conflict might be attenuated. Excessive expectation (i.e., more than is consistent with limited actuality) offers a clear prospect of doom. If, however, survival with significance means coping well and hoping reasonably, then it might be plausible to negotiate our fears about amounting to nothing, even though we will go from somethingness to ambiguity. Although unbridled optimism is inexcusable, much of our hope consists of trying to learn how will might overcome anxiety with the support of appropriate skills and courage.

Dealing with Dichotomy

Opposite ideas, inconsistent and equally tenable, pervade mental life. Dichotomies and antitheses, for that matter, pull at our very nature, sometimes tearing us apart with doubt and dilemmas. When we ask what anything means, it soon becomes evident that nothing means very much unless we can also conceive of its opposite. When a man—a father and husband—comes to a psychiatrist looking for a good reason to get a divorce so that he can marry his mistress, the counselor's first job is to piece out the problems through pairing opposites. What does he mean by his wish to be separated? How will it feel when he is alone, even with the mistress? And on the opposite side, what does the mistress provide that makes him feel like repudiating his family and marriage? In most instances like this, the patient comes with a series of claims, each one representing a wish or fear that cannot exist alongside another, yet neither will subside.

Conflict consists of paired opposite claims, including those of the body versus the spirit, mind versus instinct, rules versus repudiation of authority, and so on. It all becomes very ambiguous unless a therapist can piece opposites together in order to sharpen what each means; otherwise, everything remains blurred and highly charged with emotion. For example, the true opposite of *alienation* (a common term often used for diagnosis) is difficult to determine, because it depends on finding the relevant context. But true relevance depends, in turn, upon asking certain questions about what is and is not factual. Alienation generally means whatever puts an individual at a distance from sources of pride, support, or identity. Aboriginal peoples are often alienated from their native land by invaders; it is a case of conform or else. And even if conformity and compromise are the strategies used, skin color maintains alienation. This leads to conformity by accepting only the less prestigious and menial jobs available, thereby underscoring that the natives are undesirable because of their low work status.

There are a number of other terms that are usually given to explain what alienation truly means. But rejection, abandonment, loneliness, humiliation, and so forth do not really explain; they are consequences, or synonyms of alienation at best. In my opinion, the true antithesis of alienation which fleshes out meaning is affiliation, which implies such things as family membership, affectionate bonds, and legal association. As a pair, consequently, alien-ation/affiliation gives us a strong meaning, with metaphor.

In earlier sections, I tried to find a true paired opposite for the concept of courage, indicating that it is not (or at least not in-variably) cowardice. It is important, however, to recognize that most conflicts are not merely polarized meanings but also signify dilemmas of action: What are the consequences of one action versus another? From the therapist's viewpoint, finding an oppo-site that makes for a sharper meaning can be exceedingly difficult. But when the range of action is broadened, more meanings will emerge. For example, if a patient is in doubt about leaving an unrewarding job, the therapist will ask about alternatives and get at meaning by making extreme contrasts: "Will you quit your job and become a part-time beachcomber?" The initial question may be somewhat silly, but closer scrutiny exposes the true antithetical ideas.

The example signifies something like this: "I'm considering leaving a job that interests me not at all, except for the paycheck. But I don't know any other job better, at least any job I'm trained for. In fact, I'm not sure I want to work at a regular job, anyway. I wish I could just live for the day, the way beachcombers are supposed to do. I don't know any beachcombers, but a part-time beachcomber would work a little, and have more time to do what-ever he chose to do." The antithetical ideas are working on a treadmill for others and working at one's own pace for private purposes. Beyond the latter view of working are other notions (e.g., the idea of leisure) that the patient may have trouble with. Guilt, after all, is an enemy of freedom.

The flight from freedom is often very expensive, and fear of fallibility—if not downright failure—keeps many people from rec-ognizing their actual distress by suspending decisions in favor of equivocation. Instead of being held back by doubt, therapy should compress problem solving into short-term actions that are within reasonable reach and deal with fallibility as a natural and nonfatal contingency. This is encouraged by pressuring patients about what they might do now, disregarding long-term and irrevocable actions. Perhaps they prefer to stay stationary, equivocating indefinitely until some outside event intervenes. If true, then the suggested antithetical ideas will generate different meanings: Shall I act to be free and defy duty, or risk being ostracized and lose everything else? Just because a problem exists and is starkly clear to a therapist, there is no reason to expect that the person most involved will want to do anything about it. Contrasting meanings will clarify and develop into potential polarity for separate actions designed to cope with a problem. No one is compelled to take specific action, although some action is expected.

The existential perspective is copiously aware of dichotomies and contradictions. Dichotomy is the common thread of metaphors, paradoxes, and conflicts; emotions and intellect, chance and necessity, cause and consequence, options and obligations, and stability and change are further examples of polarized meaning. Without a true and significant opposite, there is no meaning worth tangling with. For example, the person who claims that he will tolerate only high standards among government officials is speaking nonsense, because very few people come out in favor of low standards and venality.

Dealing with dichotomy has such a long history that it is fearfully shortsighted to claim it only for psychotherapy. It is required for thinking hard about anything and then making a decision; without it, we are doomed to ambiguity and vulnerable to vague dictums. Long ago, the philosopher Empedocles divided the world according to the opposing principles of love and strife. Love, of course, brought things together, whereas strife pulled them apart. The great philosopher Ernst Cassirer later did about the same thing with symbols and forms, concluding that whatever discipline is under study, opposition and complementarity are the ruling principles.

Ultimate questions and basic concerns will obey such principles, too, at the risk of being just generalities. No more than psychotherapy itself, the existential perspective is required to glean meanings from conflict, just as it seeks a common agreement or assumption behind paradoxes. There are at least two antithetical images for this viewpoint: a relaxed hedonism that does not bother to explain itself or to find a pattern, and a fervent search for rational explanations that will surely discover how exceptions only force the rule.

A common example occurs in bereavement. Shortly after the death of some key person, hardly anyone would consider starting a new relationship; at that point, a new relationship is apparently an indication of disloyalty or plain indifference to the recent death. Here the therapeutic task is not to urge another relationship nor to counsel solitude, but to investigate meanings tactfully. How should conflict between meanings be expressed? What to do about anxiety (often a conflict about unacceptable actions, wishes, and fears)? Or about ambivalence, a clear conflict about the relationship between opposing emotions? Although I shall not pursue the psychotherapy strategies and tactics in acute bereavement, it is such a frequent existential predicament that practically everyone, sooner or later, is confronted with it. Ultimate questions are based on life-and-death matters; bereavement is as close as most people get to mourning loss of love and rising above strife.

Is There an Existential Psychotherapy?

If there is no fundamental consensus about the meaning of existentialism, anyone might opt to be or call someone else an existentialist, depending on how one meaning is paired with its opposite. There is no special merit in dubbing one mode of therapy or another existential, unless a very special meaning is given to it. I have tried to make such a meaning clear by emphasizing certain concepts, but I resist the notion of anointing certain practitioners as "existential" therapists. I hope this makes sense to the skeptical pilgrim. He or she is clear about one point: Ideas are representations of sentiments that designate something, but often not much more than redundancies and vague feelings of attachment or repulsion. Consequently, these clusters of sentiments do not always make sense, nor, in some cases, do they have to. Various disciplines, however, have systems for making sense in their own peculiar way, with appropriate language and operations to match. A skeptic who only stands at the point of decrying ambiguity and denouncing preconceptions has hardly begun.

An existential viewpoint toward ultimate questions, as well as psychotherapy, must go beyond the skeptic who stops short and promises to clear up ambiguity later on. The viewpoint advocates a number of principles in the aggregate, as well as recommending the probing question that will crystallize a relationship between therapist and patient.

The existential viewpoint that means *my* existential perspective does not list propositions and dicta as if they were floating around in an intellectual perisphere. Nor do I elevate subjectivity and irrational intuition to a principle to be practiced by therapists of uncertain aim and qualifications. I would not even push the probing question that has no specific answer to the point of tedium, or get such exquisite detail that my patient falls over in sheer vertigo. A false exactitude about meanings is like the hobgoblin that scares the unwary into a false consistency. Meanings do not direct existence so precisely; indeed, existence directs meaning, and that is why there are so many kinds of meaning (as the next chapter will, I hope, make clear). My existential viewpoint praises meaning for the sake of action, and action that gives meaning to meaning. As a unique method of relieving distress or coping with problems, existential psychotherapy has no authority. It deplores dogmatism, ignorance, complacency, and inertia for obvious reasons. It is person oriented, predicament oriented, encounter oriented, and vulnerability oriented, all within a context of courage, hope, and resiliency.

Very few therapists, including counselors and psychoanalysts, really use more than a fraction of the principles taught to them by preceptors and their textbooks. Experience, culture, and wisdom tend to do more than the most rigorous testing to smooth over the rough edges of schooling. Coping is how most problems are dealt with, not well at all times, but often enough to encourage trust in confronting anxiety about fallibility. Were there an existential psychotherapy, it would surely note well how transitory human wishes and discontents are, but also assume that people in general (and patients in particular) have residual choice, freedom, and the capacity to deal effectively with the dilemmas that agonize them.

Much of existential psychotherapy, like any psychotherapy, would depend on the personality of the therapist. What might be real and revealing for the therapist would be real and revealing for the therapy because it would emphasize the strengths and vulnerability of the therapist. The antithesis of this meaning is the meaning that emphasizes therapeutic technique, a set of prescribed instructions that, like a cookbook, tells you what to do. Technique is fine for surgeons, but rather impersonal for therapists. But my injunction against technique is not to be misconstrued: Skill is not merely technique but a judicious combination of competence and compassion, along with many other fine qualities. My existential therapist might be very skeptical, but is suspicious as well of using skepticism as a disguise for a rigid viewpoint. Also, the opposite of technique is not mere improvisation, nor is spontaneity the same as making it up as you go along. The existential viewpoint exempts no therapist from self-monitoring, which at least means competence, i.e., knowing the difference between what is real and relevant and the whims of the moment.

For therapists, too, freedom and responsibility are earned and learned. The skeptic might accept these principles while questioning the meaning of autonomy and authenticity. He or she is approximately free, within responsibility, to ask searching questions that go beyond precise answers and accurate information: "What matters most to you?" "How would you see yourself wanting to spend the rest of your life?" These questions have no precise answers, I think, but an existential therapist of quality might ask them occasionally anyway. He or she respects a patient's right to be wrong, to use denial, and to fool himself or herself egregiously, but has deep enough regard to the patient not to tolerate it for long. Thus they give the benefit of the doubt by casting a benign doubt over much that passes for truth. The therapist also does this out of respect for his or her own fallibility, and does not camouflage it by holding up overly high expectations for anyone. Nevertheless, respect for paradox will not permit the therapist to be too modest about expectations, lest they deteriorate into hardly any expectations at all. Instead, courage about confronting difficulties, with a reasonable hope of dealing with them, requires assiduous self-scrutiny and a compassionate search for an ego ideal that a vulnerable self can live with and aspire to. This aim is both paradoxical and practical, which gives it a good chance of working out.

Chapter 6

Three
Metaproblems

If there is no well-defined discipline of doctoring called existential psychotherapy, then a therapy that puts primary emphasis on self-monitoring, uncoerced choice, competent coping, vulnerability, and courage, among other ideas, will have to suffice. Furthermore, an existential viewpoint, even without a specific mode of therapy, would have to recognize certain types of problems that other viewpoints might not be so alert to.

Nature is bountiful in many respects, good and bad, that are beyond calculation. Mankind is but a prominent form in a seemingly endless parade of possibilities. So far as we presently know, these endless creations testify to the profligacy and insatiability of life and death. Between birth and death, nature—I know no better term—provides extensive problems that each of us needs to cope with in order to survive.

I suppose that everyone might agree that we could do with fewer problems. There is a superabundance, however, of things that challenge our existence, expose our vulnerability, and hinder us at almost every turn. It should not surprise us, therefore, that there are problems beneath ordinary problems that are less conspicuous and need to be demonstrated.

On Terminating Therapy

Psychotherapy deals with problems and whatever makes them so problematic. But there are reasons to question what lies beneath, whether deeper questions about existence and basic tasks inherent to survive as a person, as well as unfathomed inquiries about the tenacity of ordinary problems. Such *metaproblems* have much to do, in my opinion, with whatever structure there is to existence and its consequences.

Psychotherapy, with all its faults and contributions, must sooner or later come to an end. It does not conclude when key problems have been resolved, obliterated, or even exhausted; the end point is very practical and down-to-earth (unless, of course, the patient and therapist are stuck in an interminable bondage). Therapy should end when, in the concurrence of both doctor and patient, a patient once in need is considered capable of coping effectively with the ordinary and foreseeable problems that might arise in the course of living. In short, at the end of therapy, problems are not so acutely problematic and mysterious.

I have already cautioned that aims of psychotherapy should be neither too lofty nor too low. One extreme is visionary; the other is trivial. There are many ways of expressing the end point described above. The ability to love and work is a famous aim, and becoming more mature—whatever that means—is another. Developing ego strength and mastering the impulsiveness of the instincts is more specialized. Being able to use freedom wisely is still another objective, among many. It is reasonable to expect, however, that psychotherapy will have a constructive influence and will help patients make legitimate decisions instead of being victimized by circumstances. Although I emphasize problem solving, therapy might also end with the acquisition of the following: (a) the capacity to cope more effectively; (b) better morale most of the time, or at least not being too depressed for too long; (c) willingness to use significant support when needed and available; (d) ability to reduce threats and bring anxiety down to a manageable level; (e) development of a broader range of strategies that will help efforts to cope; and (f) cultivation of that quality or skill known as courage.

These are reasonable objectives, although very few people achieve them all, and there are other aims beyond. These aims, moreover, are also goals for the therapist to achieve. Few therapists are paragons, flawless and filled with wisdom, skill, and compassion. There are just as few who can perform therapeutic tricks that make problems disappear, like rabbits, into a hat or simply blow away. In the early years of psychoanalysis, readers were told of semimiraculous transformations of character brought about by treatment, although Freud was careful not to compare psychoanalytic cures with those of Lourdes. Later, of course, reservations about cure were even more pronounced, but even now, new therapies announce themselves by implying more and better results.

Therapists of quality are expected to be honest about themselves and their work. They will certainly pause before making extravagant promises and pronouncements. The existential viewpoint with which I am most comfortable will recommend a caution poised somewhere between skepticism and credulity. Its position is to help patients get key problems into focus and develop strategies for dealing with them. If more is accomplished, so much the better.

Many questions must go unanswered, and many problems remain undiminished. Stripping away the gauze of unrealistic expectations and exposing their dreamlike significance may be therapeutic in itself. Frequently, patients ponder problems and try to answer questions that therapists propose, and then they go on much as before. Challenge is always there, even on topics that seem far from the complaints and distress that originally were uppermost. For example, there is always the challenge of distinguishing real and relevant questions from those that are trivial or meaningless. A question such as "How can I get people to like me?" is seen as scarcely legitimate because it ostensibly has nothing to do with an underlying conflict. But it is real, nevertheless, because it points to interpersonal problems and corresponding values. Being likeable is a popular value. When someone asks what to do about being liked more, it is a request for strategies without really formulating what is wrong.

Therapists and patients, in order to be successful, must realize that they are living in a real world, which is by no means equivalent to living in a reasonable world. When therapy terminates, patients should be able to trace critical issues and trends all by themselves, and thus reach some expectations of coping well enough to be effective.

Metaproblems and Ultimate Questions

It is somewhat unique, but the existential viewpoint pays particular attention to questions or ponderings ordinarily dismissed by most therapists as too philosophical, remote, and cerebral. These questions, difficult in themselves to formulate clearly, are concerned with the basic tasks needed for significant survival, and they apply to the therapist as much as to the patient.

Metaproblems—those underlying ordinary problems that arise from pressure points of health, work, family, and so forth—have to do with establishing a point of orientation that refers to the meaning and value of everything we are concerned about. Like basic tasks, metaproblems are left incomplete and usually unanswered. Yet their worth is undeniable, provided that we are interested in ultimate questions. Ultimate questions are characteristically arcane, referring to such matters as the substance of existence, its purpose and value, and the overall consequences of what we do and are supposed to do. Is it possible to live up to potential so fully that all choices are good, and freedom always beneficial? If it is, then how shall we go about it? But if life has no special meaning for us, aside from survival, what makes us fear death? How enthusiastic can anyone be about surviving in this world, with much suffering and intangible compensations? What is the best way to live? What is the best time to die? All in all, to continue this series of unanswerable questions, what would you be if you had become what you might have been?

Not all unanswerable questions are metaproblems, but the same problems, in one form or another, have perplexed mankind throughout historical memory. Without a feeling for ultimate questions and metaproblems, however, we are, I think, unlikely to derive much value and meaning from what we do and are supposed to do. Earlier generations might have called these questions of good and evil; principles and promises of ultimate salvation—which is as good as having questions answered—have guided uncounted multitudes. Ultimate questions are part of that never-ending quest called self-monitoring, or what others call the examined life.

Metaproblems and ultimate questions may be unanswerable, but they still make abundant sense. Indeed, they establish a groundwork for making sense of other things. In psychiatry, many questions seem pointless, yet a sensible meaning for them can be found that will show how decidedly serious they are. Certain questions seem superficial, but are not; consequently, a therapist who makes sense will discourage the easy answer or an answer that trivializes the question. For example, asking a patient a question such as "Why do you feel so guilty all the time?" is not only futile but somewhat silly. A patient who knew the answer would not be seeing a psychiatrist. A similar question—"What was your childhood like?"—asks for a brief and conclusive response that no serious person could give, except a hard-core denier: "My childhood? Oh, it was fine. My parents were saints, and I had a very happy time!" The answer fits the question by being uninformative and irrelevant. Both therapist and patient thus indirectly testify that the therapy will not amount to much.

To be sure, childhood is very important; no justification is necessary. Its connection with present complaints and recent vulnerability needs to be established more clearly than is possible by asking sweeping questions that encourage superficiality and denial. Whenever a therapist asks about the past, it should have a clear significance for the here and now. Some questions pose only pseudoproblems that make no sense at all. For example, questions that start with, "Why . . . " are not requests for an opinion about origins or motivations but rhetorical appeals. A patient who asks, "Why do I think so much about myself and am so self-conscious?" is not asking a question as much as stating a position of existential despair.

Three Metaproblems: Meaning, Morale, and Mortality

The metaproblems I have chosen to discuss in this chapter represent the existential viewpoint but do not exhaust the full range of metaproblems and basic tasks. These stretch out endlessly. To ask how many metaproblems there are sounds like a nit-picking medieval question in theology. The common theme among metaproblems, though, is concern about how best to endure suffering and find some significance for our brief existence.

Search for Meaning

The meaning of meaning is an ancient and honorable problem, and the search for meaning in what we do, think, and feel is as contemporary as today. The most banal event or casual experience has abundant meanings that could be given to it. Only a few are relevant to the task or purpose we have in mind, and just as few can be communicated. Without a meaning to recognize and talk about, it would hardly be possible to ask what something is or to make an intelligible observation. Making sense implies a capacity to make use of meanings as a guide to action. What something means or meant in the past is often the reason for many pointless polemics; there is no future action for the possible meanings to be tied to. Even a skeptical pilgrim must choose among meanings in his or her search for authenticity. We need meanings as a reference point just to affirm our existence.

There is a certain type of clinician, less common these days, who insists that every event, mental or physical, has a distinct meaning that can be readily interpreted by the initiated. Dream interpretation, for instance, is a problem of decoding something hidden, and external events also mean something other than what appears. Were we only smart enough, these messages could be disclosed, because meanings are there to be found just as they are for a curious person who looks up an obscure word in the dictionary. This kind of crypto-analysis is not what I mean by the search for meaning. I do not look at facts as symbols, although every fact must belong to a context in order to be understood. In order to monitor what we do, in contrast to what we do not intend, it is necessary not only to give a relevant meaning to a cluster of related events; we also have to find an opposite that makes sense. In psychotherapy, we are concerned less about any philosophical interpretation of meaning, than about finding a context in which a number of assorted baffling events will come together.

The existential viewpoint grew out of a realization that there are no absolute meanings, nor fixed reference points, nor absolute contexts in which things make sense and give a permanent purpose to existence. Consequently, if someone were to ask about "the meaning of life," there would be no answer; the question makes no sense, because there is no sensible antithesis. Besides, "life" is itself a context without anything else to refer itself to. The therapist of quality, however, would recognize that the questioner is asking for some focus or direction, for a reference point that will certify the values he or she holds. In fact, no one is likely to ask that very broad question without being unsure that his or her values and works have been worth the effort. The questioner might have said, "I am perplexed and disappointed about my life. I am not sure I want to go on living this way indefinitely." In short, this question about the general meaning of life is a secular complaint that can be understood with a reference point. It is not a religious entreaty; it coincides, however, with an ultimate question of how best to live and which values are most valuable and worth striving for.

Although there are a few psychiatrists of fundamentally religious orientation, psychotherapy itself is a secular pursuit that deals with this world and its troubles and meanings, not the next. There is no transcendental code, except perhaps "Know thyself," which is hardly a contemporary concept. In the course of daily encounters, most therapists try to get at what patients mean, namely, the general context or reference point from which he or she sees the world (including himself or herself). For example, a very common clinical plight or existential predicament is bereavement. Simple as it seems, bereavement has several reference points that mean different things. First, there is the act of grieving or mourning, which means sadness or remorse about losing something or someone very significant. Grieving can also signify a drastic change in behavior or way of life, as happens when a death cuts off income and the remaining family must find other sources of support or a new place to live. Grieving (at least during the acute phase) is further associated with bodily symptoms such as weeping, pining, pangs, hard breathing, no appetite, poor sleeping, and a discouraged attitude. Every dimension of bereavement has its own context to which every symptom or sign can be referred for special meaning, be it emotional, physical, economic, mental, social, or religious.

In order to assess the state of a patient's inner and outer world, the search for meaning is an ongoing requirement. I cannot, for instance, be conscious of anything (whether it is an object, person, idea, or emotion) without spontaneously running through a number of possible contexts until I find a meaning that feels right, makes sense, and is consistent with what made sense before. Furthermore, without at least traces of meaning to hang onto, there is only anxiety, ambiguity, and ambivalence. For most of us who aspire to that state of being known as self-realization, the search for appropriate meaning turns into a lifelong quest for significance. It asks: How shall I measure myself, against which criteria? Who shall be the measurer and for what purpose?

Two Kinds of Meaning. How I go about understanding my inner world and the world I share with others and then try to communicate depends on two kinds of meaning. Both are called personal, because even the most detached meaning always means something to someone within a certain context. One kind of meaning is *subjective*; the other is *objective*. Subjective meaning is primarily about personal significance, namely, what I signify in situations and how I recognize what I am, am not, could be, or never will be. Its antithesis (or, better, its companion in complementarity) is objective meaning. This kind of meaning is social, cultural, factual, and to cover just about everything, categorical. It means everything about a person from the standpoint of the world rather than the inner self. Consequently, objective meaning refers to a person's categorical or generic status, in contrast to his or her personal significance. Such status is not the same as social status (i.e., where and how a person stands with respect to the community's rank ordering of worth and birth), although surely that consideration must be accounted for by some index of meaning. Significance and status belong together, because each provides a context or frame of reference for the other. Subjective significance rates the self from the inside, objective status rates the world, and each one provides a standpoint for assessing what the other means, from inside or out.

The meaning of "being human," or just the phrase "in human terms," is what metaproblems and ultimate questions are all about. We are suspended between the two poles of subjective significance and objective status. In the search for meaning, we recruit a variety of internal and external meanings referring to contexts of both significance and status, because no one starts with a clean slate devoid of any meaning.

Everyone belongs to a social context and thus is subject to many categorical meanings that define status. For example, I am an ailing patient to my doctor, because I see him only when I am sick. I am a voter to my congressman, who sends me literature from time to time calling attention to his achievements. I am a senior citizen to consumer groups and merchants who want to sell me things I can do without. I am a retired colleague to other physicians, who treat me with a mixture of deference and indifference. In short, I am many things to many people, who help establish my objective status (and theirs) with regard to certain categories that are normal and standard. What I feel like or am from the inside is quite irrelevant, except insofar as my motivations and values are topics for public use.

In categorical terms, I am only an object. My status is defined by certain social, cultural, political, and commercial reference points. When dealing with objective status, and without intending any personal disrespect, I am nothing else, and no one—including me—takes much interest in that intangible "inner me" that characterizes any person as a unique individual to significant others.

Subjective significance, of course, is not a meaning likely to affect as many people as objective status or categorical meaning. There are very few people directly involved in intimacy or first-degree emotional involvement, compared to the hordes for whom we are just another number or categorical unit.

The difference between significance and status is widely recognized, although often ignored. Medicine makes an obvious distinction between subjective complaints and objective findings, and in very modern times, third-party payers and managed medical care have tended to impersonalize doctors and other providers. In turn, patients and their personal significance have become demeaned and minimized. Everyone has become a unit belonging to a vast file system; very few have personal significance.

The gross distinction between significance and status is what perplexed me when I first became a psychiatrist, as I recounted in Chapter 2. Suffering greatly exceeded pathological facts about the body; only in psychiatry was equal status given to the significance of pain, sadness, anger, fear, and so on, all personal events that are difficult to share with others. Most of our surmises about other people are, with the best of intentions, only categorical suppositions and do not reach very far into inner mental states of personal significance. For example, a woman patient described her husband as a capable carpenter, an excellent plumber, and a superb handyman. She conceded that he was a good provider and above-average father, but as a husband, he was only a hardworking bore in every respect. This was his categorical rating: His status was to be all those occupations and roles. She had nothing to say about him as a person; his personal significance or subjective meaning was zero except to the extent he evoked a number of unpleasant feelings in her.

Psychiatrists with experience note, for example, that when a man keeps referring to his wife in categorical terms (e.g., "my wife") rather than by name, he probably has a different and more impersonal kind of relationship with her than one who uses her name and notes her personal activities and interests. Therapists spontaneously make distinctions between significance and status. Although we seldom have access to another person's private feelings and thoughts, we do value statements that refer to the inner meanings of attitudes and interests. These are "significant" in clinical terms, but few psychiatrists devote themselves exclusively to inner significance without also developing a categorical context for all the facts that constitute that patient's status. We call that "taking a history." The woman who described her husband, more or less, as a satisfactory functionary considered him a vacuous, boring person, thus reducing his significance to the vanishing point, despite his individual history.

Very sick patients do not lose the distinction between different kinds of meaning. For example, it is not unusual for a patient with cancer (a categorical assignment of status), or a person who is sick and has a diagnosis of cancer (subjective meaning and objective status), to deny the diagnosis ("I am not a cancer patient!") but complain about symptoms of subjective significance ("Why have I lost so much weight and feel so weak?"). In response, the doctors use objective meanings, such as statistics and medicines, to objectify a patient's significance further into clinical status.

There are several subgroups in the categories of both subjective significance and objective status, although both, as emphasized earlier, have personal attachments. Knowing which subgroup and category a patient and therapist are using will help clarify the ambiguity that too often muddies the field of meaning. Although different kinds of meaning help decipher vulnerability and even guide the analysis of ultimate questions, the search for meaning goes on, and remains a metaproblem of unmatched importance.

Subjective Significance. Responsive clinicians of experience learn how to identify different kinds of meaning that on the surface seem similar. Perhaps this is what being experienced means, i.e., recognizing subgroups and special meanings within a general field of communication. Listening well means paying attention to details of how a general meaning, whether subjective or objective, can be subdivided. However, meanings in natural language overlap, and may quickly shift from one group to another. Every meaning depends on the interpretation that another person gives it. Deciphering meanings behind meaning, therefore, is an art, perhaps, that resembles the criteria for a good or bad theory that I described earlier: generality, specificity, relevance, and acceptability (Chapter 3). However, concerning conflict, there is no one meaning that accounts for a patient's mistrust or misery, although cognitive therapists strive mightily to achieve such understanding. Nevertheless, in my opinion, there is no foundation for anything analogous to the germ theory of disease where one microorganism is responsible for both clinical and subjective manifestations or meaning of disease.

1. *Intrapersonal meanings.* These meanings are intended to designate seemingly objectless states of consciousness: moods, aches, pangs, yearnings, and other special sentiments couched in metaphorical language. Intrapersonal meaning is me and mine, that is, the self referring to itself and its extensions. No one gets in on intrapersonal meaning unless the primary person wants to share privacy. Examples are "I am sad [or glad, mad, or even bad]" without disclosing the reason, or "I must tell you, Doctor, how discouraged I am about my treatment." The latter means "I feel no better inside after being treated"; the patient could have said how disappointed she or he feels about the doctor, but this would give the statement an interpersonal meaning. Calling discouragement

something related only to the treatment impersonalizes the plight, as if the doctor had not been involved.

2. *Interpersonal meaning.* This meaning establishes a connection from me and mine to you and yours. Instead of the very intrapersonal I, now it is the interpersonal me and mine, an extension or collection of things that matter to me. I may know you and yours (often, you and yours are interchangeable), but you become real when there is an actual relationship between us. It is when you emerge as a distinct individual through your extensions that you acquire significance and cease to be just a categorical object (my neighbor, colleague, etc.). In psychotherapy, most observations and especially interpretations are about interpersonal relationships. In this way, a therapist hopes to get at emotions that are private: "Yes, I am mad at him. He ignores me whenever I see him, yet I still want to be his friend." Another example is shown below.

Psychiatrist: I think that you get angry and very anxious whenever you feel misunderstood. It seems to make you feel helpless, too.

Patient: I'm usually pretty cool, except when my wife criticizes me, I think without a good reason.

Psychiatrist: Your parents were seldom satisfied either. Perhaps that has something to do with feeling misunderstood and helpless, as if you can't do anything worthwhile. Your wife, as you see it, anyway, also makes you feel anxious and angry at the same time, especially when she criticizes you for no reason.

Patient: It's more complicated than that. I wanted so much more from my parents, and my wife, too. I always tried to please them, and I know I do things that are worthwhile every now and then. But getting praise, forget it! I get criticism instead. They always find something wrong.

The interpersonal significance of this man's relationship with parents and his wife is quite clear. It would, however, be difficult to deal only with relationships without speaking about anger, anxiety, and disappointment. In fact, only through knowing more about relationships with significant others can a psychiatrist get at inner feelings. Without a keen sense of relationships and roles, however, therapy would only be fine-tuning intrapersonal emotion and its very private meaning ("No, I wouldn't call it anger. I just feel a little irritable and exasperated today about nothing. Just a mood"). The therapist is remiss if he or she fails to look for a specific relationship or significant other that makes this patient so nettlesome today. This is based on the principle that when a patient says "nothing," there is usually "something" that accounts for it.

3. *Impersonal meaning.* Impersonal meaning on the basis of a subjective significance might seem like an oxymoron: How can something personal also be impersonal? In this case, *impersonal* refers to the events, objects, and things in the outside world that do not qualify as an interpersonal relationship. These impersonal things might well be classified as categorical and objective in meaning for me and mine, except that we recognize them as having a personal meaning because of a background that already means something personal. In fact, things may *become* items with wholly objective meaning by stripping them of subjective meaning and depersonalizing them into objects and things. The world is full of impersonal things: chairs and trees, birds and planes, stars and clouds, fire and wood, things that go bump, and so forth. When impersonal meanings about very personal matters come up in therapy, they are called "intellectualizations," "rationalizations," or something like that, even though the process is far from intellectual. Things have meaning, but they are just as impersonal as cabbages and kings.

Something analogous to impersonal meaning happens during a shocking event. For example, rescue workers or frontline physicians must impersonalize their emotions to get their jobs done. Doctors must "professionalize" themselves under particularly harrowing circumstances, a tactic the layman often calls "hardening." This is wrong, because what happens is that with constant exposure to distressing sounds, sights, and smells of death and catastrophe, the intrapersonal and interpersonal impact diminishes, and only the impersonal remains.

4. *Infrapersonal meaning.* Infrapersonal meaning refers to a relation of subject to object represented by a split between I and mine. For example, a patient goes to a doctor complaining that his stomach hurts, splitting his subjective distress from an impersonal localization within the body. It is actually a relation between consciousness and organs, but within private experience. The infrapersonal meaning also extends to other private experiences besides how the digestive system works. Past experience, as with memories, are distinctly mine ("What a fool I was! How could I have done that!"). Long after a death, when mourning has subsided, that body, aptly called "remains," beneath a tombstone acquires an infrapersonal meaning, or sometimes just impersonal significance. Mostly, however, infrapersonal meanings refer to private experiences that are difficult to share ("My insomnia is something no doctor really understands"). It is a partial event that distinctly belongs to me and mine.

Objective Status. Objective status is the meaning that an object has for public consumption. It is shorn as much as possible from subjective taint. Objects, people, and things, individually and collectively, have public status or conventional meaning. Otherwise, there could be little mutual agreement or disagreement, since communication would be impossible. When I point to something, it is an object; I cannot use my index finger to designate an emotion, or private meaning. When the Walrus and the Carpenter spoke of many things, it was the objective status of shoes, ships, and sealing wax, and even of the question whether pigs had wings. Dictionaries and maps, abstract and schematic though they must be, deal with public status to be real. However, each thing out there can also have subordinate meanings drawn from their more general status. We may define, say, an armadillo, whether or not we have ever seen one. Its objective status as an animal depends on what we do with it in its relation to me or you. But an armadillo is still out there, holding its own objective status, and has every right to. However, objective status also has clinical relevance in that we use the distinction between subject and object to generate the meaning of each. Status provides the reference point for personal significance, and analogously, personal significance helps enhance the proper meaning for something outside of my consciousness. If, for example, I truly believed that pigs have wings, reference to the outside world where no pigs have wings would be the basis for considering that I suffered from a delusion, i.e., a belief without external foundation.

1. *Surplus meaning.* Here is a very private attitude toward an object ordinarily considered wholly material and external. The meaning has no genuine relation to the fact or thing, except that it is mine and, therefore, surplus. For instance, I have a watch that belonged to my late father. As a mere timepiece, the watch has an objective status, but it also memorializes my father for me, making it different from any other watch I have or could have.

Another example is more familiar: A calendar date is only 1 out of 365 days. But any extra meaning of that specific date is surplus, especially if that date is uniquely personal and calls for special action. Birthdays, anniversaries, and so on represent surplus status. The surplus starts out as a material or commonly designated event (e.g., a watch or a national holiday) that works its way back into personal significance.

2. *Pragmatic meaning.* This is a common form of objective status in that it designates how we make use of an object or act upon it. It can happen to anything at all. The personal significance of me and mine is irrelevant compared with the general use; the categorical status is all that is important. For example, when I am asked to give information about my occupation or street address on a government form, the questions apply only to the status of categories I belong to, not the personal significance of my job or living arrangements. Pragmatic meaning is a set of instructions about how to behave toward almost anything, or any question, usually something mundane or very tangible—it means "Do something." It is a call to action.

3. *Generic meaning.* Objective status of this kind facilitates generalization and reduces complexity to a category. It insists that one or another common characteristic be considered typical of the individuals within a group, and this can lead to stereotyping. When a therapist asks about a patient's life and specifies a series of events (e.g., "marriage," "childhood," "job satisfaction"), the proper answer, detailing constant themes and variations, is usually too difficult and time-consuming. The patient might choose a generic meaning that encapsulates in broad outline what these events meant. ("What were your college days like?" "The best time of my life, except for studying, but I didn't do too much of that.") Actually, most conversations consist of exchanging generic meanings without getting into detailed accounts of what specifically happens that is unique or surplus. But such meaning is not entirely superficial. Without generic meaning, practically any activity could be stopped dead; we need to categorize in most situations in order to signify an attitude to adopt toward something potentially too complex. Most of the names we give to things use a generic or pragmatic meaning, as if we could expect homogeneous behavior always.

4. *Transcendental meaning.* I could appreciate an equivalent meaning between transcendental status and suprapersonal significance. But to draw a very fine point, *transcendental* refers to something beyond the everyday range of experience; *suprapersonal* might mean an inner experience of high metaphysical or theological importance. Together, the two terms indicate a strong affiliation between the "I" and the totality of whatever might be inaccessible to ordinary people using their regular senses. It has the significance and status of something unusual, perhaps the world beyond worlds where destiny and divinity meet: Perception is elevated and draws upon an ambience signifying higher, finer, better, and so forth.

No one can safely ignore this dimension of meaning, although it is fair game for many. Many people, however, use suprapersonal or transcendental meanings to guide their life and to profess validity of transmundane experience. It might belong to the realm of the artistic, to a sense of history, to appreciation of music, and so on, quite apart from religion or politics. Ethnographers, for example, call our attention to different ways in which nations (down to isolated tribes) anoint their history or culture with transcendental status and suprapersonal significance. What it also does for everyone is to allow them to claim superiority over others, "us versus them."

These subgroups are not intended to be exclusive, but they illustrate different varieties of meaning. They especially depict how meaning fluctuates from the subjective to the objective, referring now to the very interior of private experience, and then to the exterior of public categorization; here, a meaning that signifies an intimate relationship, there, a transmundane object that guides and validates experience. We regularly dazzle ourselves with ambiguity that is attributable mainly to the richness of everyday life and the facile interchange of meanings.

In the course of everyday life, however, we do not attend to everything, and we cannot parse whatever we hear and speak about into separate compartments of meaning. After all, we can speak perfectly coherently with each other without paying much attention to grammar, syntax, and secondary meanings of words. But distinguishing meaning is not simply a job for grammarians and academics; it is important in psychotherapy, and in discourse meaning often gets misinterpreted and confused and may lead to conflict.

Meaning and being are inseparable in healthy living. In other words, what feels real and right ranges from a right-now inclination and mood (intrapersonal significance) to that clock ticking away in the corner, indifferent, impersonal, and unimpressed by my efforts to make sense. But the clock also has a generic meaning or status as a clock, and a pragmatic meaning, because I use it to tell time. The gathering dusk as I write these words also calls me to heed the cycle of the seasons, watching new buds and flowers that were not visible in the garden yesterday, and to see the sunset through the branches of a tree. I must also stop to recall plans for the evening, and think about people I shall meet. So it goes, and in a scant moment I go from the intrapersonal to surplus to impersonal to pragmatic to interpersonal.

When I practice my profession, I am usually more alert to shades and modes of meaning than in ordinary exchanges. Much of what people say to each other is mundane and trivial, although without conversation we would soon lapse into being prisoners of our own consciousness. Yet few conversations grow in depth, or provide much amusement and understanding, before becoming boring and repetitious. It makes me think that when a patient comes to a psychiatrist who tries to make sense of what that person means according to the context being reported, it is truly a unique experience. Communication may be the art of being understood, but it is also a skill.

This skill is to be practiced; it is never perfected, because meanings are usually more elusive than we realize. To appreciate how interminable the search for meaning must be, begin at the hypothetical point at which one recognizes how little certainty or absolutism exists. The barest fact starts as a low-level theory, embedded in a mundane context that, in turn, is gathered up in ever-elevating spirals of significance until what anything means is merely the nebulous object of meditation, or the explicit goal of motivated action.

Meaning and being are also treated as equivalent realities in so-called cultural truths. For the society believing in them—and ours is no exception—such truths are as fixed as the North Star. In everyday life, and certainly in the practice of therapy, mixtures of meaning are so confluent that practically no one makes an effort to dissect them. Every scrap of reality has its shell of diversified meaning; a world without meaning might exist, but it is difficult to imagine. Out of our storehouse of potential meaning, though, we readily (and more often than we realize) make up worlds.

The search for meaning is truly a first-order metaproblem because it is inseparable from ultimate questions about mankind. One form of an ultimate question is how to find constancy amid flux, and there is no better example than meaning. The search is not a metaphysical mission pursued only by pedants, but as authentic a quest as could be conceived. For example, if the reader simply glances around the room in which he or she is presently seated and fixes attention on any object, this will be an introduction to a private search for meaning on a very elementary level. Give *that* object a name, then ask yourself what it is doing there. How did you get it? What does it do? Do you ever think about it other than now? Could you do without it? And so on until you recognize that even with very simple and unequivocal objects, we can subject them to scrutiny comparable to the events we live through. The prerequisite for the metaproblem is to realize how we manufacture meanings, and choose among them, manipulating what means what to whom. In turn, we are manufactured and manipulated by meanings that we come upon in our search.

Meaning and Value in Psychotherapy.   Problems are problematic only when something happens that violates the directives and standards set up by the relevant culture to which any of us belongs. Otherwise, they are just inconvenient obligations, readily dismissed. But violation of values that define our very existence (i.e., significance and status) also threatens our self-esteem, sense of normalcy, standards for success, and feeling of fulfillment. Suppose a high school student has no use whatsoever for the recondite requirement to learn algebra, but he values the prestige and reputation that comes with athletic skill. Obviously, he will spend more time and energy practicing on the sports field than in the classroom studying algebra, at least until it comes time to pass qualifying examinations for college. Varsity letters at that point help him not at all: The value of algebra goes up, and that of sports goes down. Not knowing or caring about algebra was once not problematic, but now its value has changed, and his ignorance is problematic. His vulnerable self and self-esteem are at risk because he might not get into college, and all sorts of complications and consequences would then arise.

Adaptive existence depends on keeping potential problems (job, housing, family, money, health, etc.) able to be coped with. In our society, work and worth are practically identical; one without the other is a sure formula for diminished self-esteem and open vulnerability. Work therefore is a value, and its violation is being out of a job and therefore useless. If no new job is forthcoming, perhaps as a result of age or a depressed economy, the only hope of resolving the problem is to find other activities with approximately the same desirability and standards. In therapy it is essential not only to understand codes of meaning (with corresponding values) that stand behind depression of self-esteem, but to know what the patient deems indispensable to significance and status within self and for society.

Metaproblems and ultimate questions inexorably expand to problems for society at large, so that the individual with personal problems comes to represent the whole. The most urgent problems are more likely to be constant than the feeble solutions for them that are proposed and even carried out from time to time. These problems include disease, poverty, unemployment, hunger, homelessness, crime and violence, corruption, and exploitation, all painful to recount and all qualified to be called epidemic.

It is a baffling and never-ending paradox that these epidemic problems seldom bother the people who complain most about lack of meaning in their lives. In simplest terms, their values and standards are different; indeed, they may not believe in any of the values they were taught to respect (except for the short-term values of entertainment, being dressed stylishly, etc.). It is not that these well-endowed people are harsh and calloused, but that hunger and homelessness mean very little when supermarkets are filled and homes are practically works of art. Yet values that do mean something fail to make an impression. I have interviewed a number of well-to-do patients who had complaints of no complaints. All of their so-called needs were satisfied without any effort. Except for unforeseen illness, potential pressure points for problems were mostly theoretical. They were in no great risk of anything except boredom and a sense of shame about being useless and idle.

The antithesis of a skeptical pilgrim seeking solution to metaproblems is, I suppose, a complacent burgher whose self-satisfaction is legendary. Such people have been scolded and ridiculed enough by novelists, and I need abuse them no further. I am reasonably sure, however, that if something happens to disrupt their complacency, the burghers might then have distinctive problems consistent with the way in which their values and standards have been violated. In other words, they will become more like us, for better or worse.

Although the unhappy folk who complain about lack of meaning would not be roused to motivated activity by learning more about hordes who exist in misery, it is because their own standards have not been challenged. They do not really lack values; their values have let them down by not causing sufficient problems. The search for meaning cannot be activated in lonely splendor; it requires other metaproblems forcing people to confront ultimate questions, as well as whatever proximal problems can be ignited.

Maintenance of Morale

The search for meaning would be pretty meaningless without an assurance that the long-term struggle was worthwhile. Staunch values are no guarantee that a high-minded person is willing and able to confront conflicts or use courage. It is a common clinical observation that patients with a strong sense of guilt have very high standards that hardly anyone could match. In fact, the higher the standards, the greater the self-expectation and the faster the descent into guilt. Constantly seeking self-improvement is a common avocation of the already overly virtuous. The sense of violation and failure dogs those who find it impossible to live up to self-imposed standards. In contrast, the overly virtuous admire the more or less psychopathic souls who can yield to a variety of temptations and feel neither remorse nor guilt. Any shame they feel when exposed is simply a matter of temporary embarrassment to be facilely explained away. The overly virtuous are not the only ones periodically plagued with a sense of moral failure. There are others who neither seem to suffer from high expectations nor are tempted to violate standards and values, and yet become morbidly ashamed and suffer from demoralization.

Severely depressed patients typically feel guilt out of all proportion to any offense, real or imagined. Guilt comes over them like a dark fog that obliterates their vision and leaves them powerless and vulnerable. It makes no sense, for it has no appropriate meaning.

Demoralization is not the same as depression or guilt, although they may be found together. Usually, however, a demoralized person feels hopeless and incapable of initiating any action on his or her own behalf. Some suicidal patients suffer more from demoralization, with an accompanying sense of total futility, than from guilt and remorse; "What's the use?" is their desperate and not unreasonable question. Such people differ from the aimless well-to-do person who asks the meaning of life and has no apparent values to provide a reason for having problems. Very depressed patients claim, "I am worthless, and I deserve to die!" But demoralized people might have tried at one time and become alienated from their own cultural habitat. They have learned values, but they do not believe that such standards apply to them, so deep is their self-contempt.

The concept of morale is not as commonly thought about as that of demoralization. But ask almost anyone about his or her morale and a cogent answer will come, as if morale is something readily understood (just like courage, to which it is related). It is an essential concept, because maintenance of a healthy morale is a metaproblem. It means the confidence to cope effectively and wholeheartedly with obstacles and difficult tasks.

I find it hard to imagine a healthy morale unless one is also effective, significant, and has status enough in the world. Good morale means belief in deserving adequate social support; however, it does not mean that the person with good morale needs such support for normalcy and acceptability. For example, there are many loners in the world who struggle for years in a cause that few others approve of or understand. Their rewards are meager, and their disappointments many. There are artists who never sell a painting, actors who rarely work, inventors without a patron, leaders (in many fields) without a devoted following, and so on. Most families have potentially high achievers who never make it the way that people expect. Some of the nonachievers become demoralized, others seem to accept their mediocrity, and still others struggle on, going from one failed project to another and still managing to resist demoralization.

If a person believes in the righteousness of his or her own cause and has confidence in his or her ability to cope effectively while maintaining healthy self-esteem, then morale and moral courage mean the same thing. Confidence and courage far outweigh any fears of failure, humiliation, and alienation; otherwise, every effort would seem directionless, and empty of promise. These are often the people to whom others give advice, to no avail. Existentialists call this plight one of absurdity, but there is nothing funny about it. Emptiness is also meaningless, and anything suggested to fill the void is deemed insignificant and inaccessible.

Morale and Quality of Life. A good quality of life does much to maintain morale. This truth has been long in coming to the attention of some medical practitioners, who seem to believe that if symptoms could be relieved and a chronically ill patient could accept his or her plight, then a better quality of life would certainly follow; furthermore, if the activities of everyday life were not significantly impaired during convalescence, then surely the quality of life would be good. Unfortunately, this is not so. There are many patients, for example, for whom surgery has been successful in prolonging life, but at a great cost in morale. Sometimes it is a bitter choice deciding whether to have a disfiguring operation or to accept a shorter life expectancy.

There is a difference between quality of life and morale. In fact, clinicians who now speak knowingly about quality of life—it has become a cant phrase these days—seldom think about morale. (I suspect that their own morale is often in question.) Morale refers to someone who keeps up courage despite adverse circumstances, whether of illness or any other continuing problem. Patients who have a terminal illness but live each day, hoping only for relief of pain and postponement of invalidism, are said to be very courageous. They do have a strong morale, demonstrated through positive expectations despite a poor quality of life. The reverse can also happen, namely, demoralization that overtakes a good quality of life and produces catastrophe. I am reminded of a middle-aged woman who could have been said to have it all. According to her family, she carried out her few functions exceedingly well—except that from time to time she got the blues, which no one paid particular attention to. She consulted no doctor, and apparently felt it unnecessary to see a psychiatrist. One day, however, she put on her most elegant fur coat, drove downtown, parked her car, and went to a busy subway station. Then, as bystanders looked on in horror, she dropped her coat and jumped in front of an oncoming train.

Morale, like courage, depends on subjective factors, whereas quality of life consists of factors measurable in objective terms (e.g., living conditions, security and safety of home, money, job satisfaction). The so-called good life is not always so good, but it may coincide with good feelings, confidence in coping well, and courage to confront problems, which constitute morale.

Two Kinds of Morale. Most people draw courage and morale from their affiliation with a respected group. Remember that affiliation is the antithesis of alienation, where the outside group is decidedly hostile and exploitative. As a rule, these respected groups represent favorite values and have members that the morale seeker wants to emulate. They may include teams, clubs, business firms and associations, religious groupings, and other tribal collections of people with a common purpose. Individuals who are ambitious or diffident would seek to join these groups, which are respected and socially sanctioned in some ways. Becoming a member can be expected to inflate self-esteem because the initiate acquires some of the prestige or tradition of the group. Even informal support groups tend to have a strength that individuals may lack; normalization and acceptability are still the desirable aims.

Morale can even be built up temporarily by identifying with a group representing team spirit; this infuses almost anyone sharing pride in the accomplishments of the "home team." But what about an individual who searches for accomplishment, recognition, and self-esteem without palpable support? Is he or she dedicated to unpopular causes (or simply following the unconventional) to a degree that much moral courage is needed? Can morale and courage survive in an atmosphere of ridicule, hatred, and even banishment?

The key question is whether morale and courage require cultural approval and common purpose or are simply nourished by success. I make a distinction between *primary* morale and *secondary* morale. Primary morale is confidence in the ability to cope competently, with self-esteem enough to flourish without common purpose and courage enough to confront private challenges. Secondary morale depends on affiliation and identification with organizations, whether formally organized or informally collected. It makes little difference, by the way, which kind of morale is primary or secondary, because both are important elements of the metaproblem: How essential is group affiliation in strengthening our courage and confidence? But primary morale, with its link to moral courage, seems to be more basic than the morale that acquires self-esteem and prestige through groups that share a common value.

Somewhere in our collective mind, we have a common admiration for the lone individual standing up to hostile multitudes, convinced of his or her cause and willing to face danger on its behalf; in movies, it is the solitary hero facing townspeople bent on banishing him and everything he stands for. "Stand up for what you believe in!" might as well be a slogan for a democratic society, even though countless individuals have suffered for following this advice. Some people have only contempt (or at least a lack of respect) for those who join as many clubs as possible or collect citations and certificates to hang on their walls. Even granted a streak of envy, those who enjoy the support of others and find it necessary for self-esteem are not respected as much as those who have the courage of convictions, come what may.

Nevertheless, affiliation is stronger than alienation, and although self-sufficiency may be admirable, there are few people who are wholly self-sufficient. They may be just a little less gregarious than most and a bit more self-motivated; being a loner is far from being alienated, and not at all pathological. Alienated individuals, moreover, are usually alienated only from the dominant group, and with good reason. Although they may be a minority of one, they could still feel a degree of affiliation and loyalty with their own people, whoever they are. Blood, the saying goes, is thicker than ambivalence.

For skeptical pilgrims, the metaproblem of maintaining independent, primary morale is puzzling. They would like to be autonomous and independent, free to make their own decisions and to revoke them as needed. Self-realization and authenticity are their general aims, and they are surely averse to membership in some very exclusive society that guarantees tradition and acceptance. But they are still not alone; they are intellectually affiliated with that host of independent and skeptical thinkers who have defied convention and pursued their own beliefs from ancient times. In following the crowd, morale can be preserved intact. In so doing, however, freedom might be surrendered for security.

No morale is needed for conformity to popular causes. No courage is necessary, because the risk is zero. But there are also many people, lacking sturdy morale, who have few affiliations with others and very dubious independence. I once knew a young man who shunned group activities and was afraid of authority, so he led a fairly secluded life that posed few challenges. He was expert in compromising, seldom taking a definite stand on issues. No one could have considered him either affiliated or autonomous. Every now and then, however, when visiting another city and feeling especially lonely and insignificant, he fantasized that he was a prince traveling incognito. Thus, even though he was of course unrecognized in the new city, he was very well known in his imaginary group of nobility back home. This provided secondary morale, at least in terms of self-esteem. His alienation became a royal affiliation that inflated his esteem and attenuated his loneliness. At home and work, he was unimaginative and difficult to converse with, and his relations with women were few and decidedly asexual. He had many of the characteristics of Walter Mitty that I mentioned earlier. He needed no courage; Fantasy sufficed. Though a prince in imagination to modulate his loneliness, he was in fact merely an office hack, and remained just that.

Dilemmas of Action. The choice between autonomy and conformity is not a true choice but a dilemma that draws upon the maintenance of morale. It is a problem of self-esteem and moral courage, combined with need for affiliation, acceptability, and normalcy. It was not a strange peculiarity that caused the hippies of a generation ago to rebel against standardization and conventional values; historical precedent amply documents how often rebels join up with other rebels and assert a new conventionality. Self-realization is an elusive quarry, never to be captured once and for all. Some people define themselves by wearing the latest styles, whereas others take pride in unconventional clothing. Both want to stand out from the crowd and look down on the outsider. What helps morale most?

One man I know sadly admitted, "I am nothing but my father's son, and president of his company." His morale, obviously, was low despite his business success. He had poor primary morale and unrewarding secondary morale, because his affiliates knew that he was less than the man his father was. Security can defeat itself, as successful parents' children already know.

Courage is seldom called on very directly in psychotherapy, although it is implied. When decisions are demanded, physical or moral courage is needed. What I have called pragmatic courage is close to morale, and its failures or lapses lead to questions about how best to behave (e.g., whether to yield to wishes or fears when they conflict). Primary morale, which stems from independent self-esteem, can be recognized in the motivation that many patients feel, despite chronic setbacks. The importance of maintaining morale sometimes becomes a rescue problem. One woman, mourning the loss of an aged dog that was her only uncritical friend, was more or less accustomed to being dominated by her husband and family. She opted unexpectedly for a trip to Europe, a tour with strangers that was utterly foreign to her family's custom and acceptability. Hard as it was to do something for herself, she went on the trip, anyway, and on returning found her morale again.

Progress in therapy requires moral courage on occasion when action against a strong adversary (e.g., a domineering family) seems imperative. It is much easier to comply with expectations and deny distress, or to find excuses for no action. The motive to change is supported by finding sources of secondary morale that were not previously available. Supportive groups that subtly encourage dissidence are common refuges and reasons for mobilizing the courage to resolve a dilemma of action. Success then might breed more success, strengthening primary morale. But each dilemma must be faced anew. Support groups tend to split up, and dilemmas persist. Many patients relapse, feeling that old familiar habits are best, because they fear change and regret potential isolation from and ostracism by forces that control them through withholding approval. And therapy itself seldom promises a specific reward.

Fluctuations in self-assertiveness or in confidence to cope with dilemmas of action are very common. Hence renewed emphasis on maintaining morale is required, lest people relapse into a customary sense of despair. Morale is a consequence of dealing successfully with the pragmatic pressure for doing things better. I consider morale of any kind to be the lifeblood of survival; it helps through many dark and discouraging nights when it would be far easier to relent and return to the unhappy ways things were. Long-term expectation is an entrancing lure, but perhaps only a mirage without lasting meaning or a mission without a goal. Rebellion or even deviance from routine expectation is a fearsome thing to be dreaded. Sometimes all that a person afflicted with dilemmas of action can manage are token rebellions, petty disputations of insignificance. Such tokens are but a roll of drums, not a genuine call to action.

Therapists also face dilemmas of action that sometimes corrupt judgment rather than stake out a better path: high composure, low confusion, being clear about consequences (good or bad), and opting for the better aim. But which aim shall it be, for what reasons? Are approval and security the values to be sought? Or is nonconformity worth the risk when it antagonizes others? Though autonomy is a desirable aim in the abstract, it is not equivalent to mere unconventionality, or rebellion on account of trivial causes. Nonconformity without a cause is negativism in disguise, not a value in itself. And as a disguise it is a pretty flimsy garment, scarcely able to provide much warmth of any kind.

Society has an ample supply of standards without any single code or formula. Not only are the standards contradictory, but there are double and triple standards to tantalize and beleaguer us. What to believe in, what to strive for, and how to assess the outcome are basic questions that typify dilemmas of action. Values may let us down by misleading us through double standards and hypocrisy. We seek acceptability and normalcy, but the quest for authenticity may be a long one, and long odds do not a hero make. I pointed out in discussing courage that society withholds its approval until someone acting for a purpose is successful, and then approves only if success justifies the values that society respects. In place of society put the therapist, who also has a dilemma of action about which way to lean. There is a natural urge to sanction what we already believe and to look for similar goals in our patients. Society does not tolerate failure, even for a worthy cause. Therapists, as creatures of society, like to see patients succeed at something, then get credit for helping them do it.

A common value in our contemporary society is that of competition: being number one, getting social approval, therapeutic success, and so on. Children are taught to play for keeps and to win, win, win. If approval and success depend on being number one, however, then something else is clearly wrong with the system of values, because most people are not and never will be champions of any sort. The win-only value is in direct opposition to the precept of learning how to use adversity and fallibility. The therapist of quality surely recognizes that the philosophy of winner-take-all has no place among his or her aims; therefore, he or she will come into conflict with a very popular worldview of competition and success at any cost. Pop psychology advertises that you can be anything and everything you always wanted, and its practitioners promise to show you how to be attractive, rich, successful, and so on. Not so well advertised is the antithetical notion of fallibility. Indeed, pop psychology implies that anything short of winner-take-all or number one is tantamount to failure.

I do not expect that we will soon find advertisements for acquiring modest gains, partial fulfillment, reasonable well-being, or satisfaction without total rapture. Yet psychotherapists would be jubilant if limited success like this were achieved regularly. We might derive some accessible consolation in believing that more modest gains and achievements have lasting value and are reasonably possible. Equanimity and composure, two decent values, are Stoic ideals that have not gained lasting popularity, nor are they formulas for success and winning very much. The big-bang theory of what counts most has advocates in the most unexpected places.

When all quiets down, including the extravagant claims, ultimate questions and metaproblems are still there looming ahead. If making sense is a primary commitment, then the search for meaning will surely end in futility unless it gets an unrelenting thrust from healthy morale, including moral courage. But it is equally true that morale without purpose is nothing much but empty potential. It is like moral courage that is never tested.

Negotiation with Mortality

Many people less celebrated than Schopenhauer and Camus would probably agree that death is the supreme, if not the only philosophical problem. At least, it is a universal fact that must be pondered. Moreover, because it is a common denominator of existence, coming to terms with the inevitably of extinction has to be a pervasive metaproblem and ultimate question. Any philosophy of mankind that leaves out our obligation to die is incomplete and fallacious, and any ethnography that does not have myths and legends (as well as doctrines) to explain it away is scarcely worthy of its name.

Because death is absolute as well as unavoidable, negotiation with mortality seems not only impossible but ludicrous. Negotiation with mortality, however, has a broader meaning than simply trying to deal with the end of life as we know it. The penultimate moment when the specter of death appears at an individual's own door is only one version of mortality. Bereavement, loss of all sorts, separation, loneliness, and life-threatening risks or sickness are all reminders of how tentative and tenuous are the things we hold onto. Consequently, negotiation with mortality, with its implications and impossibilities, is a lifelong task posing many ultimate questions. Every metaproblem sooner or later confronts other metaproblems, including questions about death. It scans what we do and have done, and in so doing authenticates our existence.

I have already indicated that metaproblems should combine in a single focus, even if that point is far distant. Thus meaning without morale is stagnant, hardly worth the effort at deciphering. Morale without meaning and direction is pointless, since it has no cause or value. Furthermore, without a sense of mortality implicit in much of what we do and are, morale is both blind and deaf to causes that make sense, and put value on our striving. Provided that suffering itself can be controlled, strong morale and a good sense of purpose can convince anyone that longevity is not long enough.

Regardless of the central importance of mortality as a reference point for the meaning of what we do and have not done, anyone who lives only to negotiate and contemplate mortality is totally preoccupied with transcendental status and suprapersonal significance. Nothing else has much meaning. This person, perhaps a hermit living in a remote cave, lives for the hypothetical next life, not this one. Under these circumstances, there is no place for moral courage in facing dilemmas of action or resolving conflicts, and morale must be meager indeed. I wonder if the spirit and body get much nourishment from such constant abnegation. The skeptical pilgrim who is very conscious of death finds that skepticism and pilgrimage wear exceedingly thin with the passage of years. Nevertheless, enthusiasm for life would prevent and deplore a vocation dedicated to contemplation and adoration of death as the sole and supreme value.

Negotiation with mortality means to be concerned about all things that signify the transience of life, as well as the presence of risk in whatever we contemplate doing. It contains elements of meaning, morale, and certainly courage of all kinds. But it does not mean constant meditation about death, like that of the poet in the *Rubáiyat,* or professional study of death in all forms, like that of a forensic pathologist. In the past few decades, the discipline currently called thanatology has studied some of the problems inherent to such death equivalents as separation, regret, renunciation, and grief. At present, we do not have the right combination of sperm banks, prepared ova, organ transplants, and suitable technology to make immortality a viable option; as a result, death is here to stay, and the firmest future we can negotiate about depends on the realization that life is limited, tasks are endless, people wear down, risk of all sorts is rampant, postponement is only temporary, and ultimate questions have a way of receding before they can be answered. Meanwhile, we would seek not to negotiate but to accept the signs of advancing age and disability, to let go of our ardent embrace, and to modulate the drive to survive.

The vulnerable self imagines death happening to someone else, especially when we ourselves are healthy, full of zest and anticipation. One man, after being told about an advanced cancer, simply replied, "Then I am not going to live forever, am I?" I suppose that this is a realization that is built into negotiating with mortality. We cannot accept total resignation.

Suicide, which presumably violates much of what we ordinarily hold precious, is not only pathetic but enrages as much as it baffles. It is a form of allying oneself with death, because it closes off life for someone who might feel better later on. As it is, suicide generally signifies failure to cope, combined with zero self-esteem and demoralization. Meaning and morale split and dissolve, with the only solution being to forfeit whatever remains of life. It is not for the young and healthy to decree that the aged and ill have nothing to live for and might as well be dead; this is always an arrogant judgment that dehumanizes. And just as we cannot imagine ourselves dead and yet living to tell the tale, few people could decide in advance what to do about the dilemma of action, should they suffer interminably with an illness beyond treatment. Extinction does acquire a fascination; after all, death cures all diseases. But to endow death with an irresistible magnetism may in itself be a sign of disease and its quintessence, vulnerability. After all, the skeptic says ruefully, we are going to be dead long enough.

A Befitting and Appropriate Death. A Faustian bargain with death seems out of the question. Negotiation with mortality must include accommodation to the various declines and deprivations of life. The only way to bring all these negatives together into a more acceptable whole would be to turn a bad bargain into a good death. A good death (in a preliminary, not a final, version) accepts with renunciation and regret, like an unwelcome invitation to a party one is forced to attend by outside pressure. The major task in a befitting death is to combine the inclination to die with the drive to survive.

In Chapter 4, *befitting* was defined as realization of the best one could be, which fits with a sense of harmony, responsibility, and compatibility in transactions with the world. A befitting and appropriate life is what is sought and expected from psychotherapy. In adapting this concept to negotiation with mortality, I doubt if we could do much better than to imagine a similar goal.

If it were possible to picture actually sitting down with death, as novelists and playwrights have occasionally done, I doubt if an unqualified and unlimited survival would be a satisfactory solution. This is not because death needs human sacrifice, or because prolonged existence might produce a population explosion. Rather, such survival might be more threatening than death. Legends about hellfire and damnation, along with myths of eternal and unrelieved anguish such as that of Sisyphus, presuppose no release from loneliness and suffering. Immortality of this variety would be like an interminably debilitating disease or a torture that stops short of killing outright: no repose, and no respite. There are plenty of very sick patients who want to die but cannot.

But some sick patients want desperately to recover and get on with life. Death is anything but acceptable to them, and far from appropriate. Whether a patient can actually will his or her death is still moot, though there are surely sick or disabled people who find it right and proper to die (and sometimes do). Largely, however, in our heterogeneous culture, people clutch at life on almost any terms, so intensely that the desire to die without an exceedingly unambiguous reason is scorned. With all of the current debate about physician-assisted suicide in cases of terminal illness, both the medical profession and others are dreadfully afraid of making death too easy and too attractive for some.

Negotiating with mortality implies dealing with death and its outcomes, whether the death is good, bad, equivocal, or befitting. There are people, sometimes patients, who live too long, whereas others die far too prematurely. When the right time to die occurs is an ultimate question on a par with the best way to live.

There is no better way to describe an appropriate death, than as a demise we might choose, had we a choice. Hospice care for incurable disease can have no better objective. Aside from eliminating more obvious negatives contained in suffering (whether from pain, desertion, invalidism, incontinence, poverty, or abandonment of those we love), a good death has significance and status in retaining much of what made living valuable. It might even have morale. A good death, after we have had so much of a good life, is one we could live with.

An appropriate death also has at least four outstanding characteristics: awareness, acceptance, propriety, and timeliness. My examples are drawn from the predicament of cancer patients for whom no further treatment is available, yet who have positive expectations of the future, however limited. *Awareness* of impending death comes at about the same time as learning that nothing more can be done, except for good medical and emotional care by others. There are some doctors, friends, and families who insist that telling patients about their illness, especially if no treatment is feasible, will cause hopelessness and serve no useful purpose, as if hope were contingent upon illusion. Others claim that a well-informed patient is able to participate in decisions affecting the outcome, as if coping with the prospect of death depended on knowing and being able to act upon potential consequences of that knowledge. Experience with patients who opt for hospice care indicates that awareness does not harm patients, and that denial of an incipient demise is apt to be foolhardy, given that most patients know from various clues what their situation is. Moreover, coping with the problems standing in the way of a better death does not seem compatible with denial of the outcome.

Acceptance of death is very inconstant; it may depend on the person speaking with a patient. Sometimes patients with full knowledge and seeming acceptance of the outlook will shade the truth from family and friends to spare them pain and embarrassment, as well as possibly to forestall being categorized and isolated as someone unacceptable. In contrast, some patients simulate a philosophic acceptance when they are actually frozen with terror. But one strategy for coping turns necessity into choice: "I choose to stop all transfusions, and the chemotherapy that just makes me sick!" For the very aged, death may finally be acceptable as the natural finish of the trajectory, despite no gold at the end of the rainbow. Here, as elsewhere, social support consists of normalization and acceptability.

Propriety seems harder to define than awareness and acceptance, but that is because it refers to the nonmedical features of illness that distinguish a good death from something more objectionable. But propriety is not propitious or ideal, nor does it depend on the outside judgment of someone in authority. The essentials of propriety are based on what a patient decides is right and proper and on what seems befitting according to the pertinent community's expectations and standards.

The first essential includes such matters as place of death (home or hospital), number and kind of visitors, degree of sharing decisions, and protection of individuality and decorum. Much of personal propriety for some patients is having a say and a choice in what happens to significant survivors, such as children.

The second essential might be whatever social and community standards do to guarantee respect and regard for the deceased and his or her survivors. This does not necessarily mean a standard funeral service, nor a glowing eulogy within convention and under the canopy of professed religion. An elderly, unmarried former teacher was besieged by calls from former students who wanted to visit her in a public hospital's geriatric division. They did not know or seemingly care that this very private and cultured woman was confined to a cot in the middle of a large ward, where privacy was out of the question and individuality something nonexistent. There were disturbed, confused, and moribund patients all around her, and she received little but routine care. As a result, she refused all visits, asking instead to be sent notes and postcards with good wishes. She clearly wanted to be remembered as she once was, not as she had been forced to become. Obviously her death, under these circumstances, could not be one of propriety.

"Living my own life" is a defiant motto voiced mostly by the young during a period when they are forced to comply with parental standards and codes, before they have had much chance to lead any independent life. "Dying my own death" is a somber parallel of the same thought that is not heard as frequently; it defies what those in authority think is best. Dying one's own death, however, reflects token autonomy or propriety. Many dying patients, for example, choose where and even how death will occur, together with specific funeral plans. When this happens, one can hardly doubt that the finality of the dying process requires abundant courage, both moral and physical, if morale is to be maintained.

Timeliness is the fourth characteristic of the befitting demise; it is the question (perhaps ultimate) of when is the best time to die. The question has had numerous and humorous rejoinders, but serious answers have not been much more appropriate. Nevertheless, there are some patients, not at all suicidal or depressed, who decide forthrightly that nothing more could be expected were they to live longer. Consequently, they are ripe to die, for example, following a relatively benign operation or an illness that ordinarily responds to medical treatment. In our society, almost any death is considered premature ("He had so much to live for!"), except for those viewed as richly deserving to die, or who linger too long for the best plans of potential survivors. Very aged and infirm patients often fail to die timely deaths. Instead they have hypermature deaths, the kind that Glaser and Strauss (1968) have described so well.

Theoretically, if we are to believe the conventional statements that some deaths occur too soon and others take too long, there should be numerous deaths that occur at the right moment (i.e., when the expectation ratio is 1). This might be the opportune occasion, indicating that further existence would be meaningless and that death now would be particularly significant.

The Right Time Is Now. So deeply ingrained is our notion that death always is bad, happens too soon, and could not have any liberating significance that it is seen as almost ludicrous (or at least in very bad taste) to suggest otherwise. The existential viewpoint, however, must look for circumstances and conditions in which respect and regard can be maintained or encouraged. This may be like *kairos,* the opportune or perhaps revealing moment. Although many people extol the slogan "death with dignity," it is a very chancy situation in which to preserve a dignified mien. Many dying patients are far less than comfortable and need ample sedation merely to survive until death decides that they have had enough.

In contrast, there are more than a few patients who have a surprising period of mental clarity shortly before they die. They often make largely unrealistic plans to salvage ambitions that had been put aside years before. One woman, for example, spoke about moving to another city and starting a business of her own. She had left her hometown in her youth when her husband had a job opportunity that could not be rejected. Although she was highly successful in Boston, her adopted home, she never reconciled herself to the sacrifice she had made. Another man, the father of three grown children, confessed that he had never married the mother of these children. While in the hospital, three months before his final admission for advanced cancer, he rectified the oversight in the presence of the ward staff, the hospital chaplain, and the staff physician.

These three metaproblems, samples of the others that are out there, are in fact practical tasks concerning ultimate questions. They are not mere metaphysical musings without a foundation in clinical experience and existential reality. Moreover, it is reasonable to expect that in negotiating with mortality, metaproblems tend to come together as time winds down. This is probably not so if consideration of our finitude is to be postponed until, quite literally, the last moment.

Much of the current debate about removing or continuing life supports for gravely ill, very aged, and brain-dead patients in hospitals revolves around what optimal care is and whether society can afford it. Although friends and family may contemplate what life and death mean during these waning hours, patients are beyond such issues; furthermore, more urgent matters should be taken care of. Negotiation with mortality is not a secular sacrament for the very sick. Ultimate questions should have been thought of during healthy times, when scarcely anyone thinks about death. Ethical issues may be just as important as financial considerations when thinking about terminating life supports, but the groundwork for whatever decisions are made truly begins in the form of ultimate questions. These questions are perhaps more prominent during later years, but chronology is no criterion for considering who we are and what we might become. Meaning, morale, and mortality are consistent and compatible, though circumstances may magnify one metaproblem over the others. We search for, maintain, and negotiate for something all along. It takes only a little memory to recognize a life unled, paths not taken, or potential left unfulfilled. All this can be a plausible extension of a pilgrimage that started years earlier, and this must be as true of a burgher as of a skeptic.

The arrogance of power is no stranger in the precincts of medicine. What we look for, however, is a way of tempering the excesses of technology and crudities of ambition that thwart how we think about ourselves. Respect and regard are rather elementary traits that help accept the significance of just being alive, maybe for some purpose. In negotiating with mortality, however, what is befitting and appropriate applies all along. During the latter period of life, such consideration should have become second nature. If so, it becomes a legacy for survivors, who must face similar situations in the course of time.

The ability to cope with this very private and personal predicament requires clarity and composure. It prepares us for dichotomies of meaning, of regret and rejoicing, of renunciation and acceptability, of loss and reparation, and of somethingness and nothingness. Perhaps it is only another version of a grand illusion to believe that ultimate questions can be voiced even in appropriate form, and that befitting answers may be found. But an awareness of metaproblems might bring us to the point where the metamorphosis that is death makes enough sense to be faced with good morale.

Chapter 7

The Pilgrim Who Stayed Home

Vulnerability and the Skeptical Pilgrim

It is the vulnerable self that first gave rise to the skeptical pilgrim. The pilgrimage is not, however, a case of spiritual wanderlust, nor is skepticism other than a quest for authenticity. Indeed, the self is not a diaphanous thing but a combination of meaning and being that struggles to cope with distress and meaninglessness by making sense and keeping strong morale. The ultimate aim of the vulnerable self is to function better, to have less anxiety and depression, and to discover traces of purpose and significance in being alive.

The skeptical pilgrim knows that vulnerability is defined by the anxiety and despair associated with unfulfilled potential and unplumbed possibilities. He or she is intimidated by frustration and calls upon all the courage and coping capacity that can be mustered. When potential is not fulfilled and responsibility to live up to it is eroded, then the pilgrim's fate is to suffer from existential guilt, which is nothing less than self-betrayal. Faith in the effectiveness of courage, the mastery of will over dread, makes pilgrims realize that they might have done more, but at the same time, certain situations were insurmountable and inescapable.

I have described skeptical pilgrims at great length, indicating that they are both vulnerable and resilient, tough and tender, and sentimental and intellectual, as well as other antithetical possibilities. But they are neither cynics nor crusaders. Both of these are products of failure; because freedom has been forsaken, choice has been reduced, and responsibility deferred to something or someone else. A crusader gives himself or herself up to a cause; a cynic has no cause or reason to seek something to believe in.

Skeptical pilgrims find that they must become pilgrims in order to focus their skepticism and turn vulnerability into authenticity. Without a strong corrective effort, the vulnerable self will surrender to mankind's conformist tendencies to fit in, to acquiesce to convention, to be collected and categorized. If this occurs, the pilgrimage ends automatically. Pilgrims settling into established positions with others who are oblivious to the mutual mystery all around are likely to mistake mystification for inspiration, because they have stopped searching. What remains is only a selection of the latest fictions and myths that claim to be true and individual. The pilgrim is now a follower, not really an insider but an outsider without any particular purpose.

Even the vulnerable self tries to make sense out of mystery; it is not wholly given over to distress, and it retains a degree of resiliency and coping capacity. As a skeptic and pilgrim, one of the pressing tasks of understanding human nature is to find good reasons why people do outlandish and self-defeating things. By being linked with reasons that are acceptable, the actions themselves acquire a kind of normality and acceptability. This is the essence of the social and emotional support that good therapists strive for. The hoped-for consequence is that actions against the self may be redirected toward those better suited to an existence of coping well and making sense, instead of vulnerability, self-defeat, and guilt.

Self-deception is a common failing that enables people to deny, procrastinate, exaggerate, rationalize, romanticize, and do many other things that give the vulnerable self the benefit of doubt and protection from suffering. Skepticism doubts, sometimes, its own search for authenticity. When this occurs, facts turn into artifacts that are then confused with something the vulnerable self thrives on, namely, a manufactured reality. We already know that reality has much make-believe in it, but a reality consisting principally of make-believe nourishes self-deception and is poison for the vulnerable self.

There is a pivotal existential struggle between the will to believe, which is strong, and the will to be deceived, which is usually much stronger. Sometimes it is hard to tell the difference between the two. The skeptical pilgrim, in seeking authenticity, is committed to finding out how to tell the genuine from the counterfeit. Manufactured articles and artifacts have varying value, and some, like works of art, are exceedingly precious. In psychotherapy there is a similar problem. Authenticity is hardly the absence of suffering; loss of freedom implies lack of genuine choice. But to realize basic factors that have undermined freedom does not automatically restore it. The parallel about telling the real from the counterfeit in psychotherapy is to perceive whether what is talked about as if it were authentic really is, and if it has any bearing on life as it might be lived by a real person. Freedom must not only be understood in proper context, but prove itself to have pragmatic value. Its relevance to authenticity and vulnerability needs to be established. Freedom with responsibility that we can live with comes close to the purpose of being alive.

It is easy to prattle about vacuous abstractions. But some abstractions are very real indeed, even in the absence of careful definition. Abstractions govern our lives more than those entities that logic and reason prescribe. Self, authenticity, freedom, vulnerability, and other concepts that gave meaning to much in previous chapters are facts of living experience, with a sense of reality all their own. We characterize, but we cannot define.

The self, for example, is an abstraction, but in reality, the experience of the self is consciousness thinking and wondering about itself. The vulnerable self is the same, except that here, self-consciousness worries about itself and suffers from uncertainty and meaninglessness. Furthermore, the vulnerable self perpetuates itself through self-deception, finding obstacles that impede authenticity. Resolution of dilemmas and clarification of meanings are very rare until a person feels better, at which point the vulnerable self will manage to cope somewhat more competently. The hallmark of the vulnerable self is a kind of nostalgia for the future when nothing whatsoever has changed. Freedom to change through autonomous action is unimaginable; after all, innovation is risky. People are accustomed to the tried and true, and they raise no objection if it turns out to be tried and false. Familiarity is best, if for no apparent reason other than that custom lends authority and casts a shadow of truth over what is merely a matter of culture and convenience. Agreeable innovations manufacture facts that are taken to be true because they are consistent with what is already firmly credible. Self-deception thrives, and questions are seldom asked; we usually get along by going along. This ancient bit of practical wisdom assumes our collective worth and avoids answering the question of where we are headed. Going along is a clear case of secondary morale, in which making sense is put aside and replaced by consensus. Because custom and convention decide what is trustworthy, skepticism finds little to recommend being skeptical.

Even the skeptic needs to borrow morale at times just to believe in his or her own beliefs, which must survive challenges. As a result, the vulnerable self is destined to dangle between alternatives, without full confidence in any pole of meaning. Actually, the image of a disembodied self (whether vulnerable or authentic) that makes judgments, sustains reasons, undergoes emotions, and even invents itself is a favorite ghost. It is ephemeral to the grasp, but indispensable to a way of life that examines options and copes as best it can. We are ready to manufacture or embrace any mystery in order to make the monumental leap from private and subjective to the real world, where tangible action makes sense and we make a difference. This truly is consciousness—call it the self—at work.

The sense of reality grasps both ends of this mystery: the insubstantial self and the outside world of consensus. Reality testing, a collection of procedures that validate reality sense, has a simple aim: harmonizing the inner and outer worlds. Nowhere is this more prominent than in psychotherapy, where the disembodied self is considered the spokesman for every event. But the therapist is also the corrective for the more one-sided judgments of the self-as-spokesman. The everyday experience of other people and other things that occupy the world demands reconciliation. This is a vast task, filled with risk and deception; all we are reasonably sure about is our sense of presence in the here and now.

Mystery Loves Company

The sense of presence, being, here, now, is firmly linked to the ultimate question of being alive. This is an abiding mystery; how we make any sense of an ultimate reference point is strictly philosophical. Every other discipline assumes it. The existential viewpoint, which challenges so much that is traditional, often seems pretty discouraged, even apocalyptic about the state and fate of mankind. But mankind, which is a collective of all collectives, seems unaware of how bewildered and meaningless it is supposed to be.

It is hard to refute the charge of existential vulnerability, because mankind—in the urbanized collective, at least—is deeply distressed and in despair, although seemingly indifferent to his state of bewilderment. After all, one can simultaneously suffer and be in grave risk despite an abundance of material goods and a disconcerting array of prophets, each with disparate promises to make things right. Vulnerable points of pressure are widely disseminated. Prone to violence, mankind is secularized beyond redemption, but all too ready to go to war for some religious belief when told to do so. We are strangers who cannot stand being alone, yet with others, we are in conflict.

That this is far from an ideal world should surprise no one. It is easy to be cynical; pessimists always have a point. Part of the general mystery about being alive is that there is nowhere to file a complaint about the misery and evil in the world. I find it pointless, however, to agonize philosophically about what the world is coming to. It is scarcely an ultimate question, but more like an agreeable topic for cool discussion on a summer night. Diatribes accomplish very little except to get one alarmed, which leads to more diatribes. Heavy-handed hectorings are nothing but diagnoses without a cure, a situation not unfamiliar in medicine and psychiatry. Although those with a share of optimism are often wrong, they seem to be no worse for it. Consequently, even in our ignorance, it is feasible to believe that we are not altogether a lost cause, a failed project, or a tragic fraud (though a good case could be made for any of these).

Mankind's collective strategies are often pitifully weak or exceedingly destructive, at times in epidemic proportions. But the vast majority of people—except for those dying by millions from war, disease, and other disasters—seem to cope pretty well, judging at least by what optimists piously claim. On occasion, they recognize the other person's right to be wrong even before they punish or destroy him or her for it. It takes a little more insight to recognize one's own right to be wrong and to admit it fearlessly.

Despite all the pronouncements by eminent psychiatrists, psychiatry has very limited influence and capacity to cope with the world's ills, and in my opinion, it is not supposed to usurp the functions of government. It has all it can do to manage the maladies afflicting patients who are deeply distressed. Other disciplines are even more peripherally concerned with the broader perils of humanity. The vulnerable self is essentially alone in facing a host of dilemmas; there are no nostrums to resolve conflict, and no magical pill to rectify the aberrations of the brain. Because we are essentially alone, the vulnerable self has few places to turn and must monitor what happens with the feeble powers it possesses. The web of mortality holds many strange behaviors within it. Seeking "salvation" in some form is certainly no sin, as a rule, but it takes many bizarre forms.

How, in fact, do we manage to survive, and do so well enough to accomplish what we do and achieve a befitting concordance between the vulnerable self and a very imperfect world? Therapy does not save people from themselves, although it does try, given that people are often their worst enemies and severest critics. Occasionally, however, therapy does have a glimmering of what it could do, had its practitioners enough power and wisdom.

The stream of vulnerability defies order and classification, let alone control and guidance. People are entangled in mysteries that are impossible to dispel. Official mental disorders are, in effect, notations for office use only, so diversified are the ways in which we can go wrong. Nevertheless, all the vulnerable self needs is better coping and clearer assessment of key problems—admittedly a strong need, because with these attributes, authenticity would not be very far.

The quest for authenticity is like looking for other virtues. But to measure these other virtues, authenticity reaches for itself as the standard and therefore deplores whatever makes people betray themselves or feel inordinately guilty. It is morale that establishes a balance between opposing meanings or forces that tend to split people apart. Morale is sustained by a promise of fulfillment, or authenticity, in whatever we elect to do. To avoid defeat and erosion, we join with others in the inflation of secondary morale that makes us feel bigger than we are. Mystery does love company, if just to normalize a group and make it feel greater than the sum of its parts. Because facts are hard to find and even harder to interpret, comfortable fictions make for a better night's sleep; myths and mysteries create comfort out of complexity.

It is just another existential dilemma how we manage to rue solitude and the privacy of individual decision, to pine for the solicitude of others, while struggling to achieve an autonomous and authentic existence that elevates our self-esteem. The shared solace of mutual mystification often results in a strong attitude of being special or anointed in some sacred fashion. Few like crowds, and few escape them, but there are scant experiences worse than being ignored or found wanting. Particularly painful is the distress/dilemma of a vulnerable person who searches for the strength of numbers, as well as normality and acceptance, and yet is doomed to the solitude or anonymity of the outsider. The vulnerable self can feel the dizziness of freedom, yet suffer the chill of loneliness.

Is There a Supervalue?

Among the platitudes voiced by members of this generation is that we lack value and purpose, as well as a number of other things once held synonymous with virtue. I have heard these complaints over and over. What the voices mean, however, is that this generation—how many generations can stand on a pin of time?—does not share values and purpose, and we seem altogether indifferent to each other.

Actually, this generation, or these generations, spread out over fifty or sixty years but living at the same time, have an overabundant supply of values. The current term is *life-styles,* but this means simply different ways of life, marked by different standards of appreciation and effort. I can conjecture that within a radius of a mile or two from just about anywhere in an urban or suburban setting, there are hedonists, puritans, stoics, epicureans, idealists, materialists, believers, nonbelievers, feel-gooders, feel-nothings, narcissists, altruists, paranoids, and of course, a goodly supply of depressives. Many are mixed, if not most, depending on mood and mentality. For every value, there is an opposite (but not always equal) value; similarly, for every value there is a corresponding problem when that value fails. I must also surmise that every problem has its opposite, too, depending on which value is ascendant. The best way to get rid of a problem is to get rid of the value that makes it painful and problematic.

This generation may lack many things, but many other things it has to a saturation point. For example, it is overburdened with troubles that seem to be piling up. But it does not lack values and purposes, only the means to make a selection and act upon them. Contradiction tends to blur genuine alternatives. It would be useful to have a road map of purpose and the most effective strategies for getting from here to there, but a road map is not much good if the directions are reversed and guidelines crisscross, then cross again. The result is a tangle of destinations.

Normalcy is often confused with conformity to ruling values and strategies, called a way of life. Conformity is both necessary at times and stultifying at others, but it does offer a certain security, provided that much else is forsaken. Normalcy, however, is a value predominantly. It is often used as a reference point to decide what is true and worth believing, what is approved to act upon, and what limits to put on boundaries. To be normal is a judgment that hastens acceptance, success, and all the good things that go with these. Each culture, I suppose, has its own version of normality; subcultures exist in order to accommodate differences within the larger range. Each difference, however, implies conformity and conventionality.

The concept of normalcy will, in other words, accommodate conformity, conventionality, and beliefs that signify value for a particular culture, group, or subculture. For example, one of the common beliefs that is well established in our culture is that work and worth go together. Self-esteem depends on work that is worthy; it is considered distinctly aberrant not to work at a gainful occupation, even if such labor is not financially necessary. If work ceases, worth also may decline, as it does with some retired executives or professional people. Fear of obsolescence seems to permeate the marketplace. Its occurrence will not only cause a drop in self-esteem but an overall perception of failure, uselessness, and abnormality that is beyond the limits of acceptability for an autonomous person formerly worthy of respect. The wisdom that a superannuated citizen is reputed to have is seldom sought out, and there would not be much consolation if it were.

We grow up with abundant standards, only one of which is that work and worth are synonymous. We assume the beliefs that circumscribe normality, and then we spend years complaining about conformity and conventionality. Much depends on interpretation of what is deemed normal and good, or abnormal and bad. Success is certainly a criterion of normalcy and value that most everyone believes in. But although earning a good living is mandatory, sometimes making too much money is misinterpreted to mean something evil. If love of money is the root of all evil, there will nonetheless be some who would begin with a lot of money and take their chances with evil. It is the ascribed meaning of money that misleads.

Another social value that circumscribes the meaning of success is that of individualism, having personal tastes that are distinctive and admirable. Success in developing individualism is wholly normal until we begin to analyze what it means and does not mean, what is normal and acceptable and what is abnormal and deplorable. Guidelines go in different directions. If too much money can be tempered by substantial benefactions, then those who are so altruistic are guaranteed success and admiration. If individualism means to domineer regardless of how others feel, however, then giving in excess would not be compatible with the individualism that autonomous people seek.

Values and standards that seem identical, therefore, do not guarantee self-esteem, success, or normality. They may mean entirely antithetical things. As already indicated, psychotherapy is not at all value free; certain standards are implicitly recommended. The problem with the goal of getting what you want is that there may be a conflict between your meaning of success and the limits set by society. How is this conflict to be resolved? It used to be true that practically every therapist of quality would refrain from urging patients to do one thing rather than another as a matter of principle. I am not sure now that conscientious therapists are so evenhanded, also as a matter of principle.

Some patients plead primarily for approval, asking over and over, "Is the way I feel normal? Am I crazy?" Normalcy and acceptability rule the day, regardless of other considerations. It is a conflict of values, a choice among alternatives, or an undesired consequence of a well-intentioned action that leads to guilt and impaired self-esteem. Patients are seldom plagued by so-called moral questions; they already feel guilty, ashamed, selfish, and so forth. What were once moral questions are now questions of normality and acceptability. If wishes interfere with normality and acceptability (i.e., norms and requirements of accepted culture), then the customary compromise is to try and have both. For example, when a man comes to a psychiatrist and confesses infidelity, he will not ask if adultery is moral or immoral. But he will ask if his suffering is acceptable (i.e., understandable) because he is not a bad person, but usually a good father and husband. The question he asks in effect is, "Under what circumstances is a double life tolerable and acceptable, even approved?"

It comes down to the ultimate question of authenticity and what it means. The therapist of quality does not, I hope, pass judgment on the morality of normalcy, but tries to examine the set of assumptions, values, and standards that the patient brings to therapy. It is such considerations that make appreciation of meta-problems essential: what things mean, how to keep up morale, control betrayal and guilt, and deal with the restrictions of mortality and its manifestations (e.g., bereavement, loss, abandonment).

In selecting a therapist, it is wise and prudent not to choose one whose values are too much or too little like those of the patient. A therapist needs to understand a viewpoint without sponsoring it or disagreeing so adamantly that all communication is artificial and arid. The quest for authenticity requires looking for points of vulnerability, areas of suffering, and indications of doubt and dismay. The therapist recalls the differences in levels of threat, types of anxiety, kinds of motivation, and values among *must, can/could, should, need,* and *want. Ought* is a frequent indication of unspoken guilt. A good therapist examines the differences between what is then needed for health and safety (a must), what a person is capable of or competent to do (can/could do), and what is socially approved and required (should/ought).

The man consulting a psychiatrist because of an extramarital affair is subject to different levels of interpretation. The therapist could differentiate various meanings; indeed, he or she must understand what the patient is in conflict about. Is his conflict within normality, or does its value fall outside approval? Another less contemporary and outdated dilemma may show how different kinds of suffering seem to stem from similar-sounding conflicts. For example, we are not now concerned about the reasons people fight duels; that might have been important a hundred years ago. But suppose a man came to a psychiatrist today asking under what circumstances he should, could, or must fight a duel? Because dueling is not part of our modern strategy for seeking retribution, honor, or domination, the psychiatrist would obviously not take the question literally. The therapist's task, however, stays the same: understanding the circumstances that led to this antiquated question, as well as the grievances that besmirch the patient's self-esteem. What wrongs need redressing? What is needed to gain acceptance and normality again?

The vulnerable self is always exposed to conflict (or other kinds of challenges and danger, on any level) to various degrees, regardless of time and custom. The authentic self, its presumed complement, understands how standards and values differentiate themselves within subcultures, and how stereotyped some responses are. Authenticity includes knowing the conditions that decide for approval and success versus disapproval and shame. Skeptical pilgrims are caught in the middle, between conventionality and custom and deviation, resistance and innovation. Because they resemble traditional pilgrims seeking spiritual certitude as well as intellectual integrity, they are balanced between looking for an absolute, trustworthy value or standard to calculate by and a judicious adaptation to the uncertainty of most absolutes.

If there were no reckoning of values or common basis for comparing differences between ways to behave, psychotherapy would have no purpose. It would merely consist of differential indoctrination for no specific purpose except persuasion. But the quest for an absolute standard to measure man by is an ultimate question; if it exists, it would serve notice on all other values that it alone is the standard that no one disputes. The absolute standard of standards would be a supervalue. This could be an enormous simplification, because conflicts then are transformed into dilemmas, and dilemmas become alternative choices that a person is free to act upon. Unfortunately, I know of no supervalue other than expressed in God's will, which few people know much about but many borrow to prop up their own beliefs and demands. Choices are things we could or can do; a supervalue is a must that cannot be avoided, compromised, or contradicted.

Ordinarily in psychotherapy, if all goes well, conflict is converted into choices. In tracing the roots of conflict, however, it will often turn out that conflict began with different and possibly opposing choices that for one reason or another a patient could not act on or resolve. By comparing antithetical problems, the therapist is able to see which set of standards or values seems to apply. From an existential viewpoint, choice is limited by responsibility, which I define as the best (or ego ideal) that is necessary for feeling authentic. Responsibility, however, is not a supervalue, because there are a number of values that go into making up an ego ideal. Moreover, not everyone can attain fulfillment of the ego ideal; goals may be contradictory, and consequences are not always consistent. Instead of continuing to look for a panacea that offers a supervalue to measure everything else by, the therapist avoids a sense of failure by lowering expectations and stressing flexibility and pragmatism.

Options in Psychotherapy

We are caught between conformity and independence, between hard necessity and soft choice. We are not at all homogeneous, but as a rule, we agree in fearing deviation from the norm. Deviation from the norm takes many forms, which can be summarized as the practice of making bad choices that offend prevailing customs and standards. I have emphasized how important it is for most people to feel that they are within the bounds of normality. Deviance, however, is as intimidating as anonymity or extinction, although few people are willing to call themselves conformist. This is because, just as deviance is feared, so is utter compliance with expectations.

Change is hard to bring about. The vulnerable self characteristically sticks to old values and conventional expectations, thus drawing upon secondary morale. Some patients, for example, are very conformist on the outside but rebellious and deviant inside. When conflict ensues, what is produced is a symptom, emotional or physical, that spares a patient from consequences; but genuine change is doubtful. Passions can be held in check, for example, but as a result, corresponding fantasies become harder to tolerate. Sooner or later, impulses and conduct contrary to expectations boil over. The pilgrim who ventures not very far or stays home is apt to retain old and original values (contrary to what he or she expects) unless new experiences, different evaluations, and exceptional relationships make a difference. Even maturity, that virtue supposedly conferred on the aged, cannot be counted on. Issues and matters that rouse enthusiasm or indignation now, however, may not be so relevant later on; wisdom is also helped by recognizing the special circumstances that make certain demands irresistible. A more mature and possibly wiser head and heart have a wider range of feasible options to call upon, and more resourceful ways of preserving morale. The nature of wisdom, I suppose, depends on being able to keep new ideas near enough to examine them carefully without being overly afraid of change and while realizing that not all change is better. This is not beyond the capability of a skeptic, who needs courage and morale as much as anyone. His or her faith, as time goes on, finds more entrenched beliefs than he or she is comfortable with.

During psychotherapy, few patients actually admit that they are afraid of having more options or are in danger of changing anything at all. Indeed, most patients overtly yearn for more options, and suffer because they are convinced that only unsatisfactory choices are available ("Oh, I could not do that! Must I? Should I?"). Options once put into place ease conflict and help patients normalize themselves. Self-blame is the sense of failure resulting from lack of ample autonomy. Patients either believe that they have failed their world, i.e., expectations, or that the world has failed them and withheld its approval, i.e., unrequited love. Between these two kinds of failure is the vulnerable self, defenseless and distressed. Sometimes, in order to rally itself, the vulnerable self will seek a solution so urgently that what is feared is realized. Psychiatry calls this "acting out"—deplorable behavior that has no compensation in healing or successfully externalizing a conflict. Usually it has shock value for the interested community (sometimes a community of one, i.e., the therapist), and it discloses a conflict too intense to retain unexpressed. It assumes protean forms, sometimes spoken of as if the entire personality consisted of specific aberrations: impulsive, aggressive, paranoid, depressive, erotic, obsessive, and so on. Part of the reason is because acting out seems to have a life of its own and is no more controllable than the same objectionable behavior in someone else.

There are other forms of so-called misconduct that stay inside, seldom expressed, and are controlled mainly through fantasies, avoidance, and inhibition. The effect is not overtly harmful except in the form of passivity, which favors victimization. Some people find joy in negativism, in silence instead of communication, and in inability to take action, a kind of catatonia of choice. Words are weapons that must be sheathed; life may imitate death; and patients hesitate or even seem immobilized about doing anything to cope with problems.

Sometimes the two seeming opposites are found in the same person. I once had a woman patient who periodically visited rundown bars, drank to excess, and picked up working-class or unemployed men. She then engaged them in explicit and vivid sexual conversation as if she were the most promiscuous and wanton slut, promising anything. When it came to doing what the men had been led to expect, however, she stopped abruptly and withdrew, excusing herself by saying, for example, that she was just getting over a venereal disease.

I cite her situation because her barroom behavior contrasted diametrically with her regular life. It fit most criteria for acting out and certainly violated customary standards. In fact, her sluttish acting out caused great pain and shame; it contradicted the very values she wanted to live by. Nevertheless, the barroom behavior could not be resisted. If, however, she desisted at these moments of high vulnerability, in her mind she was just as culpable because of the temptation to violate her own beliefs. In other words, whether she acted out egregiously or stayed at home, inhibited, emotionless, and depersonalized, she was incapable of coping with her various dilemmas.

This was not a case of multiple personality. But without going further into earlier history or precipitating events leading up to each new sortie, her conduct had two meanings. First, it was an effort to normalize herself by abnormal means (i.e., antisocial, deviant behavior by her standards). While pretending (and she always knew it was a charade) to be a drunken whore, she refused to come across to the men she picked up. This made her feel a little less humiliated and ashamed, because she protected what was left of her preferred ego ideal. Even the excuse of having a venereal disease was a kind of punishment for her fantasized promiscuity. The second meaning was that by visiting the seediest pickup joints, she felt at one with the other patrons. In a way, she adopted their standards, and thus did not feel guilty at that time. Her low self-esteem could not sink any lower, and she became less depressed and more in control in her role as the slut. The others expected very little from her; she was essentially anonymous, and her vulnerability was protected in a peculiar sense, because sexual acts with these men were always considered wholly unacceptable. She feigned availability in order to reassure herself.

But it was not as easy as all that. Although she gained some control by withholding herself, on several occasions she risked rape and was slapped around. Nevertheless, her self-betrayal was averted, and even her bruises testified in her favor. We could not deny, however, that for those few hours in a tawdry and disreputable world, she felt herself to be in a befitting situation, where there was little discrepancy between what she actually felt like being and what she only pretended to be. Some of her acting out was a protest against conformity: Her dramatization of being a slut was a wish to free herself from moral coercion and further restriction. She reserved the right to refuse and resisted total surrender in both worlds. To have sex with any of these men, she asserted, would have defiled her indelibly.

Many people are afraid of both freedom and coercion, moral and physical. This dilemma makes it difficult for the therapist, to say nothing of the patient in psychotherapy. There is conflict between wish and fear, wish and wish, or fear and fear, depending on how a predicament is formulated. Freedom and coercion are natural antitheses, but one is not always good, nor is the other invariably bad. Coercion is reputedly bad and freedom good, but only because we think of them in these contexts. Many fears and wishes have different directives and prohibitions, and if a therapist waits until each reveals itself, less confusion will result. In a sense, my woman patient sought freedom from coercion in her visits to the seedy saloons; in this case, freedom was more inimical than coercion through moral prohibitions in her regular world. Coercion meant protection, even at a price, from her viewpoint, but it provided a basis for psychotherapy, in contrast to the make-believe freedom from guilt she concocted in the barrooms.

Options in psychotherapy imply that by choosing one option rather than another, a distressed patient will find testimony about freedom and thus feel better. Although the ability to choose dispassionately and without coercion is a signal or prerequisite for better coping, actually changing values or directives is a very recalcitrant achievement. Values constitute much of what any person understands by his own personality, and they are not given up readily. Behavior can be changed, to a degree, but the reference points that identify values and problems are pretty fixed, because they decide what is good or bad, with little room for compromise. Making sense is imperative, especially for understanding the context that gives any behavior, however reprehensible, its meaning and motivation. Moral censure is unlikely to change that same behavior, only to drive it underground and sometimes accelerate the problems it implies.

A therapist of quality appreciates both sides of a dilemma, making sense out of antitheses (although he or she may tilt toward underscoring what is harmful and self-defeating). Sometimes compromises are possible; for example, trying to distinguish for the woman patient the considerable difference between her fantasies and the overt actions that risked trouble might encourage reconciliation of opposites. It could also show that each pole has its share of truth.

A skeptical therapist will not hesitate to point out discrepancies between what a patient does and what he or she professes to want. This is like exposing a denial outright, or revealing a fabrication. But abrupt disclosures are shortsighted, since they usually have no discernible effect. Not even skillful therapists can pick out and destroy the values that a person needs, wants, or professes only to violate them over and over again; values and standards are the person, for better or worse. What a wise therapist does, however, is to recognize what is significantly harmful, not merely deviant and unconventional. Self-betrayal is as deplorable as its less conspicuous cousin, self-deception. A rich man's son who prefers to work in a very low-paying service job instead of following his family's directives and values cannot be faulted, even if he risks disapproval and disappointment. He is not specifically betraying himself, only respecting other values.

Freedom and responsibility can either work together or be in conflict. There is freedom that truly liberates, and responsibility that keeps freedom honest and justifies it. Nevertheless, the therapist of quality minds his or her business and makes no choices for anyone else. Otherwise he or she deprives the patient of the right to be wrong and refutes the ostensible therapeutic goals of authenticity and autonomy.

Occasionally a patient has such bizarre behavior that it is difficult to refrain from revealing a certain consternation, if not disapproval. Freedom and responsibility sometimes take a curious turn. One man was in the habit of putting leaves and small twigs into his girlfriend's vagina after intercourse. He saw nothing especially wrong, given that she did not object and neither of them was hurt in any way. What this strange (to me) behavior symbolized, I could never be sure. It seemed to exist side by side with other unconventional behavior, so perhaps he had a point in considering his sexual practices wholly within normality.

Clarifying what behavior means is like clarifying any other contingency. But in therapy, it risks the moralistic stance that forbids by explaining behavior as abnormal to begin with. Similarly, finding a good reason for everything is equivalent to approving just about anything, which is absurd and makes a fool of the therapist. To judge is to dichotomize, making an action wholly one way or another without allowing for partial truths or qualifications that make sense of both poles of meaning. Because the aim is to bring opposites together, not to obliterate them, therapists are advised to abstain from making decisions about which is right or wrong unless pushed to it by self-destructive considerations.

What about the skeptical pilgrim who stays home and only makes a pilgrimage within himself or herself, according to the precincts of custom and conventionality? Surely he or she wants authenticity and autonomy, and is unhappy about making compromises or enduring coercion. Like many such characters, he or she frets about finding the "true" self amid an assortment of false selves. But to be true to an avowal of skepticism, he or she ought to ask how a true self differs from a false self, and what differences it makes. Distinctions between true and false selves are about as valid as any other moralistic pronouncements. From a skeptical viewpoint it is valid to declare, as one man did, that his true self was false to him; he much preferred his false self, because the "true" self seemed too self-righteous for his taste.

Does an authentic self lie, steal, or do such things that most people would disapprove of? Who does it harm? Is self-betrayal an indispensable ingredient of a vulnerable self? Is authenticity just a state of feeling comfortable and at home in the world, with stress down and self-esteem up? The pilgrim who travels transcends the boundaries of his or her customary haunts. He or she seeks an absolute in some form, such as a panacea, a messiah, a flawless method for disclosing truth, or a supervalue that judges but is not itself judged. In some perverse way, my woman patient who sought salvation in a saloon to rescue her self-esteem, and feel less guilt in the process, was herself making a pilgrimage, seeking a compromise that would not besmirch her.

The existential viewpoint makes an ethical point of avoiding judgments whenever possible. But because it is unlikely that judgments can be indefinitely avoided, they are usually identified and then held at arm's length. Not all judgments, therefore, are bad; however, categorical judgments that ignore special contingencies risk being bad judgments in the sense that they are secretly moralistic. Categorical judgments would have scorned this woman more than she did herself. Such judgments inflict pain and little else. Moreover, by ignoring contingencies that make sense, categorical judgments without qualification overlook the nature of vulnerability; instead, secret moralisms idealize evil by making it something absolute. We would understand this woman no better by calling her names or making sweeping diagnostic judgments, which amount to the same thing.

Problem solving is prolonged and often complicated, but it can be cut short at almost any time by deciding that enough is enough. This happens frequently in psychotherapy, where to pursue a problem endlessly defeats the central purpose of learning how to cope independently. Old-fashioned dream interpretation, for example, went on and on, seeking out every fragment of recollected dream material. Meanwhile, the patient's life went on, and because time was necessarily short, dream interpretation at length avoided the realities of other events that occurred. Finally, in some cases, patients were so pleased to be able to interest their analyst that they brought in dream after dream, and nothing else. (For whatever it meant, such problem solving at least solved the problem of intriguing the analyst.) Usually problems are not solved, but brought to a compromise that is befitting. Much of this type of problem solving depends on deciding which problems are worth solving and, in fact, are solvable.

When therapy fails, it can be for any of several reasons. It is not always attributable to the incompetence of the therapist or the recalcitrance and resistance of the patient; sometimes the illness is just too fixed and cannot be moved. It is not always because therapist and patients have different values or have tried to work on insoluble problems. There are compromises, but it takes a certain sensitivity and experience to know which problems should be compromised or are resolvable up to a point. Reduction of distress, like reduction of pain, is not considered a reliable indication of lasting relief or resolution. Whether or not therapy has a positive result, furthermore, is almost as unreliable an index as and more difficult to measure than reduction of distress. Achieving authenticity and autonomy is very subjective; few patients fully appreciate an expanded range of choice, and therapists are perhaps the last to ask critically about their results.

The end point of therapy, as mentioned earlier, has no specific measurement. Ordinary criteria for social acceptability (e.g., getting a promotion or keeping a faltering marriage intact) are within the range of normality, but hardly a sign of being able to cope better, with less distress. Therapy does not promise a promotion, guarantee success, find love, or endow anyone with a skill they never had before, but it is reasonable to anticipate the presence of courage, morale, and better coping. Respect and regard, which are necessary for the progress of therapy, also must be there at its conclusion, and they sometimes ensure a successful parting.

If these nebulous criteria for termination apply to other quests, what will be the outcome of the skeptic's pilgrimage? How will it differ for the skeptic who stays home? A wise skeptic expects to compromise, cut losses, lower standards somewhat, and acquire what is euphemistically called maturity, if not resignation. This kind of compromise is befitting and congenial, because distress declines and, strangely enough, certain values do change. He or she may have no creed and always be an outsider, but he or she might have some degree of faith in the value of the mission. It is something like a dedicated artist who sells very few pictures and gets disproportionately little recognition during her lifetime. How worthwhile is her mission? Will her faith in the artistic venture endure? I do not believe that faith belongs exclusively to religion. Faith does more than move mountains; it is a mountain in itself, especially when the question of faith is never raised.

Skepticism is a position requiring faith. Its faith is to refuse judgments that claim universality and, therefore, to rend them open to question if knowledge permits. But if everything is open to question and nothing is considered closed, then it might seem reasonable to sanction any action. But not all actions are equally or even conceivably permissible. The skeptic, therefore, can maintain skepticism without frustration by adopting a few constant reference points that give meaning to many things, just in order to make sense. He or she does not need declarations of universality to feel autonomous. The skill of courage enables the skeptic to select causes worth believing in, and for most purposes, this is faith enough. It is difficult to cope competently with problems that refuse to define themselves; therapists (or skeptics, for that matter) distinguish reality from metaphors used to describe it and do not always accept the word for the deed.

There are articles of faith in any discipline which are beliefs and practices established so long that hardly anyone questions their veracity. In so-called classical psychoanalysis, for example, there was a belief amounting to a consensus that the analyst ought to be a "blank screen" of nonjudgmental silence and receptivity, except when pronouncing interpretations of the unconscious gathered from unimpeded free association. Here were metaphors equated with reality, prob lems that refused to define themselves, and words standing in place of deeds. These beliefs were based on the foundation of the curative or corrective powers of psychoanalysis, practiced precisely.

These were noble declarations of faith, particularly in an era when psychiatric patients were treated less than humanely. No one is capable of being a blank screen, however, passively registering an uncritical flow of words called associations (which, in fact, they are not). The requirement of being nonjudgmental is equally disingenuous. No person coming into psychoanalysis would be able to divest himself or herself of a fear of being harshly judged simply by a reassurance that most analysts, I suspect, did not grant.

The metaphor of a blank screen encourages the unwary to assume the mien of the "great stone face," unwilling to respond even to very pathetic entreaties or, in some instances, precarious plights. The blank screen is no worthy substitute for a compassionate and comprehending analyst, who must prove himself or herself over time. If the metaphor were taken literally, as it was by some classical types who were entirely detached and only listened, the therapist would be a tape recorder, not a person. The method could not possibly be compatible with wisdom, culture, and experience.

Views about the world cannot be shunted aside or held in suspension. Instead of pretending to a false objectivity, a therapist holds to a standard which itself can be critically examined and applied selectively, case by case, just as a benevolent skeptic might. In this way, it becomes possible to distinguish standards and expectations that are most influential in understanding patients. For example, if I dogmatically claim that only an examined life is worth living, then I would fail to respect patients who for a variety of reasons, including that of education, do not themselves honor self-examination as a way of life. In recognizing the elitism behind the precept, I make allowances for my false universality and appreciate that not every person values self-inquiry, perhaps to their detriment but not necessarily. Having a purposeful existence, moreover, is a trait treasured largely by a certain group of literate, educated people. A far larger majority lives from day to day, following limited goals and mundane appetites. Therapists cannot insist that these people become something other than what they are.

Learning how to cope better with more specific problems, however, does not require such far-ranging analysis. I might be able to follow my own precepts at times and instead show many faults and shortcomings to myself. Although this is not necessarily a cause for alarm or guilt, I will recognize that my insistence on the value of an examined life is only my viewpoint, not a universal principle, and that even the most thorough self-examination is not always followed by good coping, compassion, respect, and regard. I have no more inkling of supervalues than anyone else.

The classical democratic ideal influences me, too. Therefore it insists upon a fair hearing for divergent viewpoints, although frankness requires me to admit that I might not always insist on equal time or credence. I should also specify that not all biases are created equal, nor do they have the same consequences. An excess of virtue is very seductive, but it distorts the purpose of self-understanding. The evil inherent in virtue is that it encourages self-righteousness, whose principal purpose is to enjoy its own splendor. In more down-to-earth terms, the practitioner of quality simply puts whatever skill and knowledge are available at the disposal of someone in need; in return, the patient offers respect and regard, which is reciprocated. The therapist should not offer an image of infallibility, because it draws upon all those defects of rectitude that interfere with good understanding. In the society that entitles him or her to practice, a therapist is given many rewards, more than enough compensation for relinquishing the infallibly expert and authoritarian role. The image of the magical expert, prevalent just a few generations ago and lingering somewhat even now, arose in response to mutual mystification in the presence of problems too large to comprehend, and with remedies too empirical to be more than symbols. Nevertheless, some patients and a goodly proportion of people at large yearn for an infallible leader or expert; this does not mean that a therapist should yield to such fantasies.

Impossible Goals, Proximal Problems, and Ultimate Questions

The past cannot be renounced, but we hope it can be neutralized. Limitations are a distinct heritage, and therefore an unavoidable part of the human conditional. I use the term *human conditional* because it signifies a certain uniqueness to any individual's situation. It also implies that change is possible, that we have suffered a soft fate, not a hard doom, in becoming what we are. Third, a "conditional" status offers some hope of becoming an option that can be chosen rather than coerced.

Any option is better than none. For example, bedridden patients are helped substantially by having meager choices that might not seem very significant to the healthy but are better than lying helplessly dependent on the decisions of others. Even the very healthy have limited options, though they may not care as much. Expanding the range of clearly understood options has to be a central rationale for coping with distress from demanding problems. We have to recognize limitations and accept limited options; psychotherapy only adds that perhaps the options we recognize can be used more effectively.

If we expect to find absolute self-validation as the end point of pilgrimages, we shall certainly be disappointed at our failure. The skeptic's purpose will be particularly soured, because we suspect that he or she had faith in some more substantial outcome all along. The pursuit of any pilgrimage, even one that remains in place, is energized by a magical belief in rationality and a rational belief in magic. This is why pilgrims start out believing in causes that are unspecified. Rationality and magic come together by accepting the reality of impossible goals and ultimate questions.

To reconsider the vulnerable self, its plight comprises few options, poor choices, absence of hope beyond a pious wish, limited coping, thin morale, and a pervasive sense of worthlessness. If there is no purpose in making sense, it is because the vulnerable self believes in advance that nothing means very much, and that if it did, nothing could be done about it. Vulnerability sometimes takes refuge in an unapologetic cynicism, as well as unqualified fundamentalism.

The existential pilgrimage is based on belief in the attainability of an authentic self that copes well. More than this, however, for a pilgrimage to make sense, belief in magic and belief in rationality must find themselves together. Their conjoint conclusion is that ultimate questions and metaproblems pull everything else together, clustering because of passion and principles set down long ago. Otherwise, we are all attending a meeting without an agenda, and merely waiting for an arbitrary adjournment without taking a vote. What about a hypothetical skeptical pilgrim, who is surely a mixture of vulnerability and authenticity? By forever questioning, he has little to advocate and recommend. Let him turn his interrogations against himself. How does he propose to know and heal himself? Is an indefinite pilgrimage itself therapeutic, like the reputed benefits of a long sea voyage or a hot, dry climate? Maybe he is heading nowhere. Perhaps he is like the man without a country, unceasing in quest of a port that will not turn him away. Maybe he is more like the wandering Jew, waiting patiently for the return of the Messiah to make things right; if so, then his mission turns out to be in search of a strange autonomy. Is this all that authenticity means? Alternatively, I cannot believe that authenticity is but an illusion, spawned by rebellion against conventionality and coercion. If wisdom, culture, and experience are ends in themselves, they have a certain mature value, like a cautious investment, that should have practical significance in some version of a payoff.

Ultimate questions are not impossible goals, just largely unanswerable without a host of contingencies and conditions. Proximal problems, however, are those that are nearby, reasonable, and capable of resolution. We solve them every day, mostly without realizing it. But for patients, proximal problems are very urgent and not at all easily solved. If therapy is even partially successful in bringing about increased coping ability, it will help in finding practical solutions to proximal problems and let ultimate questions subside. The latter will always be there, anyway.

Proximal problems require a sturdy morale and optimism that renders itself a sense of purpose. It helps to have a capacity for courage, too. If enough proximal problems can be solved, then there is much gain. Ironically, patients who best accomplish the pursuit of and triumph over proximal problems sometimes wonder if they needed much help in the first place, or else voice complaints that they were helped not enough, if at all. Although the conscientious therapist may feel a sting of rebuke or depreciation, he or she might recognize that this attitude may be a tribute to the patient's newly acquired autonomy, if not to authenticity and sense of history.

Solving proximal problems gets people off dead center. It shows that some strategies work better than others, and that some problems are more amenable than others when approached with suitable options and enough courage. But the ultimate question of which value is most valuable, which option is most worthy, and so forth is not proximal at all; it is a metaproblem that each person adapts. In the long run, for example, is it better to play the piano or to play pool? Specific instances of proximal and pragmatic pertinence are hemmed in by possibility and preference, not decided by absolute criteria.

The general aspirations I cited earlier, however, are success, normalcy, security, sustenance, and self-esteem, among others. These are somewhere intermediate between the solution of proximal problems and addressing wholly impossible goals. They are close to the ultimate questions that catch us up in uncertainty and the quest for authenticity, but no ultimate question proposes to tell if playing pool is better than playing the piano, provided that both are done well. Should this, for example, ever be a significant problem, resolution is helped by knowing that pool and piano playing are not opposites at all but separate skills, wholly consistent with each other, like a variety of other skills. Their opposition comes only when we give each skill a meaning or context that betrays a bias for one or the other.

Ultimate questions are those that pertain to the justification or purpose of being alive. To ask, as I did, why there is something instead of nothing is a silly question that is not ultimate but merely ambiguous, like asking what the universe was like before it was created. Such questions do sound silly, certainly are very ambiguous, and are for that reason unanswerable. From a slightly different viewpoint, however, in our efforts to make sense out of mystery it is our fate to be something that inexorably turns into nothing, or at least not very much. Although it is phrased awkwardly, this question sounds like something rather ultimate. Our knowledge is so scanty that we really have no basis for asking such a question; nevertheless, it corners mankind and forces us to wonder.

Only in logic and in the pieties of philosophers is mankind a rational animal. Humans are beasts, prone to violence, subject to vulnerability, stretched between proximal problems and ultimate solutions. No skeptic worth his or her salt can escape wondering if insistent probing into mystery and cant produces results or simply avoids proximal problems. Like playing pool versus the piano, I do not believe that there is any inconsistency between dealing with pragmatic problems and considering ultimate questions about the significance of survival. After all, in resolving proximal problems, we also manage to visualize a world we would hope to live in, whether it is feasible or not. Like it or not, feasibility of a better world is also the concern of ultimate questions.

We should not be too mystified by ultimate questions, although they attach themselves unavoidably to Tillich's ultimate concerns or the other kinds of remote issues. I visualize an entire range of ultimate questions, not all concerned with the metaphysics of life and death, but maintaining a link to proximal and pragmatic questions that concern us here and now. At one extreme are questions about the purpose of life; at the other are questions that challenge what can be done about suffering, disease, famine, hatred, poverty, war, and all those seemingly insoluble matters that keep us from being truly humane. Thanatologists study questions like the best time to die and the best way to capitulate to incurable illness. If anyone doubts that these are both ultimate and proximal questions, consider the heated debates now going on about abortion, euthanasia, optimal care, custodial supervision of the very aged, and so forth.

There are still other questions that are grounded in ultimate wonder about the world and our dismay about how painful and purposeless existence seems to be. Our secular inclinations, for example, keep us from asking questions that perplexed mankind for centuries: How likely is immortality? What are the chances of reincarnation? How can we explain the curious experiences of people on the verge of dying? Some questions are embarrassing in their naïveté; others seem scientifically worth investigating. We may not, for example, fret about the nature of evil as much as generations past; but when we look around and witness the horrors of this century, up to the present day's news, we cannot be sure that ultimate questions about evil have even been settled to a minute degree. Ultimate questions are not child's questions, but adults may be no more qualified to offer an answer than a bright child. Theologians and many others manage to perplex the rest of us by asking, What is the ultimate thing for the sake of which everything else was created? This is pretty close to asking about a supervalue of such absolute significance that it usurps all possible questions about being alive.

Having posed a number of sample metaproblems and suggested a range of ultimate questions, I wonder if either metaproblems or ultimate questions have to be put into words. The pendulum swings wide, and time runs short; unvoiced concerns persist, and we return again and again to questions that only seem to lose their relevance with the passing of generations.

Most people want safe conduct, not tedious explanations, particularly because explanations in this area are so dubious and parochial. Making sense is only part of the monumental task; coping courageously is another. Meanwhile, skeptics and certainly many others undertake pilgrimages of all kinds. It is very likely that whatever answers might be found for ultimate questions, the relevant method rests on making them more proximal and pragmatic. This does not, however, mean that such questions should be disregarded. The other part of finding adequate answers to pragmatic and proximal problems is to consider them against the background of ultimate values and metaproblems. Two examples are as follows: How should we deal with vulnerability in order to construct something positive and useful? What contributes most to our quest for authenticity?

Metaproblems raise ultimate questions about suffering and

diminished self-esteem. Searching for a satisfactory meaning will surely enhance morale, and with it the confidence to cope more effectively. The basic task, as I see it, is to turn vulnerability to our advantage. In so doing, therefore, questions that seem unworldly and abstract become very proximal, urgent, and practical. This is what is meant by *ultimate.*

Chapter 8

Coda without Conclusion

In bringing this book to a close, I must ask myself a variety of questions that in themselves constitute an open-ended viewpoint about the vulnerable self, its confrontation with ultimate questions, and its quest for authenticity. This means that there are certain things I am sure about and recommend highly for your serious consideration, and other things that require a high order of skepticism. For example, hardly anyone escapes having a view that colors the world as he or she sees and imagines it. This view rank orders the various things met with that seem better or worse than others, according to very intrinsic criteria which are more or less real and reliable. Most of the time, however, we are oblivious in any formal sense to having a definite worldview; unless we have an explicit creed handed down from predecessors, we are rather uncertain about the principles we think are worth acting upon. We are not completely blank, but we have a point of view and standard of judgment already in place, just plastic enough to be influenced.

I began by asking about the meaning and purpose of suffering, especially when in sick people there seems to be no acceptable foundation or justification for it. This enigma is no different, however, than why suffering exists at all, and why misfortune dogs existence from its onset to extinction. Considering the troubles and tragedies that afflict so many, and have perplexed generations

227

beyond count, it is not surprising that although specific problems come and go (depending on the viewpoint and phraseology of their times), not only are they resurrected again in full bloom, but certain ultimate questions remain unchanged.

What a Vulnerable Self Needs Most

If there is no satisfactory answer as to why there is suffering—and I anticipate none—then our life task, which is reflected in metaproblems, is to cope with distress and, in so doing, to preserve and enhance as much morale as feasible. In order to cope with distress (an overall generic term covering painful emotions from mild dismay to intolerable suffering), people have always sought out, depended upon, and in many cases surrendered themselves to various acknowledged sources of authority, whether divine or temporal, professional or priestly, opportunistic or established. What it is that qualifies an authority is determined by the values and traditions of the society that the supplicant lives in and defines himself or herself by. In any case, the general goals in relieving distress are guidance, healing, catharsis, and regaining acceptance. All these things are what a vulnerable self needs most.

In the arduous path that the vulnerable self must take in reaching potential authenticity, the following are some of the most distressing means of identification:

1. Impaired self-esteem
2. Defective coping skills
3. Inability to make sense out of personal existence or the world
4. Inadequacy in meeting acceptable standards and demands
5. Difficulty in enduring prolonged distress
6. Absence of support that confers respect and regard

These are rather universal signs of vulnerability; specific individual complaints tend to be more convoluted and diversified. Psychotherapy is only one feasible strategy out of many intended to help distressed people gain or regain a sense of authenticity. A recognized and established source of authenticity helps people at least feel more capable of coping with the problems posed by a perplexing world.

A potentially authentic self needs both a capacity for making sense and skill in coping well enough to ensure survival. Feeling at home in and around existence requires a sturdy morale; this means being confident about holding one's own and coping effectively with unforeseen problems. Because it takes the help of a great many people and institutions just to feel completely self-reliant, an authentic person is willing to seek out and use reliable, trustworthy information, based on his or her own selective powers.

Using such information is by no means synonymous with giving up autonomy to please someone else, or being passively compliant to the loudest voice or most persuasive plea. Because normalcy and acceptability are two of the objectives sought by most people who feel outside the mainstream, respect and regard (based on befitting support) are qualities of health that few can do without.

What authenticity requires above all, given the uncertainties in being alive and the pervasiveness of vulnerability, is a large supply of courage and hope. Courage is defined in many ways, but I see it as the potential for self-assertion and confidence despite significant dread. It is a skill beyond that of merely declaring a plan of action or a bold viewpoint. This type of courage is not equivalent to a natural gift from on high, or some sign of bravery on a battlefield that may be temporary. Not every battlefield is bloody; office buildings are full of them. I tend to link courage with hope, because both deal with unknown risks and threats that endanger everything. At any moment, achievements as well as individuals can be obliterated; courage and hope must recognize this bleak existential fact. Hope does not need unlimited options, nor does courage require unconditional means to surpass everyone else. Both, though, need a simple faith that we can do something in bringing about a positive outcome to a task.

The quest for authenticity starts with a candid appraisal of vulnerability. It is, however, an entirely reasonable and realistic aim, not at all requiring some resplendent realization. Authenticity, however, can be a cliché, as if it were there to be taken like a hat on a rack. The authentic self will use skill, effort, hope, courage, and a sense of purpose, combined with just about any other virtue within reach. Having options, an authentic self is able to choose carefully, whereas a vulnerable self suffers from woefully depleted options. Authenticity knows that skepticism can be abused and has its own limitations. It encourages autonomy, and even rebellion at times, but wisdom is cautiously selective about which authority to rebel against or how far to test autonomy. Hope does require a certain optimism, but pessimists are not pariahs who are doomed by their own deeds. A healthy pessimism knows, for example, that despair is not a virtue and therefore should not be cultivated.

Virtues of an Authentic Self

The concept of virtue has a singular durability, resisting cynics and moralists alike. Each age has its own version of virtue, just as it has a special vision of vice and evil. Rather than being fixed character traits, however, virtues are hard-won talents for living up to potential and gaining approval of the society that puts value where virtue strives to be. Consequently virtue is a tool for doing good, whether for the skeptic who stays home or the traveler who makes his or her home everywhere.

Virtue is an implicit aim of psychotherapy, although most therapists would hesitate to breathe its name. I find that modern-day virtues are a number of desirable traits that most people approve of, look for in themselves, and appreciate in their heroes. Most of all, having such traits helps in managing vulnerability, although many upright and "virtuous" patients seem to suffer from an excess of doing good. But virtues do not seem to have much effect on clarifying ultimate questions. I can clarify, however, a number of practical virtues that may have more substance than many of the traditional and nonspecific virtues (bravery, knowledge, temperance, thrift, righteousness, etc.) proposed by sages.

1. *Care and caution.* An authentic person, in my opinion, is capable of caring and being cared about without feeling threatened or compromised. These traits are befitting experiences that put a stamp of humanity on a person. The exercise of care, however, needs the ameliorating and protective antithesis of caution. "Give till it hurts" may be an effective slogan until one asks who is being helped and who is hurt; moreover, care and caring for can be misnomers used to excuse other shortcomings. For example, many of those who "choose" to surrender their personal life in order to care for an aging, infirm parent may not have had a choice at all. The purpose of caution is to ward off just such surrender and failure. Pitiful is the person who cares not for anything, for such an existence is like being permanently demoralized. But tragic, too, is the person who cares too much, because too often what they care most about is their own power and prestige.

2. *Control, choice, and decision.* These virtues are not likely to make any other list, because they seem all too typical of self-seeking and small-time tyrants who trample anyone standing in their way. Nevertheless, having the capacity to exercise good options and make wise decisions is one of the better measures of physical and emotional health. Here, too, caution is advisable, because virtue taken to an extreme is an embodiment of evil. Society, prizing passivity and compliance, intrudes enough to make decision and choice very limited for all but a chosen few who deem themselves immune. Repetitiously choosing what seems best, however, can only go in one direction: boredom and routine. We cannot escape from our own fallibility, which makes having faults a kind of non-beneficial virtue. Routine virtue is a bore because existence confronts us constantly with new and perhaps insurmountable challenges to what only seems best.

3. *Composure.* I like this stoic virtue. It seems to imply poise and disinclination to panic; it need not include that soporific called

serenity. Perhaps the best thing about cultivating composure is that its lack has such painful consequences: anger, bad judgment, and distortions of all kinds that only encourage fear and ignorance. Most of the exercises that counsel relaxation and deep breathing through various techniques are based on the virtue of composure, and it has been hallowed by such eminent persons as Ralph Waldo Emerson and Sir William Osler. Perhaps composure receives such near-unanimous approval because it has few if any significant opposites. Even qualities such as vigilance imply concentration of forces consistent with high-tension composure and single-mindedness.

4. *Credibility.* When I depend or rely on someone, I trust that my confidence is warranted. Such a belief seldom needs documentation, although a past history of loyalty and competence helps. If my confidence is given to someone in authority who is not well-known to me, I may still rely on his or her counsel, but I am not sure why. Credibility refers to willingness to believe in another's integrity. Nevertheless, for anyone wishing to be a credible skeptic, my advice is to begin by challenging the pretenders who claim to know and, by their claims, take away our choices and our own credibility.

5. *Character.* This virtue is hard to leave out because it has a self-evident worth that transcends difficulties in definition and recognition. It implies reliability, integrity, and other quiet assets that are not at all derived from any role or relationship that the person happens to be playing. Though just as vague as the term *personality,* having character usually means that an admirable person exemplifies the values we prize most highly.

6. *Candor, clarity, and communication.* Although this is an age of communication (as if other ages were not), candor and clarity in what gets communicated put a suitable edge on communication. Despite the virtue of catharsis and open discussion, which are so dearly advocated by many therapists, not everything benefits from unqualified talk. Half-truths, for example, may be more merciful and tactful than full disclosure. A half-lie is another matter that is much more deplorable; this is what we tend to tell ourselves

when we pass judgment on an act we already know was unworthy. Candor with ourselves is a skill that must be learned and practiced, provided that we realize that it is not necessarily best, or accurate, to believe the worst about ourselves. Denial and rationalization are habitual and entrenched, so cultivating candor about oneself and claiming to achieve it is a favorite illusion. Although self-candor has much to overcome, candor in dealing with others is not often appreciated; it must be blended with tact and euphemisms if it is used at all. Candor is useful, however, when clarifying genuine points of difference when distinctions do matter. So much has been written about communication that there is hardly any reason to praise it, except to note that what ordinarily passes for communication between people is merely a device for covering up significant differences or contentiousness.

7. *Compassion.* Compassion is as universally praised as composure, but for different reasons. Composure is cultivated primarily for the sake of an orderly and effective self striving for its own betterment. Compassion means to appreciate the suffering and distress of other people; we seldom hear about compassion for another person's pleasures and successes. Respect and regard are, as might be expected, indispensable to compassion. For example, while I can imagine what it is like to be a prisoner with no chance for parole, I cannot truly experience the hopeless plight of such a person. If I claim to feel compassion, it can only be because I suffer in his place, a most unlikely event. Compassion, therefore, is an exceedingly rare commodity, often confused with pity, imagination, and secret self-congratulation for not being in a painful predicament. This occurs regularly when bemoaning the disasters that occur to anonymous people in faraway countries or in neighborhoods we are unlikely to visit.

Yet compassion is very real, though it is more uncommon than often thought. It is a direct confrontation with suffering and may be a prerequisite virtue enabling negotiation and compromise between opposing factions that otherwise might never agree. Like courage, compassion can be cultivated, but I have no intention of telling you how. For the most part, what passes for compassion is something like closing your eyes and pretending to be blind.

8. *Competence and effectiveness.* Though it is possible to be both competent and ineffective, for some reason it is highly unusual, because a successful and effective person is assumed also to be competent, which is a very singular and pragmatic virtue. I have alluded to coping strategies that seem ill-advised (e.g., leaping to an impulsive judgment) and yet are successful in managing a problem. It is hard, however, to imagine a strategy based entirely on impulse, or no strategy at all. Consequently, if a person regularly is effective despite having no recognizable strategy except arbitrary impulses, perhaps there is more method than we appreciate. Sometimes competent people minimize their abilities, attributing success to luck, but I cannot believe that luck occurs to anyone regularly, even to one who professes that virtue out of modesty. I regard competence, however, as a distinct virtue that an effective person can hardly do without. Obviously, competence is not automatic, but must be acquired diligently. It is not enough to hold high a banner proclaiming the virtue of virtue; something good must be done well, and perhaps within the grasp of most people.

9. *Continuity and closure.* I am sure that few of the sages of old would regard continuity and closure as significant virtues that people ought to practice and become adept at. What I refer to, however, is a talent for making a satisfactory assessment of a problematic situation and then following through on a feasible solution. It includes foreseeing consequences, exploring both real and remote alternatives, and rehearsing and revising strategies persistently and with a sense of positive purpose. It is not entirely equivalent to problem solving because continuity and closure come from a desire to complete a task, not just to do it successfully. This kind of stick-to-it adherence to duty may seem very hackneyed. No one could praise dabbling at a problem, breaking off an effort frivolously, or not foreseeing consequences, nor should continuity and closure be considered worth doggedly pursuing for their own sake without regard for new considerations.

Impromptu guesses and unwarranted surmises about ends and means are, of course, antithetical to serious continuity and closure. Giving up easily is permissible for unimportant decisions, but not for regular practice; it might become habitual. In contemplating different courses of action, asking oneself "What if?" or "If . . . then?" draws upon experience and shows that the problematic situation does matter enough to pursue its resolution.

10. ???? No list should have more than ten items. In this instance, the tenth item is open, to be filled by whatever virtue seems to have been left out and has practical significance. I have not named the previous nine virtues in any particular order of importance; perhaps the unknown remaining virtue is the super-value that so far has eluded most of us.

Skepticism and Ultimate Questions about Closure

A somewhat well-known passage from "Little Gidding," a poem by T. S. Eliot, is curiously apt:

> What we call the beginning is often the end
> And to make an end is to make a beginning.
> The end is where we start from. And every phrase
> And sentence that is right . . .
> Every phrase and every sentence is an end and a
>   beginning,
> Every poem an epitaph . . .
> We shall not cease from exploration
> And the end of all our exploring
> Will be to arrive where we started
> And know the place for the first time.
> Through the unknown, remembered gate
> When the last of earth left to discover
> Is that which was the beginning.

On the surface, these words reflect a predetermined, even dismal conclusion that any skeptic might embrace. But if I were to do that, I would undermine much of this book's positive message about coping, hoping, and courage. The life cycle is itself a metaphor holding within it many other images and analogies, some of which are mistaken for unadorned truths. My metaphors about the vulnerable self and the pilgrimage toward authenticity are intended to offer hope in the genuine possibility of ameliorating vulnerability and suffering. An enlightened skepticism is one strategy among many for bringing this about.

We are accustomed to reading articles and books where, after a long discussion, the author announces that no final answers are possible. He or she must know a lot to make such a statement; after all, do we need final answers? Courage and hope, as well as respect and regard, exact no such conditions. I have assumed that experience, culture, and wisdom are precious enough residues, even prizes, in the quest for authenticity. By its very nature, this pilgrimage has no ultimate conclusions except to beware of those who seem too cocksure or too anointed with authority. Skepticism helps make people more reliant on their own strategies and maybe become better copers, with a rich understanding of the metaproblems that all humanity faces.

A long time ago, in another book, I wrote that "only by discovering how the sense of reality combines with the sense of responsibility for the self in its quest for authenticity can an individual define . . . the world he contends with and creates." In short, we test our reality and, in turn, are tested by it. Like T. S. Eliot in the passage quoted above, I was struggling with the dilemmas of the vulnerable self, whose very agility and protean ingenuity lead so often to blind alleys of regret and disappointment.

The sense of reality for the world has to be synchronized and synthesized with the sense of responsibility for the vulnerable self, so that when authenticity seems within reach, we can turn a healthy skepticism upon it and lower our expectations. There are conditionals and contingencies for everything; limitations and compromises are always plentiful. But Eliot's message reflects only the disappointment of a pilgrim with lack of absolutes.

We are still dependent on a sense of reality, without the

confirmation of reality testing, for the ultimate questions and metaproblems that permeate existence. Consequently I see a confident prospect for continuity, but perhaps not closure, in the steady accumulation of experience, culture, and wisdom that shall prepare us for the inroads and inexorability of time. This would be an authentic achievement, a fitting closure, and surely not a closed circle that finds us at the end of life just as innocent and uninformed as at its inception.

Considering the hokum and horror that this world puts forth without stinting, skepticism needs no excuse for its healthy cultivation. But a caution is needed: Skepticism can be endangered by its potential for capturing itself and being dragged into a doubting compulsion or generalized cynicism. Confronting ultimate questions has to be combined with an aptitude for courageously assessing and coping with problems that matter. Far more accessible than spurious "final answers," this is an achievement or legacy that authenticity bequeaths itself.

It is not as mere reminiscence that I recall the period I was immersed in the practice of regular daily psychoanalysis (of myself as well as others), when I realized how vulnerability obligated us to recognize the inexorability of death and suffering. Indeed, there were no adequate names for this existential predicament. Furthermore, despite all my patients' difficulties and distress, underneath it all was an unceasing task, which is to look for significance in survival itself. Not even the most interminable psychoanalysis could hide this elemental fact of potential dislocation and absolute extinction.

This was by no means a passing philosophical rumination fostered by a sedentary occupation. It was a very practical understanding, if not insight, into the urgency of coping effectively with what we have. I could no longer conduct my practice in a timeless cloister in which the rush of events amounted to a bland and somewhat irrelevant background. Times change, and people age; the quest for significance goes on. Mine, too, was an existential plight, somewhere between absurdity and annihilation on one side and affirmation with courage on the other. I compared the difficulty with that of a man wandering at night in a strange city, unsure of whether he is to deliver a message or to receive one. In a way this describes the plight of the skeptical pilgrim, seeking authenticity, confronting ultimate questions, and getting no answer whatsoever.

I am reasonably confident at this point, however, that the man need not worry. Although I am still not sure what that message might be, I think he is expected to deliver it *and* receive one in return. But whatever the messages are, I do not know who gave him the assignment in the first place. This much the pilgrim surmises, and the skeptic knows. Furthermore, it is distinctly unwise to wander at night in any of our modern cities, with and without a message. Knowing that you can get in much trouble by knocking on the wrong door, even solitude is better. Contemplation has its compensation.

The skeptical pilgrim has his own vulnerability to contend with, and he expects obstacles to beset his course. Because he is forced in the interest of authenticity to learn how to cope courageously, but not recklessly, he realizes that his mission, if any, is mastery of the vulnerable self. When time loses its meaning, morale must provide the impetus to continue this endless task. I find an unlikely ally in the Dalai Lama, who once wrote that no pilgrimage is a required act; it is not a duty except to the extent that it is self-imposed.

Nevertheless, the purpose of a pilgrimage, even (or especially) that of a skeptic seeking authenticity, is to communicate about virtue and, as a result, gain some merit. That is how I paraphrase the Dalai Lama's words, and I yield to his authority. For me, however, virtue and merit—both strong objectives—are not far removed from the courage to cope. I think that the ancient Stoics could agree about this, although they were inclined to dispute so much else. At least they might concur that courage is a virtue not confined to bravery in battle, but that it is mandatory in meeting the challenge of the unknown. We need courage for the unknown that may be tomorrow, despite or because of our apprehension.

Skepticism always has a say in confronting existence and its ultimate questions. In fact, without a healthy skeptical longevity, ultimate questions and metaproblems probably could not be formulated at all; entrenched authority, conventional wisdom, and axiomatic precepts would take over and abolish questions. As it is, we know that vulnerability can be managed in part by knowing the limitations of time and our coping capacity.

Uncertainty is a challenge, or at least it is much of the time in dealing with important matters. Perhaps this is what helps make them important. We can accept uncertainty as a skeptic does, as a signal of hope rather than despair. The precarious conditions of existence keep us vulnerable; of that we can be sure. But in confronting these conditionals, we gain in stature and certainly can contend while complying. What it comes down to is narrowing the unfathomed chasm between our symbols, artifacts, and institutions and a vast universe of truths that manage to transcend us.

For Further Reading

Adams, James, et al. (eds.), *The Thought of Paul Tillich* (San Francisco: Harper & Row, 1985).

Binswanger, Ludwig, *Being-in-the-World*, ed. Jacob Needleman (New York: Basic Books, 1963).

Birley, J. L., "The Psychology of Courage," *Lancet* 1, 1923, pp. 779–789.

Boss, Medard, *Psychoanalysis and Daseinsanalysis* (New York: Basic Books, 1963).

Buber, Martin, *I and Thou*, trans. Walter Kaufmann (New York: Charles Scribner's Sons, 1970).

Camus, Albert, *The Myth of Sisyphus* (New York: Alfred A. Knopf, 1955).

Cannon, W. B., *The Wisdom of the Body* (New York: W. W. Norton, 1936).

Capongri, A. Robert, *A History of Western Philosophy, Vol. V: Philosophy From the Age of Positivism to Age of Analysis* (Notre Dame: Indiana University Press, 1971).

Cassell, Eric, *The Healer's Art: A New Approach to the Doctor-Patient Relationship* (New York: Penguin Books, 1978).

Cassirer, Ernst, *An Essay on Man: An Introduction to a Philosophy of Human Culture* (Garden City, NY: Doubleday Anchor Books, 1953).

Cobb, Stanley, *Borderlands of Psychiatry* (Cambridge, MA: Harvard University Press, 1943).

Coelho, George, David Hamburg, and John Adams (eds.), *Coping and Adaptation* (New York: Basic Books, 1974).

Collingwood, R. G., *An Essay on Philosophic Method* (Oxford: Clarendon Press, 1933).

Dewey, John, *Reconstruction in Philosophy* (New York: Henry Holt and Company, 1920).

Dougherty, Flavian (ed.), *The Meaning of Human Suffering* (New York: Human Sciences Press, 1982).

Edelstein, Elihu, Donald Nathanson, and A. Stone (eds.), *Denial: A Clarification of Concepts and Research* (New York: Plenum Press, 1989).

Ellenberger, Henri, *Discovery of the Unconscious: The History and Evolution of Dynamic Psychiatry* (New York: Basic Books, 1970).

Eliot, T. S., "Little Gidding" (London: Faber and Faber, 1944).

Feifel, Herman (ed.), *New Meanings of Death* (New York: McGraw-Hill Book Company, 1977).

Frank, Jerome D., *Persuasion and Healing: A Comparative Study of Psychotherapy* (New York: Schocken Books, 1963).

Frank, Jerome D., *Psychotherapy and the Human Predicament: A Psychosocial Approach,* ed. Park Dietz (New York: Schocken Books, 1978).

Frankl, Viktor, *The Will to Meaning: Foundations and Applications of Logotherapy* (New York: New American Library, 1969).

Fromm, Erich, *Escape From Freedom* (New York: Rinehart & Company, 1941).

Gaylin, Willard (ed.), *The Meaning of Despair: Psychoanalytic Contributions to the Understanding of Depression* (New York: Human Sciences Press, 1982).

Glaser, Barney, and Anselm Strauss, *Time for Dying* (Chicago: Aldine, 1968).

Haley, Jay, *Strategies of Psychotherapy* (New York: Grune & Stratton, 1963).

Heinemann, F. H., *Existentialism and the Modern Predicament* (New York: Harper and Brothers, 1958).

Holt, Herbert, "Existential Psychoanalysis," in *Comprehensive Textbook of Psychiatry,* ed. Alfred Freedman, Harold Kaplan, and Benjamin Sadock (Baltimore: Williams & Wilkins, 1975), pp. 661–668.

James, William, *The Meaning of Truth* (Cambridge, MA: Harvard University Press, 1975).

Janis, Irving, and Leon Mann, *Decision Making: A Psychological Analysis of Conflict, Choice, and Commitment* (New York: Free Press, 1977).

Josephson, Eric, and Mary Josephson (eds.), *Man Alone: Alienation in Modern Society* (New York: Dell Publishing, 1962).

Kastenbaum, Robert, *Death, Society, and Human Experience* (St. Louis: C. V. Mosby Company, 1981), 2nd ed.

Kaufmann, Walter (ed.), *Existentialism from Dostoevsky to Sartre* (New York: Meridian Books, 1957).

Kuhn, Thomas, *The Structure of Scientific Revolutions* (Chicago: University of Chicago Press, 1970), 2nd ed.

Lakoff, George, and Mark Johnson, *Metaphors We Live By* (Chicago: University of Chicago Press, 1980).

Lifton, Robert, *The Broken Connection: On Death and the Continuity of Life* (New York: Simon and Schuster, 1979).

MacCurdy, John, *The Structure of Morale* (New York: Doubleday, 1943).

Mackenzie, Compton, *Certain Aspects of Moral Courage* (New York: Doubleday, 1962).

Maris, Ronald (ed.), *Pathways to Suicide: A Survey of Self-Destructive Behaviors* (Baltimore: Johns Hopkins University Press, 1981).

May, Rollo, *The Meaning of Anxiety* (New York: Ronald Press, 1950).

Mayeroff, Milton, *On Caring* (New York: Harper & Row, 1971).

Moos, Rudolf (ed.), *Human Adaptation: Coping With Life Crises* (Lexington, MA: D. C. Heath and Company, 1976).

Osler, William, *Aequanimitas and Other Addresses* (Philadelphia: The Blakiston Co., 1906), 2nd ed.

Parkes, C. Murray, *Bereavement: Studies of Grief in Adult Life* (New York: International Universities Press, 1972).

Polanyi, Michael, *Personal Knowledge: Toward a Post-Critical Philosophy* (New York: Harper, 1964).

Rachman, Stanley, *Fear and Courage* (San Francisco: W. H. Freeman and Company, 1978).

Rapoport, Anatol, *Operational Philosophy: Integrating Knowledge and Action* (New York: Harper & Brothers Publishers, 1954).

Reichenbach, Hans, *The Rise of Scientific Philosophy* (Berkeley: University of California Press, 1951).

Rothenberg, Albert, "Empathy as a Creative Process," *International Review of Psychoanalysis* 14, 1987, pp. 445–463.

Russell, Bertrand, *A History of Western Philosophy* (New York: Simon and Schuster, 1945).

Schopenhauer, Arthur, *The World as Will and Idea* (London: Routledge & Kegan Paul, 1948), Vol. 3.

Strupp, Hans, and Grady Blackwood, "Recent Methods of Psychotherapy," in *Comprehensive Textbook of Psychiatry*, ed. Alfred Freedman, Harold Kaplan, and Benjamin Sadock (Baltimore: Williams & Wilkins, 1975), pp. 1909–1920.

Tillich, Paul, *The Courage to Be* (New Haven, CT: Yale University Press, 1952).

Tillich, Paul, *The Eternal Now* (New York: Charles Scribner's Sons, 1963).

Torrey, E. Fuller, *Witchdoctors and Psychiatrists: The Common Roots of Psychotherapy and Its Future* (Northvale, NJ: Jason Aronson, 1986).

Wahl, Jean, *A Short History of Existentialism*, trans. F. Williams and S. Maron (New York: Philosophical Library, 1949).

Watzlawick, Paul, Janet Beavin, and Don Jackson, *Pragmatics of Human Communication: A Study of Interactional Patterns, Pathologies, and Paradoxes* (New York: W. W. Norton & Company, 1967).

Weisman, Avery D., "Coping with Illness," in *Handbook of General Hospital Psychiatry*, ed. Ned Cassem (St. Louis: Mosby Year Book, 1991), 3rd ed., pp. 309–319.

Weisman, Avery D., *The Existential Core of Psychoanalysis: Reality Sense and Responsibility* (Boston: Little, Brown and Company, 1965).

Weisman, Avery D., "Terminality and Interminable Psychoanalysis," *Psychotherapy and Psychosomatics* 45(1), 1986, pp. 23–32.

Weisman, Avery D., *The Coping Capacity: On the Nature of Being Mortal* (New York: Human Sciences Press, 1984).

Widinger, Thomas, et al., "The DSM-III-R Personality Disorders: An Overview," *American Journal of Psychiatry* 145(7), 1988, pp. 786–793.

Wild, John, *The Challenge of Existentialism* (Bloomington: Indiana University Press, 1955).

Wisdom, John, *Philosophy and Psychoanalysis* (Oxford: Basil Blackwell, 1957).

Worden, J. William, *Grief Counseling and Grief Therapy: A Handbook for the Mental Health Practitioner* (New York: Springer Publishing Company, 1991), 2nd ed.

Wortman, Camilla, and Roxane Silver, "The Myths of Coping with Loss," *Journal of Counseling and Clinical Psychology* 57(3), 1989, pp. 349–357.

Index

Absurdity, 92
Acting out, 211–213
Adams, Raymond, 22
Affiliation, group, courage and, 181
Alcoholism, attitudes toward, 27
Alienation, 183
  examples of, 82–83
  meaning of, 150–151
Analyst. *See* Therapist
Anger, depression and, 37
Anti-intellectualism, 147–148
Anxiety
  coping and, 113
  existential. *See* Existential anxiety
  reducing, as psychotherapy goal, 158
Authentic self, 208
  belief in, 221–222
  candor, clarity, and communication in, 232–233
  care and caution in, 231
  character of, 232
  compassion in, 233–234

Authentic self *(cont.)*
  competence and effectiveness of, 234
  composure in, 231–232
  continuity and closure in, 234–235
  control, choice, and decision in, 231
  credibility of, 232
  versus false self, 215–216
  needs of, 229
  virtues of, 230–235
Authenticity, 1–19, 207, 208
  characteristics of, 8–9
  requirements for, 229
  search for, 203, 230
Autonomy, 186
  versus conformity, 184

Behavior
  aberrant, 7–8
  appropriate, therapist's role in encouraging, 132
  context of, 8

Behavior *(cont.)*
  meaning of, risks of clarifying,
    215
Bereavement, 153, 164, 188
Bonhoeffer, Dietrich, 103

Cancer patients
  Project Omega study of, xii
  resiliency of, 12–13
Cassem, Ned, xviii
Cassirer, Ernst, 152
Character, in authentic self, 232
Clinical judgment, versus moral
  judgment, 99
Closure
  authentic self and, 234–235
  ultimate questions about,
    235–239
Cobb, Stanley, 21
Communication
  and authentic self, 232–233
  as skill, 175
Compassion, 135
  in authentic self, 233–234
Competence, defined, 98
Competition, 186–187
Composure, in authentic self,
  231–232
Condemnation, and Tillich's
  concept of existential anxiety,
    94
Conflict
  nature of, 149–153
  vulnerable self and, 208
Conformity, 210
  acting out as protest against,
    212–213
  versus autonomy, 184
  versus normalcy, 205

Consciousness, 143
Consumer advocacy, 130
Coping, 14, 154
  anxiety and, 113
  competence in, 96–97
  courage in, 85–120
  effect on respect and regard,
    106
  good
    versus bad, 105–114, 106
    characteristics of, 109–111
    moral context of, 107
  improved capacity for, as
    psychotherapy goal, 158
  morale and, 179
  negative
    characteristics of, 111–114
    versus positive, 80–81
  Project Omega study of, xii
  as psychotherapy goal, 160
  through denial, 81
Coping Capacity, The, xi
Coping with Cancer, xi
Counseling
  defined, 141
  in psychotherapy, 139–141
Counselor. *See* Therapist
Countertransference, 99
  and double standard in
    psychotherapy, 101
  ignoring of, 100
Courage, 85–88, 180, 236
  absence of, 86–87
  to become, 95
  characteristics of, 87–91
  of coping, 85–120
  cultivation of, as psychotherapy
    goal, 159
  defined, 229

Courage (cont.)
   existential, in psychotherapy,
     94–99, 95
   existential anxiety and, 98–99
   group affiliation and, 181–183
   moral, 90
   in psychotherapy, 184–185
   rationality of, 88–91
   versus recklessness, 87
   selective occurrence of, 106
   Stoic view of, 91
   of therapist, 102
   Tillich's view of, 91
   vulnerability and, 90–91
Courage to Be, The, 91–94
Credentials, therapist, 135
Credibility
   of authentic self, 232
   of therapist, 135
Culture, 47–53
   psychotherapy and, 128–129
Custer, George Armstrong, 87

Dalai Lama, 238
Darmstadt, Frank, xviii
Death. See also Mortality
   acceptance of, 192
   befitting and appropriate,
     190–194
   coping with, 187–196
   denial of, 192
   as focal point for meaning,
     188–189
   negotiation with, 16
   propriety in, 192–193
   and Tillich's concept of
     existential anxiety, 93
   timeliness of, 194
Decisions, informed, 109

Decisions, informed (cont.)
   in authentic self, 231
Demoralization, 179
   as motivating force, 133
Denial
   of death, 192
   exposure of, 214
   function of, 81
Depression
   anger and, 37
   attitudes toward, 27
   as contagious illness, 28
   guilt and, 179
   reducing, as psychotherapy
     goal, 158
Deviance, fear of, 209–210
Diagnostic and Statistical Manual of
     Mental Disorders, Axis II of,
     80
Dichotomy, 215
   nature of, 149–153
Disease, emotion and, 26–27
Donoghue, Deirdre, xviii
Dreams, interpretation of, 163,
   216
Drugs, psychotropic, 28, 29

Ego ideal, 98
Ego strength, 80, 158
Eliot, T.S., 235, 236
Emerson, Ralph Waldo, 232
Emotion, physical disease and,
   26–27
Empedocles, 152
Emptiness, and Tillich's concept
   of existential anxiety, 93
Estrangement, 94
Evil, 225
   existential attitude toward, 104

Existential anxiety, 95–96
  courage and, 98–99
  emptiness and meaninglessness
    as, 93
  fate and death as, 93
  guilt and condemnation as, 94
  issues in, 96
  Tillich's forms of, 92–93
  of vulnerable self, 98
Existential foolishness, 92
Existential vulnerability, 75–79, 80
  examples of, 78–79
  personality classification
    according to, 80
Existentialism, viii, 17
  post-World War II, 145–146
  and search for meaning, 163
  and setting therapy goals, 159
  and ultimate questions in
    psychotherapy, 142–144, 154,
    160
Experience, 47–53

Faith
  psychology of, 60
  in psychotherapy, 218–219
Fallibility, fear of, 136–137,
    151–152
Fate, and Tillich's concept of
    existential anxiety, 93
Feifel, Herman, xviii
Finesinger, Jacob, 21
Flexibility, 109
Fox, Norma, xviii
Frank, Jerome, 133
Freedom
  fear of, 151–152, 210–211
  responsibility and, 214–215
  use of, 158

Freud, Sigmund, 105, 159
Fromm, Erich, 136

Grieving, 164
Group, affiliation with, courage
    and, 181–183
Guilt, 38
  existential versus neurotic, 97
  and Tillich's concept of
    existential anxiety, 94
  values and, 178

Hackett, Thomas, xviii
Healing, 16
Heidegger, Martin, 103
Hope
  courage and, 229
  versus optimism, 119
Human conditional, 220–221

Illness
  emotion and, 26–27
  meaning of, 32–33
Individualism, 206
Insight, in psychodynamic
    therapy, 41
Instincts, impulsiveness of, 158
Integrity, 232
Intellectualization, 170
Intuition, 5
  in psychotherapy, 126–127

James, William, 146
Judgment
  avoiding, 215, 216
  categorical, 216
  moral
    versus clinical, 99
    in psychotherapy, 100–102

Kairos, 68–69, 73
Kastenbaum, Robert, xviii

Lewis, C.S., xvi
Life-style, 204
Lindemann, Erich, xvii, 21
"Little Gidding," 235

Meaning
  of behavior, risks of clarifying,
    215
  generic, 173
  impersonal, 170–171
  infrapersonal, 171
  interpersonal, 169–170
  intrapersonal, 168–169
  kinds of, 164–168
  loss of, 115
  in patients' reports, 40–47
  pragmatic, 172
  in psychotherapy, 176–178
  search for, 16, 162–178
  subjective, versus objective, 28,
    165
  suprapersonal, 173
  surplus, 172
  transcendental, 173–174
Meaninglessness, and Tillich's
    concept of existential anxiety,
    93
Medical specialties, social
    significance of, 32
Medication, psychotropic, 28, 29
Mental health professionals, 124
Metaproblems, xii, 16–17
  defined, 158
  life task and, 228
  suffering and, 225–226
  ultimate questions and, 160–162

Midlife crisis, 83
Mitty, Walter, 108
Moral standards, 100–102
Morale
  enhancement of, as life task,
    228
  group affiliation and, 181–184
  healthy, 179–180
  defined, 179
  kinds of, 181–184
  maintenance of, 16, 178–187,
    203
    as psychotherapy goal, 159
  primary, 185
    versus secondary, 182
  quality of life and, 180–181
  self-realization and, 133
Mortality. *See also* Death
  coping with, 187–196
  as focal point for meaning,
    188–189
  negotiation with, 16
Motivation, 127
Mourning, 164

Neurosis, attitudes toward, 27
Neurotic patient, 24–25
Nonconformity, 186
Normalcy, 209
  concept of, 205
  versus conformity, 205
  patient focus on, 206–207
  as psychotherapy goal, 131, 132

Objectivity, illusory nature of, 59
Optimism, 109, 110
  versus hope, 119
Options
  fear of, 210–211

Options *(cont.)*
  importance of, 221
Osler, William, 232

Paradox, deciphering, 45–47
Paranoia, 37, 70
Patient
  cancer
    Project Omega study of, xii
    resiliency of, 12–13
  and fear of fallibility, 136–137
  "good," 107–108
  motivation of, 127
  respect and regard for, 102–105
  support of, 137–139
  therapist attitudes toward, 107
  therapist "fit" with, 114
  therapist judgment of, 99–102
Personality
  self-enclosed, 79–83
  of therapist, 33, 155
Phobia, attitudes toward, 27
Pilgrim, skeptical. *See* Skeptical
    pilgrim
Pilgrimage, 13
  internal, 215–216
  purpose of, 238
Plato, xv, xvi
Problem solving, 216
  as goal of psychotherapy, 158
Problems, proximal, versus
    ultimate questions, 222–223
Project Omega, xii, xviii
Psychiatry, attitudes toward, 25
Psychoanalysis, 14–15
  authoritarian nature of, 130
  classical, 129–130
  democratization of, 130

Psychodynamic therapy, insight
    in, 41
Psychopathology, neurological
    basis of, 21–22
Psychopharmacology, xii
Psychotherapist. *See* Therapist
Psychotherapy
  acceptibility in, 69
  articles of faith in, 218–219
  counseling in, 139–141
  courage required in, 95–96
  cultural relativism in, 128–129
  definitions of, 124–125
  double standard in, 101
  effectiveness of, 126
  evaluation of, 217
  existential, 16, 153–156
  existential courage in, 94–99
  failure of, 216–217
  goals of, 131, 132, 158–159, 223
    virtue as, 230–231
  historical perspective on, xv
  intuition in, 126–127
  meaning and value in, 176–
    178
  moral judgments in, 100–102
  motivation in, 127
  options in, 209–220
  pathological emphasis in, 86,
    104–105
  philosophies of, 9–10
  quality control of, 130–131
  schools of, 121
  secular nature of, 163–164
  short-term, 131
  skepticism in, 121–156
  subjectivity in, 125–127
  teaching of, 6–7
  terminating, 158–160, 217–218

Psychotherapy *(cont.)*
    ultimate questions in, 142–144,
        154, 160–162
Psychotropic medication, 28, 29
Pyrrho, 58

Quality of life, morale and,
        100–101
Questions, ultimate
    about closure, 235–239
    metaproblems and, 160–162
    versus proximal problems,
        222–224
    in psychotherapy, 142–144, 154,
        160–162
    virtue and, 230–231

Rationality, 5, 133
Rationalization, 170
Relationship, interpersonal
    significance of, 169–170
Resistance, as manifestation of
    vulnerability, 78–79
Responsibility, 96
    defined, 97, 98
    freedom and, 214–215
Risk, minimizing, 109
Risk taking, 109, 136–137

Sachs, Hanns, 21
Self
    authentic. *See* Authentic self
    healthy, versus vulnerable self,
        34
Self-affirmation
    courage and, 91–92
    courage for, 96
Self-betrayal, 214, 215
Self-deception, 198–199

Self-esteem, impaired, 37–38
Selfhood, of therapist and patient,
        33
Self-realization
    befitting outcomes and, 119
    morale and, 133
Self-respect, coping and, 110
Self-righteousness, 215, 220
Self-sufficiency, 183
Shame, 178–179
    existential versus neurotic, 97
Shneidman, Edwin, xviii
Significance. *See also* Meaning
    versus status, 166–167
    subjective, 165, 166, 168–171
        and impersonal meaning,
            170–171
        and infrapersonal meaning,
            171
        and interpersonal meaning,
            169–170
        and intrapersonal meaning,
            168–169
Significant survival, xii, xiv, xv
Skeptical pilgrim, 55–83, 162
    antithesis of, 177–178
    death and, 189
    maintaining morale and, 183
    and questioning about
        psychotherapy, 122–123
    vulnerability and, 197–201
Skepticism, 13
    versus cynicism, 237
    enlightened, 4–5
    faith required for, 218
    in psychotherapy, 121–156
Sobel, Harry, xviii
Standards. *See also* Values
    absolute, search for, 208–209

Standards (cont.)
contradictory, 186
moral, 100–102
Status
objective, 171–176
and generic meaning, 173
and pragmatic meaning, 172
and surplus meaning, 172
and transcendental meaning,
173–174
versus significance, 166–167
Stoics, 238
attitude toward courage, 91
Subjectivity, in psychotherapy,
125–127
Suffering, 25–26
attitudes toward, 23–24
categories of, 23
compassion toward, 233–234
demoralization and, 133
endurance of, 162
enigmas of, 52
interpretations of, 31–32
meaning of, 33, 37, 75–76, 227
metaproblems and, 225–226
nonphysical, 166
persistence of, 148–149
pressure points of, 141–142
privacy of, 28
in psychiatric patients, 28
religious interpretations of, 32
vulnerability and, 29–30, 75, 92
Suicidal patient, demoralization
in, 179
Suicide, 190
Superman, 108
Supervalues, 208–209, 220, 225
Support, of patient, 137–139
Support groups, 185

Survival, 98
existential meaning of, 96

Temperament, 3
Theory, 62–75
acceptability of, 68–75
application of, 71–74
generality in, 64
in psychotherapy, 63
relevance of, 66–67
specificity of, 65–66
Therapist
attitudes toward patients, 107
authenticity of, 1–19
authoritarian, 130
background of, 124–125
courage in, 102
credentials of, 135
credibility of, 135
and encouragement of
appropriate behavior, 132
fallibility of, 137
honesty of, 159
motivation of, 127
patient "fit" with, 114
patient judgment by, 99–102
personality differences of, 33
personality of, 155
quality of, 134–136
respect and regard for patient
by, 102–105
role of, 17
self-analysis of, 2
significance in healing, 2
temperament of, 3
values of, 207
Tillich, Paul, 91–94
Transference
and double standard in

Transference *(cont.)*
    psychotherapy, 101
    as manifestation of
        vulnerability, 78–79
    therapist's attitude toward, 99

Values, 18–19, 51. *See also*
    Standards
    in psychotherapy, 176–178
    sharing of, 204–205
    violation of, 176
Virtue
    authentic self and, 230–235
    changing attitudes toward,
        88–89
    definitions of, xv–xvi
    excess, 178–179, 220
    as goal of psychotherapy,
        230–231
    neglect of, 86, 104–105
    ultimate questions and, 230–231

Vulnerability, 31–36, 74
    actual, 36–37
    appraisal of, 230
    courage and, 90–91
    existential, 75–79, 80
        examples of, 78–79
        personality classification
            according to, 80
    kinds of, 36–40
    potential, 37–40
    skeptical pilgrim and, 197–201
    suffering and, 29–30, 75
Vulnerable self, xiv, xvi–xvii
    characteristics of, 228–229
    conflict and, 208
    existential anxiety of, 98
    limitations of, 221
    needs of, 228–230

Wisdom, 47–53
Worden, J. William, xviii